Legalizing Moves

Legalizing Moves

Salvadoran Immigrants' Struggle for U.S. Residency

Susan Bibler Coutin

Ann Arbor

THE UNIVERSITY OF MICHIGAN PRESS

2003   2002   2001   2000   4   3   2   1

A CIP catalog record for this book is available
from the British Library.

Library of Congress Cataloging-in-Publication Data

Coutin, Susan Bibler.
    Legalizing moves : Salvadoran immigrants' struggle for U.S.
residency / Susan Bibler Coutin.
        p.   cm.
    Includes bibliographical references and index.
    ISBN 0-472-11012-8 (acid-free paper)
    1. Refugees—Government policy—United States.   2. Asylum, Right
of—United States.   3. Emigration and immigration law—United
States.   4. Salvadorans—United States.   5. El Salvador—Emigration
and immigration.   6. United States—Emigration and immigration.
I. Title.
JV6601   .C68   1999
325'.21'0972840973—dc21   99-6550
                                                                     CIP

To Jordy (it's your turn!)
and
In memory of my grandfather,
Roy J. Burson

Contents

Preface

The title of this book, *Legalizing Moves,* is an effort to evoke the multiplicitous and shifting nature of Salvadorans' legal goals and strategies. Applying for political asylum is a means of legitimizing Salvadoran immigrants' entry into the United States. Recognizing Salvadorans as refugees would suggest that these immigrants had to come here and are entitled to safe haven. Legalization would also legitimize other moves, enabling asylum applicants who are currently "trapped" within U.S. borders by their pending asylum applications to visit family members in their homelands. Undocumented immigrants who legalize acquire greater mobility within the United States in that they are able to pass through checkpoints that previously restricted their movements. Changing policies to permit legalization has required various political and legal moves, such as filing class-action lawsuits, mobilizing constituencies, and creating the sanctuary movement. Each movement on the part of activists and policymakers has also provoked a countermovement, much like a game of chess. Individual asylum seekers and their legal representatives have also made moves, such as seeking legal expertise, filing papers, and making motions in court. The title's shifting meanings—"movements that legalize" and "legalizing one's movements"—are intended to evoke the spatial movement of immigrants, the ambiguity of their physical presence, and the continual refinement of their legal strategies.

This book could not have been written without the assistance of many people and institutions. It truly has been a collaborative effort. My colleagues at North Adams State College were supportive when I first proposed to take an extended leave from teaching to conduct the research for this book. I am particularly grateful to Joe DeOrdio, Sumi Colligan, Michelle Ethier, Steve Green, and Deb Foss.

In Los Angeles, Central American activists, advocates, immigrants, and community organizations allowed me to hang around, ask questions, use some of their limited time, and sit in on many activities. These experiences have redefined Los Angeles for me. ASOSAL, CARECEN and El Rescate became homes away from home for me, and I am immeasurably indebted to each of these organizations and their staff members. I thank Robert Foss, Juan Carlos Cristales, Elena Fernandez, Tim Everett, Ricardo Quintanilla, Teresa Cruz, Jaime Peñate, Judy London, Raquel Fonte, Edgardo Quintanilla, Sandra Nieto, Carlos Alvarado, Luis Hernandez, Nelson Lopez, Claudia M. Godoy, and Myrna Toulet. CHIRLA staff (particularly Susan Alva) were also of assistance. To the Coalición Centroamericana, ¡muchísimas gracias por permitirme estar presente! The many people who participated in interviews for this project gave of their time and their words, allowing me to visit them in their homes, workplaces, and neighborhoods. I hope that this analysis does justice to their experiences, y les deseo mucha suerte en los años que vienen.

This book would not have been written or would have turned out worse were it not for the advice and assistance of numerous colleagues. Sue Hirsch and Rebecca French provided invaluable suggestions when the project was still in the planning stage. Bill Maurer read the entire manuscript despite having been previously inundated with drafts of the (aptly named) "Papeles" chapter. I am particularly indebted to his suggestions and insights. Barbara Yngvesson also read the entire manuscript and provided extremely helpful comments. Carol Greenhouse, Sally Merry, Don Brenneis, David Engel, Phyllis Chock, Mindie Lazarus-Black, Eve Darian-Smith, Michael Musheno, Peter Fitzpatrick, Christine Harrington, Robert Foss, Beth Baker-Cristales, Ester Hernandez, and George Collier read and commented on chapters in their various incarnations. The ideas expressed in this manuscript also benefited from my conversations with Richard Perry, Rosemary Coombe, Nahum Chandler, and Teresa Caldeira.

Numerous institutions provided support throughout this project. My research regarding Central Americans' legal strategies was funded by a grant from the National Science Foundation's Law and Social Science Program (grant SBR-9423023). I am also grateful to North Adams State College for its support for this project and to Joe DeOrdio of NASC's Office of Grants and Institutional Research for his help. In 1997, during the final stages of research and the initial stages of writing, I was a visiting professor in the Department of Criminology, Law, and Society at the University of California, Irvine. I would like to thank Richard Perry for inviting me to participate in this intellectual community. I spent some of 1997 and most of 1998 as a visiting scholar at the Center for Multiethnic and Transnational Studies at the University of Southern California, and there I completed my research and wrote this manuscript. I am grateful to CMTS's director, Michael Preston, for this invaluable opportunity and to Clare Walker for her support and assistance. Two USC students, Daniel Rodriguez and Mauricio Alanis, also helped to transcribe interviews.

It has been wonderful working with Susan Whitlock and the editorial staff of the University of Michigan Press. I am grateful to them for their support and for making this a smooth process.

Finally, I thank my family. The year that I wrote this book was difficult due to my grandfather's illness and to other blows. I am grateful for the support of my grandparents, my mother, Jim, Juanita, Judy, my father, my sister, and my cousin, Pam. Thank you also to Luxy and Cherie for their encouragement. To Olga, ¡gracias por *todo lo que hiciste!* I am grateful to my husband, Curt, for coming along on the circuitous route that I have taken, and to my children, Jesse and Jordy, for their infectious joy. This book is dedicated to Jordy, who was born when I began this research, and to my grandfather, Roy Burson, who died as I was completing the manuscript.

Chronology of Political and Legal Events
Affecting Salvadoran Asylum Seekers

March 1980	Salvadoran Archbishop Oscar Romero assassinated during Mass.
January 1981	Salvadoran guerrilla forces launch their first major offensive of the civil war.
March 1982	Handful of congregations around the United States declare themselves sanctuaries for Salvadoran and Guatemalan refugees.
January 1985	Fourteen sanctuary activists indicted in Tucson, Arizona, on alien-smuggling and conspiracy charges.
May 1985	Religious and refugee-service organizations sue the U.S. government, charging it with discriminating against Salvadoran and Guatemalan asylum seekers. This suit came to be known as *American Baptist Churches v. Thornburgh* (ABC).
May 1986	Eight of the eleven sanctuary activists who stand trial are convicted.
November 1986	Passage of the Immigration Reform and Control Act (IRCA), which permits certain undocumented immigrants to legalize their presence and imposes sanctions on employers who hire undocumented workers.
November 1989	Salvadoran guerrilla forces launch their "final offensive" in the civil war. During the offensive, Salvadoran death squads assassinate six Jesuit priests, their housekeeper, and her daughter.
November 1990	Passage of the 1990 Immigration Act, which creates Temporary Protected Status (TPS) and designates Salvadorans as its first recipients. Salvadorans' TPS status is scheduled to expire in June 1992.

January 1991	Negotiated settlement reached in the ABC case. Settlement gives ABC class members the right to de novo asylum hearings under special rules designed to ensure a fair hearing of their claims.
January 1992	Salvadoran guerrilla forces and the Salvadoran government sign peace accords.
June 1992	Bush administration permits Salvadoran TPS recipients to register for Deferred Enforced Departure (DED) status. Salvadorans' DED status is scheduled to expire in June 1993 but is extended until March 1996.
January 1996	End of period during which Salvadoran TPS recipients could apply for the benefits of the ABC agreement.
September 1996	Passage of the Illegal Immigration Reform and Immigrant Responsibility Act (IIRIRA), which eliminates many of the remedies for which ABC class members could have applied in the event that their asylum applications were denied.
April 1997	Asylum interviews of ABC class members commence.
November 1997	Passage of the Nicaraguan Adjustment and Central American Relief Act (NACARA), which creates an amnesty for certain Nicaraguans and permits certain Salvadorans and Guatemalans to apply for U.S. residency (suspension of deportation) under pre-IIRIRA terms.

Chapter 1
Negotiating Identities

November 14, 1997. After circling several times in search of parking, I walk past bystanders, a record store playing lively dance music, bustling shops, traffic, and a man asking for a handout to MacArthur Park, near downtown Los Angeles. About sixty Central Americans have gathered at the busy intersection of Seventh and Alvarado. Holding signs that read, "Permanent residency for ABC class members," they shout their demand of "¡Residencia permanente!" to curious onlookers and passing drivers who occasionally honk their support. I quickly take my place in the middle of the group and join in the chanting. The night is unusually cold for Los Angeles, and participants alternate between clustering in small groups to discuss events and rejoining the chanting. I recognize many of those present. There are activists from Central American community organizations and hometown associations in Los Angeles, paralegals who filled out asylum applications for Salvadorans and Guatemalans who fled political violence in their homelands, women who participated in a fast at the Los Angeles Federal Building the previous week, and people whom I do not recognize but I assume to be clients of these organizations—"affected families," as the activists who organized this event sometimes call them. Noting the absence of press, I wonder whether this event will be deemed a success or a failure by its organizers.

The occasion for this protest is the news that President Bill Clinton is about to sign the Nicaraguan Adjustment and Central American Relief Act[1] (NACARA, previously termed the Victims of Communism Relief Act), which the U.S. Congress passed only a few days

FIG. 1.   Protesters at MacArthur Park rally, November 1997.
(Photo by author.)

earlier (Wilgoren and McDonnell 1997). This act creates an amnesty
for Nicaraguans who entered the United States prior to December 1,
1995, and allows certain Salvadorans and Guatemalan asylum seekers
and their relatives to apply for suspension of deportation, a form of
legal relief that had been eliminated by immigration reform in
1996.[2] I find it amazing that NACARA has passed at all. As recently as
January 1997, local activists' contacts in Congress had advised them
that any form of legislative relief for Salvadoran and Guatemalan asylum applicants was out of the question. Despite the fact that obtaining favorable legislation might be characterized as a victory, the
mood of those gathered in MacArthur Park is defiant rather than
jubilant. Activists and supporters are outraged at the lack of parity
between Nicaraguans (who were granted an "amnesty") and other
Central Americans (who received the right to apply for suspension of
deportation). Suspension cases are difficult to win. Most applicants
can easily satisfy the first two requirements—seven years of continuous presence in the United States and good moral character. But the

third requirement—proving that deportation would constitute an "extreme hardship" to the applicant or the applicant's legal permanent resident or U.S. citizen relative(s)—constitutes a formidable hurdle in many cases. As many as 80 percent of the Salvadorans and Guatemalans affected by the legislation could be denied suspension and ordered deported, leading to anguishing separations of family members who have legal status from those who do not; economic deprivation for relatives back home who depend on the remittances of an immigrant wage earner; the pain of being wrenched from one's home, job, school, and community; and in some cases, the terror of being returned to a place where one was persecuted. "¡Clinton! ¡Escucha! ¡Estamos en la lucha!" protestors chant. "Clinton! Listen! We are fighting!" Activists hope that President Clinton, who promised to treat Nicaraguans, Salvadorans, and Guatemalans equitably, will discover or create an administrative mechanism for stipulating that the Salvadorans and Guatemalans affected by the legislation would suffer extreme hardship if deported. Such a policy would create a de facto amnesty for these immigrants.

A complex course of events led to this moment and to my presence at this rally. In September 1986, I had attended a much larger demonstration in Washington, D.C. At that time, civil wars raged in El Salvador and Guatemala, and the U.S. government had just obtained conspiracy and alien-smuggling convictions against eight religious activists who had declared their congregations sanctuaries for Salvadoran and Guatemalan refugees. In response to the convictions, sanctuary activists from around the United States had gathered in Washington, D.C., for a National Sanctuary Celebration. At the time, I was a graduate student in anthropology at Stanford University and had decided to make the sanctuary movement the subject of my doctoral research, so I accompanied northern California sanctuary workers to Washington for the celebration. During three days of prayer, worship, and protest, I joined other participants in lobbying congressional representatives to pass what was then known as the Moakley-DeConcini bill—legislation that would grant Central Americans safe haven in the United States (Fiederlein 1992; Rubin 1991). It would be another four years before this goal was achieved in the form of the 1990 Immigration Act,[3] which created temporary protected status (TPS) and designated Salvadorans as its first recipients (see Frelick and Kohnen 1994; *Interpreter Releases* 1990a, 1990b;

Wasem n.d.). Though I was unaware of it at the time, sanctuary congregations and refugee-service organizations had responded to the
1985 indictments of movement members by suing the U.S. government for discriminating against Salvadoran and Guatemalan asylum
applicants. This lawsuit, which came to be known as the ABC case
after the American Baptist Churches, the lead plaintiff in the suit,
resulted in an out-of-court settlement in 1991.[4] The settlement
granted many Salvadoran and Guatemalan asylum seekers the right
to de novo asylum interviews under special rules designed to ensure
a fair consideration of their claims.

My first contact with Central American community organizations
in Los Angeles was in the late 1980s. I had just returned from Tucson,
Arizona, where I had spent eight months working with sanctuary
activists as part of my doctoral research. Feeling a bit burned out on
political activism and legal risks, I decided that as I wrote my doctoral
dissertation, I would work directly with the legal-services programs of
Central American community organizations rather than with sanctuary groups. I approached the Central American Refugee Center
(CARECEN), which at that time was located on Bonnie Brae in a
somewhat dilapidated building that also housed the People's College
of Law. I was assigned the task of preparing the asylum application of
a woman who, along with her husband, had been active in the peasant movement in El Salvador. I interviewed the woman repeatedly
over a period of several weeks, drafting and revising the declaration
that would be submitted along with her asylum application. During
one particularly painful interview she admitted that her torture at the
hands of Salvadoran security forces had included being raped—a fact
that she had not revealed to her own husband. Though I was not new
to this process, I resented the legal system's emphasis on details and
consistency as measures of credibility. The woman with whom I was
working remembered events but not dates. After she described the
brutal assassination of a family member or another equally tragic
event, I often had to ask what I thought she would consider an
extremely irrelevant and insensitive question: "And on what *date* was
your brother killed?"

Over the next few years, I continued to volunteer with CARE-
CEN from time to time when asked to do so. I took depositions from
asylum applicants for the Mendez case[5]—a class-action suit that
addressed the inadequacy of the Immigration and Naturalization

Service's (INS's) asylum interviews as means of determining the merits of an applicant's case (see Murphy 1989; Oliver 1989). I heard countless stories of individuals being interviewed for five to ten minutes in cubicles that lacked privacy by officials who did not ask applicants about the persecution they had experienced. When Salvadorans were permitted to apply for TPS, I helped applicants fill out the forms. And I occasionally met with other volunteers on Saturday afternoons to stuff envelopes for mailings.

As I did volunteer work and followed Central Americans' legal situation in the news, I formulated the idea for my next major research project, a study of Central Americans' efforts to negotiate their legal status in the United States. In 1993, before moving to Massachusetts to accept a faculty position, I conducted several preliminary interviews with CARECEN staff regarding this project. By this time, peace accords had been signed in El Salvador and TPS had expired, giving rise to a campaign for its extension. This campaign had proven successful, as the Bush administration had granted TPS recipients the right to apply for a new temporary legal status known as deferred enforced departure status (DED). During these preliminary interviews, I was intrigued to note that staff members' discourse about Central Americans had changed. Instead of referring to them as "refugees," staff members now referred to Central Americans as "immigrants" (Coutin 1998b). In fact, CARECEN was in the process of changing its name from the Central American Refugee Center to the Central American Resource Center. A staff member explained, "'Refugee' didn't do much for Central Americans. 'Refugees' didn't get aid. The term didn't do much for people within the community. What we're trying to do by using 'immigrant' is to point out that all people deserve to be treated with dignity and respect." By doing research on Central Americans' legal strategies, I would be able to examine the reasons that *immigrant* came to be an empowering term, the interconnections and/or contradictions between Salvadoran activists' political and legal goals, and the ways that Central Americans' legal strategies drew on and reformulated U.S. immigration law.

In June 1995, after obtaining funding from the National Science Foundation's Law and Social Science Program, I returned to Los Angeles to conduct full-time research regarding Salvadorans' efforts to define their legal status in the United States. I then first met many of the activists present at the MacArthur Park protest. By 1995, Salvadorans' DED status was scheduled to expire, which meant that applying for asylum under the terms of the ABC settlement was the only way for TPS/DED recipients to maintain their temporary legal status and their right to a work permit. I began working with three Salvadoran community organizations that prepared ABC class members' asylum applications: the Association of Salvadorans of Los Angeles (ASOSAL), an organization that grew out of the effort to extend TPS; CARECEN, where I had worked earlier as a volunteer; and El Rescate (Spanish for "the Rescue"), a refugee-service organization that had formed in Los Angeles in the early 1980s and whose work was similar to that of CARECEN. Each of these organizations had devoted considerable staffing and resources to the ABC application effort, only to discover that over the summer and early fall of 1995, the numbers of applicants dropped (most likely due to a false rumor that June 30, 1995, was the deadline for applying). It was during this slow period that I began to volunteer with these organizations, preparing asylum applications, filling out INS forms, writing declarations, and translating applicants' accounts of persecution. I also interviewed staff members, legal-service providers, activists, and ABC class members about their experiences, strategies, and goals. By January 1996, when the application period was scheduled to end, the pace at each of these organizations was frenzied. I stopped doing interviews and devoted myself full-time to volunteer work, as organizations struggled to register as many applicants as possible before the deadline. I recall driving home close to midnight on January 31, 1996, the final day of the application period, wondering what would happen to all of the knowledge and expertise devised specifically for processing these applications—rules about which relatives could be included in an application, decisions about how to report brief absences from the United States, and so on. On that rainy night, a dedicated staff member of one organization persuaded the Los Angeles post office to remain open until 3:00 A.M., as long lines of ABC applicants sought to obtain the coveted January 31 postmark on their application packets.

And now, almost two years later, many of the people involved in this almost superhuman application effort are gathered in MacArthur Park, demanding residency for ABC class members. This call for residency is a response to a series of predicted and unpredicted events. Activists' efforts to register large numbers of Salvadorans for the benefits of the ABC settlement had been grounded in activists' and service providers' conclusion that Salvadorans were an immigrant rather than a refugee community (Coutin 1998). Although the settlement agreement merely promised fair asylum interviews, not residency, advocates hoped that by the time that their cases were adjudicated, most ABC class members would have developed strong suspension claims. Activists planned that if asylum applications were denied, class members could then apply for suspension of deportation. In 1996, this strategy was jeopardized by the passage of the Illegal Immigration Reform and Immigrant Responsibility Act (IIRIRA).[6] IIRIRA replaced suspension of deportation with a new form of relief, called cancellation of removal. Cancellation required proving ten years of continuous presence rather than seven and proving that deportation would pose an "extreme and exceptional hardship" to an applicant's U.S. citizen or legal permanent resident spouse, parent, or child. Hardship to the applicant was irrelevant. Moreover, an annual cap of four thousand was placed on the approval of suspension or cancellation cases, making it unlikely that the 260,000 ABC class members with pending cases could resolve their situations through this avenue. To make matters worse for applicants, the INS chose to commence ABC class members' asylum interviews in this much more restrictive legal context. The first interviews took place in April 1997.

Hence the protest. Beginning in January 1997, Salvadoran, Guatemalan, and Nicaraguan community organizations had joined forces to demand residency for Central Americans who had fled to the United States during periods of civil conflict. Though legislators were initially cool to their efforts, the support of Central American leaders concerned about the impact of mass deportations (McDonnell 1997b) and the assistance of Republican members of Congress who feared that immigration reform was alienating Latino voters resulted in a bill (Wilgoren and McDonnell 1997). On learning of the amnesty proposed for Nicaraguans, Salvadoran and Guatemalan activists demanded parity. Because such equal treatment was not forthcoming, the law that restored Salvadoran and Guatemalan asylum applicants' suspension eligibility and exempted them from the four thousand-per-year cap was denounced by one activist as "a law that mistreats us more than we were mistreated in our countries."

After the protesters in MacArthur Park chant for about an hour, a paralegal takes the megaphone and explains the details of the legislation. "This is a partial victory," he concludes, "an example that our cries were heard, but perhaps we haven't shouted enough." One activist after another takes the megaphone, denouncing the legislation and urging others to take action: "We want to send a message to Clinton that we will not rest until all Central Americans—the Nicaraguans, the Guatemalans, the Salvadorans—have amnesty and permanent residency." "This is not over!" "Now it's not Congress. Now it's Clinton and the Department of Justice." "The fight is just beginning!" "Congress more or less has done what Herod did in his time: order the boys to be killed and leave the girls alive. And here they are killing our desire to be able to convert ourselves into useful citizens of this nation. We want to send a message to Congress: stop playing with our lives!"

At about 9:00 P.M., the rally breaks up. Participants write their names on the backs of signs to be notified of future actions. I walk over to some of the organizers to find out when their next meeting is. I also pick up a flyer about an upcoming dinner with and presentation by the mayor of San Salvador, who is to visit Los Angeles in two weeks. The mayor is the first leftist candidate to be elected the city's mayor, and local activists have arranged for him to visit the expatriate Salvadoran community here.

As I leave the rally, I wonder whether the campaign for a de facto amnesty will succeed. If so, what sort of political impact will the legalization of several hundred thousand Central Americans have? If not, how will ABC class members negotiate the suspension process? And regardless of the outcome of this particular campaign, what role will the expatriate Salvadoran community continue to play in Salvadoran politics? How do undocumented immigration and illegal sojourn redefine not only the nation but citizenship, movement, and existence itself?

Redefinitions

This book recounts Salvadorans' efforts to define their legal status in the United States from the early 1980s to the present. In so doing, it addresses five interrelated legal issues: the senses in which immigra-

FIG. 2.   Children holding sign at MacArthur Park rally,
November 1997. (Photo by author.)

tion law is powerful, the role of law in constructing and/or challenging identities, the processes through which law is negotiated, the
political implications of legal proceedings, and the ways that immigration redefines citizenship and the state. This book is not, however,
exclusively about law. It is also about ethnicity, gender, violence, illegality, and political struggle. I hope that this ethnography of a complex and multifaceted legal process will reveal not only how law is
implicated in struggles over personhood and legitimacy but also how
movement, boundaries, persons, and nations are constructed
through debates over immigration policies and individual status.

Attention to such processes can shed light on the fluid but stubbornly persistent boundaries between nations, regions, and regional scholarship such as American studies and Latin American studies. As individuals' legalization cases are assessed, so too are criteria for inclusion and exclusion, the meanings of borders and crossings, and the significance of belonging. Legal ethnography therefore provides insight into phenomena that are not, on the surface, legal.

Immigration and immigration law are almost inseparable, as law defines the legitimacy and nature of movements and persons. Law delimits the borders of national territories, establishes criteria for passage, creates categories of sojourn and of sojourners, defines the nature of citizenship, legitimizes states, and criminalizes unauthorized entry. Without law, the movements that are deemed immigration might be perceived and characterized differently. Despite their inseparability, law and immigration have often been juxtaposed by scholars who ask whether law can prevent illegal immigration (Briggs 1984; Calavita 1992, 1994; Hamilton and Chinchilla 1991; Poitras 1983; Portes 1978). Implicit in this juxtaposition are the assumptions that immigration could exist without law; that immigration obeys other "nonlegal" economic and historical forces; and that the "power" of immigration law is best measured by its ability to "control" immigration. Though I agree that legislation even combined with stringent enforcement efforts is unlikely to prevent undocumented migrants from trying their luck along U.S. borders (see also Harwood 1984, 1985; Heyman 1995), I believe that a more fruitful approach to assessing the relationship between law and immigration is to examine how law produces citizens, illegal aliens, legal permanent residents, legal immigration, illicit travel, and even territories and the state (see Foucault 1977, 1980). Individuals are situated within immigration categories through a variety of practices, including court hearings, requests for proof of work authorization, determinations of eligibility for services, and detention and deportation. Such practices negotiate not only the statuses of the individuals in question but also the relationship between states and citizenries, the nature of movement, the meaning of presence, and the legitimacy of existence. The outcomes of these negotiations have material effects on individual lives, transnational relations, and national futures.

Because of the high stakes involved in their definition, negotiations of legal identities are highly contested. Immigration categories, such as "political asylee"[7] or "suspension of deportation" are predefined; therefore, to qualify for particular forms of legalization, immigrants must redefine these categories and/or make their own life narratives conform to a "deserving" prototype (see Yngvesson 1993b). Debates over immigrants' legal deservingness therefore entail judgments regarding the morality and legitimacy of family relationships (Maurer 1995; Yanagisako and Delaney 1995), the nature of persecution and terrorism, the components of civic responsibility, the meanings of Americanness, and the limits of state authority. Powerful claims about gender, race, class, ethnicity, nationality, and historical reality are implicitly and sometimes explicitly at stake in immigration hearings (see Chock 1991, 1995; Coutin and Chock 1995). Aware of the potentially far-reaching implications of assessments of legal status, legal identities have sometimes become a focus of immigrants' activism (Bousquet 1991; Castles and Miller 1993; Hammar 1990; Miller 1981). For example, in the case of Salvadorans, efforts to obtain refugee status during the 1980s were not only intended to prevent deportations but also to problematize continued U.S. military aid to the Salvadoran government, thus potentially facilitating a guerrilla victory in the civil conflict (Coutin 1993, 1998b). Contests over immigration policy thus have the potential to affect the conditions that initially cause people to emigrate.

The legal processes that immigrants must negotiate as they seek to define their legal status are politically complex and contextually diverse. In the case of immigration, legal proceedings are not limited to formal court hearings or official interviews. As U.S. policy has increasingly made private citizens accountable for the legal status of those with whom they interact, employers, college admissions officials, social workers, public housing officials, Department of Motor Vehicles clerks, and others must assess others' legal status in the course of rendering rights and services.[8] As immigrants negotiate these processes, they devise their own understandings of what legal status consists of and how to get it. This "legal consciousness" (Merry 1990)—which, from the perspective of attorneys and other legal experts, is factually incorrect—provides an account of law as seen from the realm of "illegality" in which the undocumented are located. Like immigration and law, legality and illegality are intrinsically interconnected (Fitzpatrick 1992; Holston 1991). Law defines that which is illegal and thus demarcates the boundaries of illegality.

Similarly, illegality gives rise to law in that the definition and limits of the illicit can be refined each time an individual seeks to legalize. The complexity and multiplicity of immigration "law" situate immigrants and those who advocate on their behalf in contradictory subject positions. On the one hand, applying for legal status reproduces immigration categories in that the undocumented claim to have met predefined criteria for deservingness. On the other hand, seeking to include another individual case in the subset of the "deserving" requires further refining and sometimes redefining these criteria.

It is difficult to definitively locate power and resistance within immigrants' legalization struggles. It is tempting to view immigrants' legal consciousnesses, their alternative accounts of immigration law, as a subversive discourse. Yet if this discourse is intrinsically connected to and in some ways reproduces law, which in turn justifies the social and physical exclusion of the undocumented, then immigrants' legal notions are less a form of resistance than an account of law narrated from a particular subject position. Likewise, though law makes legal status a prerequisite for particular rights and services, law simultaneously creates mechanisms through which the illicit can regularize their status. As a result, law cannot be characterized as exclusively hegemonic.[9] In my account of Salvadorans' legalization strategies, I therefore strive to convey the political complexity of various actions and subject positions, including those of immigrants, activists, attorneys, judges and others. This approach is not intended to suggest cynically that all political actors and institutions have somehow been co-opted in furtherance of disciplinary power or to flatten out accounts of political action by implying that power and resistance ultimately balance each other out. Rather, I seek to problematize theories of action that equate agency with resistance, independence, sovereignty, escape from social control, and so forth (see also Maurer 1998). Both agency and resistance (which I do not view as the same)[10] can reside in clever manipulations of a system as well as in challenges to that system. Moreover, as Feldman (1991) notes, agency can be the effect of rather than a precondition for action. Negotiating a political or legal system requires innovation and adjustment, knowing when to stay the course and when to try a new tack. But multiple negotiations can cumulatively alter the course itself.

In constructing arguments about legal identity, Salvadoran

immigrants and activists are manipulating notions of citizenship and legitimacy in ways that could transform commonly accepted definitions of the state, the nation, borders, and movement. Just as agency can be an effect of action, so too can subject positions and the structures in which they are embedded be products of as well as bases for social analysis. Much has been made recently of transnational communities as entities that defy the state-based notion that immigration consists of movement from one nation to another (Basch, Schiller, and Blanc 1994; Chavez 1991, 1992; Hagan 1994, Kearney 1991; Rouse 1991; Schiller, Basch, and Blanc 1995; Wilson 1993). Less has been said, however, about the structures and assumptions that make it possible to perceive people, groups, and places as national, local, transnational, global, mobile, and so forth (Featherstone 1995; Gupta and Ferguson 1997; McMichael 1996; Robertson 1995). One advantage of examining immigrants' struggles to legalize is that they bring such structures and assumptions into sharp relief (Sassen 1996). For example, an individual who left El Salvador, spent two years in Mexico, and then entered the United States may be deemed by immigration officials to have "firmly resettled" in Mexico and to therefore be ineligible for asylum in the United States. This example reveals that within immigration law, traveling and residing are a dichotomy (see also Clifford 1997) and that this dichotomy precludes the possibility that the purpose and meaning of being in a particular place could be ambiguous. When immigrants seek to create subject positions that would legitimize their prior experiences (such as a two-year stay in Mexico), they reveal the types of political structures—including new notions of citizenship, legality, and movement—that could characterize a more globally just future. At the same time, the criteria that are used to legitimize and/or delegitimize these subject positions and prior experiences shed light on how spaces, movements, persons, and states are currently delimited. It is worthwhile to examine Salvadorans' legalization strategies not because immigrants are somehow intrinsically transnational or because they are choosing between national allegiances but rather because these strategies shed light on how the local and the global, the national and the transnational, are simultaneously constituted and deconstructed in the process of immigration.

Salvadoran immigrants confronted these questions about

belonging, exclusion, location, and identity in the 1980s, when the onset of civil war made continued existence in their country of origin precarious.

Salvadoran Immigrants

The Salvadoran civil war began in the late 1970s and early 1980s. Although the January 1981 Frente Farabundo Martí para la Liberación Nacional (FMLN, Farabundo Martí National Liberation Front) offensive is sometimes defined as the action that marks the beginning of war (Byrne 1996), I prefer a more imprecise date because that is how Salvadorans whom I have interviewed have described the war: as violence and repression that intensified until they became unbearable. For example, one Salvadoran man who fled to the United States in 1984 recalled, "In '79, already the situation was beginning to get pretty bad in El Salvador." Regardless of when the war began, it, like all wars, was destructive. The army (and eventually the guerrilla forces) practiced forced recruitment, civilians were caught in cross fire, and bombs destroyed jobs, homes, limbs, and lives (Byrne 1996; Montgomery 1995). Even many of those who left El Salvador as young children can remember hiding under their beds during the fighting or seeing bodies in the streets. From 1981 to 1984, the guerrillas sought an immediate military victory and fought accordingly. When a victory was not forthcoming, the insurgents devised an alternative strategy of wearing away at the Salvadoran Armed Forces through prolonged war. To counter this effort, the Salvadoran military strafed areas that were deemed zones of guerrilla support. This strategy, which was called "draining the sea" (Byrne 1996:130) caused high levels of civilian casualties. Throughout the war, human rights violations—the bulk of which were committed by Salvadoran military and paramilitary units rather than by the guerrillas (Montgomery 1995)—terrorized the populace. These violations included surveillance, interrogation, the destruction of property, abduction, torture, rape, assassination, and dismemberment. Victims were sometimes chosen arbitrarily, on the basis of an informant's denunciation or a personal vendetta, as well as for clearly political reasons (Green 1994; Paul and Demarest 1988; Schirmer 1985,

1988; Stephen 1995). It became difficult for even those who were "uninvolved" in the conflict to ensure their own safety.

Given this violence, it is not surprising that the civil war produced a massive dislocation of people. Rural populations moved to urban centers to escape bombings and battles, those who were targeted by death squads moved around the country in search of safety, and many who were threatened by the war left El Salvador for Guatemala, Honduras, Mexico, Costa Rica, Belize, the United States, Canada, Australia, and Europe (Aguayo and Fagen 1988). By the time that peace accords were signed in 1992, 25 percent of the Salvadoran population had been displaced (Byrne 1996), and Salvadoran activists in Los Angeles estimated that approximately one million of these individuals were in the United States (personal communication).

During the early 1980s, when the influx of Salvadorans to the United States began, official papers were not as important as they have since come to be. Few of the Salvadorans who came to the United States during this period had permission to be in this country. Only those who owned property or were well educated could obtain visas, so most migrants hired smugglers, known as *coyotes,* to bring them through Guatemala and Mexico and into the United States. On arrival, these illicit travelers became illegal aliens, persons whose presence is unauthorized and who are subject to detention and deportation if apprehended by the INS. Though they lacked green cards and travel permits, these immigrants were able to work, attend school, rent apartments, obtain drivers licenses or identification cards, and so forth. It is true that their jobs were often low paying, that the need to work extra jobs made it difficult to go to school, and that housing was often cramped and of poor quality, but work permits did not exist, and papers, though helpful, were not a necessity. For these early immigrants, the chief drawback of their undocumented status was the risk of being caught by the INS. Most therefore avoided government officials, if possible. Because many of these people intended to return to El Salvador in a year or two, by which time the political situation would surely have calmed, legal status in the United States would be unnecessary. If they were apprehended and if they were either knowledgeable or lucky enough to obtain legal advice, Salvadorans sometimes did apply for political asylum.

Though such petitions had little chance of being granted—the approval rate was only 2 percent during this period (USCR 1986)—an asylum application would delay deportation until a case was decided, a process that, including appeals, could take years.

This (in retrospect) relatively tolerable situation[11] changed in 1986 with the passage of the Immigration Reform and Control Act (IRCA).[12] IRCA imposed sanctions on employers who knowingly hired undocumented workers, called for the creation of an employment authorization document (EAD), and established an amnesty program through which individuals who had been continuously and illegally present in the United States since January 1, 1982, could apply for permanent residency. The earliest Salvadoran immigrants qualified for the amnesty program and were able to obtain residency and eventually citizenship. For the bulk of the Salvadoran immigrant population, however, the law had primarily adverse effects. Although employer sanctions have not been fully enforced and therefore have not prevented illegal immigration (Bean, Edmonston, and Passel 1990; Calavita 1990),[13] IRCA has made it more difficult for the undocumented to find work. Employer sanctions unofficially codified distinctions between working in the primary and secondary labor markets,[14] in that established firms have required proof of work authorization as part of their hiring processes, whereas businesses (such as restaurants, hotels, and factories) that employ unskilled workers on a temporary or part-time basis are less particular about employees' immigration status. Those who lack EADs (also known as *permisos* [work permits]) therefore have more restricted work options and less job security.

The implementation of IRCA's employer-sanctions provisions led to a demand for work authorization among the undocumented and to a proliferation of public notaries advertising themselves as immigration specialists. Though such quasi-legal "law offices" were not new—particularly in Spanish-speaking areas, where migrants are misled by the fact that *notario,* a Spanish word for "attorney," has a different meaning in English—the amnesty program, with its complex application forms and documentation requirements, gave these institutions a boost (Mahler 1995). When immigrants who could not qualify for amnesty began seeking a means to avoid the impact of employer sanctions, these public notaries responded. Because asylum applicants were entitled to work permits while their applications were pending, notaries began filing asylum applications for clients who sought work permits. These applications, which were poorly prepared and often blatantly fraudulent, did generate work permits for applicants,[15] many of whom thought that they had applied only for work authorization, not for asylum. As the number of asylum applicants increased, so too did the time needed to process their cases, meaning that asylum applications sometimes bought years of temporary legal status in the United States.[16]

As U.S. immigration policy became more restrictive, the civil war in El Salvador dragged on. Efforts to negotiate a peace agreement faltered (Aguilera Peralta 1988; Córdova Macías 1988), and in 1989 the guerrilla forces launched a "final offensive," designed to demonstrate their military strength. During this offensive, Salvadoran death squads assassinated six Jesuit priests, their housekeeper, and her daughter. International condemnation of the assassinations was swift and severe, and peace negotiations resumed in 1990.

The early 1990s were watershed years for the Salvadoran populace. In the United States, years of struggling for refugee status finally resulted in legislation that granted TPS to Salvadorans who had entered the United States before September 19, 1990. At the same time, an out-of-court settlement was reached in *American Baptist Churches v. Thornburgh,* the lawsuit filed against the U.S. government by religious and refugee-service organizations in 1985. The agreement acknowledged that foreign policy and other ideological considerations were irrelevant to the merits of an asylum claim and granted Salvadorans who had entered the United States before September 19, 1990, and Guatemalans who had entered before October 1, 1990, the right to de novo asylum interviews under special rules designed to ensure fear hearings. Then in 1992, peace negotiations resulted in an agreement that officially ended the Salvadoran civil war (see Córdova Macías 1993). With the signing of the peace accords, it was safe (on paper, at least) for Salvadoran émigrés in the United States to return home. By this time, however, many had established themselves in the United States and fully intended to stay.

Salvadorans who wished to legalize their sojourn in the United States had to negotiate a complex set of obstacles and dilemmas. TPS and the ABC settlement agreement were designed to address the needs of refugees who were fleeing civil war and political persecution. Could these remedies be renegotiated to serve an immigrant community whose most compelling reasons for seeking residency were the lives that they had established in the United States? Despite the peace accords, the civil war produced indelible wounds and ongoing psychological traumas in many of its victims. Would these victims be able to persuade U.S. officials that it would be unjust to return them to the sites of their persecution? Anti-immigrant sentiment rose and U.S. immigration policy became more restrictive in the mid-1990s, precisely when Salvadorans' temporary permission to remain in the United States was running out. How would Salvadorans attempt to counter this sentiment? Would they define themselves as an exceptional case, distinct from the mass of undocumented migrants seeking legitimacy? Or would they challenge anti-immigrant discourse itself, suggesting that policies that exclude people on the basis of their immigration status are unjust? These were among the questions that I set out to investigate in June 1995, when I returned to Los Angeles, funding in hand, to do ethnographic research about Salvadorans' legalization strategies.

Ethnography

In the course of my research regarding Salvadorans' efforts to negotiate their legal identities, I spent countless hours sitting in the lobbies or waiting areas of the organizations where I did fieldwork when someone whom I had come to see was delayed in a meeting or when a client whom I had been asked to assist arrived late. Staff members who passed through would laugh with surprise, and say, "Susan! You look just like a client!" Eventually, I learned to bring reading or other work, spend this unanticipated "extra" time leafing through organizations' asylum manuals, and sit at an unoccupied desk (like a staff member) instead of in the waiting area (like a client). This extra time and the ambiguity of my presence in the waiting areas nonetheless reveal something of the position that I occupied during research. Like a client, I had to contend with the tactics through which community organizations managed the onslaught of clients seeking their services as well as with the realities of nonprofit organizations that lacked funding for secretaries, full-time receptionists, good computer systems, and other such infrastructure. Clients and visiting researchers (of which I was not the only one) who wished to meet with staff members had to telephone repeatedly to get past answering machines, wait around until overworked staff could find a spare moment, learn which times of day people were most likely to be in their offices, and accept the possibility that a scheduled meeting could fall through unexpectedly. Like a staff member, I learned to negotiate organizational spaces, moving past waiting areas directly to the offices where staff members were actually working. I was eventually given direct phone numbers so that I could bypass recorded phone systems. I learned that the counterpart of scheduled appointments falling through was the possibility of spur-of-the moment meetings. And, like a staff person, I worked directly with clients in preparing their immigration cases.

My time in waiting areas was not wasted, however, as the history of these organizations' political struggles was to be seen on the walls. Various posters commemorated the assassination of Archbishop Romero, proclaimed that Central Americans were refugees, featured the Statue of Liberty, promoted naturalization, announced that no human being is illegal, and advertised the scenic beauty and archaeological wealth of Central America. Bulletin boards (which I had ample opportunity to study) contained announcements about upcoming events, protest marches, services available to low-income people, and job and educational opportunities. Flyers from local Central American restaurants, entertainers, and courier services were available on tables, along with Salvadoran free weekly newspapers, brochures about organizations, and information about U.S. immigration law. Detailed maps of Central America were also often prominently displayed, as were crafts and other products available for purchase. This material sometimes sparked conversations among waiting clients, who reminisced about life in El Salvador, their trips to the United States, and their legal experiences, while their children wandered around playing with whatever they happened to find or disappeared into bathrooms or down hallways only to be retrieved by their parents. Though staff members maintained a pleasant and professional atmosphere, these organizations had an air of warm dishevelment that made it clear that they were nonprofit entities rather than corporate offices.

The bulk of my time during fieldwork was not, of course, spent in waiting areas but rather in conducting interviews, attending meetings and events, observing interaction between clients and legal-service providers, sitting in on court hearings, doing volunteer work, and attending training sessions regarding immigration law. I worked primarily with three organizations during my research: ASOSAL, El Rescate, and CARECEN. These were the three most prominent Salvadoran community organizations that provided legal services in Los Angeles. I focused on these groups because they were located at the intersection of law and politics, in multiple senses. Each of these organizations grew out of the political struggle in El Salvador, and each pursued political change in the United States as well. El Rescate and CARECEN were founded in the early 1980s by activists associated with different popular organizations in El Salvador. ASOSAL, which grew out of CARECEN, was founded much more recently, in the early 1990s, as part of the campaign to extend TPS for Salvadorans. Though organizations' strategies and philosophies have differed somewhat over the years, each of these groups strives to improve the situation of Salvadorans in the United States as well as to promote human rights and economic development in El Salvador. Learning about these organizations' legal-services programs as well as the ways that these programs were connected to other goals of the organizations, enabled me to understand how Salvadoran community activists were interpreting and applying U.S. immigration law, the political significance of immigration policies, and the outcomes of Salvadorans' legal strategies. I was also able to observe how clients represented their own legal histories and legal needs to service providers who clients hoped would accept their cases.

In addition to my fieldwork within community organizations, I interviewed a total of ninety community activists, legal-service providers, and Central Americans with pending immigration cases. When interviewees granted permission, interviews were tape-recorded.[17] When interviewees preferred not to be recorded, I transcribed the interview from notes as soon as possible after each interview was completed. Pseudonyms have been used for all interviewees throughout this text as well as in my own notes and interview transcripts. In the cases of activists and legal-service providers, I used a "snowball" approach to locating potential interviewees—that is, I began with activists and service providers whom I met in the course of my fieldwork and then asked these individuals to suggest other people to interview. Interviews with activists covered the history of their own and their organizations' activism, their journeys to the

United States and their own legalization experiences, their strategies and goals as activists, and their opinions about the nature of and changes within the Salvadoran immigrant community. Interviews with legal-service providers—some of whom were Central American but many of whom were not—focused on their strategies in representing clients, the goals of their legal work, their opinions of U.S. immigration law and policy, and the dilemmas that they had confronted as legal advocates. I attempted to use a snowball approach in interviewing clients of community organizations, but it proved unsuccessful. Given the current public uproar about immigration policy, individuals whom I had not met personally were unwilling to risk talking to a stranger about their immigration situations. Therefore, to interview people who were attempting to legalize, I had to rely primarily on direct contacts with clients whom I met at community organizations. Interviews with organizations' clients were generally conducted at locations of their choosing—homes, restaurants, public parks, or community organizations' offices. These interviews usually lasted two or three hours and covered immigrants' reasons for leaving their home countries, their journey to the United States, their experiences of U.S. immigration law, and their goals and plans.

To round out the perspective that I developed through interviews and fieldwork in community organizations, I participated in a variety of other events. When possible, I attended the court hearings of people I had interviewed or of other clients on whose cases I had worked. I participated in demonstrations and other political campaigns and coalitions regarding Central Americans' legal status. When permitted to do so, I attended meetings between legal advocates and the INS. I attended meetings and events of Comunidades (Communities), a federation of Salvadoran hometown associations in Los Angeles. I participated in training sessions and meetings sponsored by such groups as CHIRLA (Coalition for Humane Immigrant Rights of Los Angeles) and NILC (National Immigration Law Center). These gatherings were intended for legal-service providers and provided technical information about developments in immigration law and policy. I also attended community events, such as the Central American Independence Day Parade, Central American festivals, and so forth. Through these methods, I sought to become better informed about the meanings, significance, and relevance of immigration law and legal status within the establishment and political enfranchisement of the Salvadoran community in Los Angeles.

The fact that my research coincided with a period of immigration reform made this project simultaneously easier and more difficult. The project was easier in that immigration reform was being debated in the press, activists were discussing strategies, coalitions were forming, and campaigns were being launched. I was able to witness firsthand the ways that legislative changes affected immigrants' chances of legalization. The project was more difficult in that people with pending legalization cases were more fearful of being deported and therefore more nervous about talking to me. At El Rescate and CARECEN, where I was working directly with clients in the preparation of their cases, attorneys asked me not to use information for research purposes unless I first obtained clients' written consent. In consultation with attorneys, I developed a consent form that I asked clients to sign if they were willing for me to use information about their cases for this study. Many balked, as they were already nervous about applying for political asylum or about the outcome of their immigration cases. One woman who agreed to sign the form told me that if I had been doing this project in El Salvador, merely the words with which the consent form began ("I am investigating . . .") would have endangered my life. When clients were reluctant to sign the form, I did not press them but rather set the form aside and simply worked on their cases. When I was sitting in on attorney-client interviews, attorneys usually only asked for client's oral consent, which was almost always forthcoming—though some clients first wanted attorneys' assurances that the *gringa* (my word, not theirs) sitting in front of them did not work for the INS. I was extremely careful regarding the confidentiality of research materials and, to the detriment of my own filing system, used pseudonyms in all notes, interview transcripts, and quotations. I also changed information that could potentially identify individuals, such as the names of their hometowns. I was careful about my note taking and set my notebook aside whenever politically or emotionally sensitive topics, such as accounts of the inner workings of Salvadoran political groups or the assassination of family members, arose. When individuals agreed to be interviewed, they were usually quite open. Nonetheless, I was careful not to ask questions that might be deemed too invasive, such as whether an individual had been tortured.

My decision to focus on the legal and political activities of Salvadoran community organizations had advantages and disadvantages. Unlike community-based studies, which generally focus either on a particular community of origin or a particular residential community in the United States (see, e.g., Hagan 1994), the individuals whom I interviewed about their pending immigration cases were scattered around Los Angeles, and few of them knew each other. (The activists and legal-service providers whom I interviewed usually did know each other and participated in overlapping social and professional networks.) In addition to spending time in waiting areas, I spent quite a bit of time driving. I did not get to participate in as many informal conversations among people with pending legalization cases, interview as broad a cross section of the immigrant community, or follow the nuances of individuals' cases as closely as I might have had I focused on a particular community. Conversely, I did follow certain legalization cases from applications for asylum or suspension of deportation through court hearings to the ultimate outcome. Because I focused on community organizations and their clientele, I tended to meet people who wanted legal status rather than those who were uninterested in work permits or green cards and who therefore never sought the services of community organizations. Also, the people whose hearings I attended tended to be those whose cases had been accepted by community organizations on the grounds that they had a good chance of winning. This potential bias was countered by the fact that, when I was in court, I observed other cases that were not necessarily strong. Moreover, because I was interested in the criteria used to allocate legal status, learning how the strength of a case is determined was an important part of this research.

In short, I viewed my research as an ethnography of a legal process rather than of a particular group of people. This legal process begins when individuals cross the U.S.-Mexico border, continues through their various formal and informal encounters with immigration law, and concludes (temporarily, at least) with their deportation or legalization. The individuals involved in this process include immigrants themselves, the authorities and other individuals whose actions led them to emigrate, activists who sought to influence U.S. immigration and foreign policies, public notaries who probably performed the majority of immigration-related legal work, community organizations that sought to educate immigrants about the law and to provide low-cost or free legal services, attorneys who represented clients on a pro bono basis, private attorneys who had their own practices, trial attorneys who represented the U.S. government during immigration proceedings, judges and other officials who decided immigration cases, employers who evaluated job applicants' work eligibility, legislators and other officials who formulated immigration law and policy, and legal advocates who monitored immigration policies and challenged those they considered unjust. My research methodology allowed me to obtain detailed and nuanced understandings of the perspectives of immigrants, activists, and the attorneys and staff associated with community organizations. My understandings of the perspectives of other actors, such as trial attorneys, notaries, judges, and legislators, is more secondhand, though I did have occasion to observe some of these people in court.[18] My own perspective on immigration law most closely resembles that of a paralegal, as I did not have the legal training that attorneys do, I did not have a pending legalization case as their clients do, I did not have the formal organizational affiliations that activists do, and I did not decide cases as judges do. Like paralegals, however, I learned how to prepare individuals' cases, complete forms, assemble documentation packets, prepare declarations in support of an application, evaluate individuals' legalization options, and so forth. Unlike paralegals, I also had the opportunity to work with multiple community organizations, interview legalization applicants in their homes, and attend numerous immigration hearings. This book attempts to convey and analyze the perspectives of the various people I came to know during this process.

Each of the following chapters details a different aspect of Salvadoran immigrants' efforts to negotiate their legal identities in the United States from the early 1980s through 1997. Chapter 2, the theoretical heart of the book, analyzes U.S. immigration law as a system that exceeds its institutional form and that simultaneously produces and erases "persons." The third, fourth, and fifth chapters are the ethnographic heart of the book, as each describes the negotiation of immigration law in a different context. Chapter 3 focuses on the understandings of immigration law that are produced through the enforcement of immigration law as well as on the legal strategies that these understandings suggest. Chapter 4 examines the interpretations of law and of legal identities that are produced through interaction between community organizations that provide free legal services to immigrants and the clients of these organizations. Chapter 5 turns to the formal legal arena, examining how immigrants' and advocates' legal strategies fare when confronted with official law in the form of officials' decisions and judges' rulings. Together, these three chapters follow individuals' legal experiences from their entries into the United States, through their various formal and informal encounters with immigration law, to either a deportation order or a grant of legal status. Chapter 6 turns from a microanalysis of the dynamics of these legal processes to the big picture—namely, the significance of Salvadorans' legal strategies given political events in El Salvador, immigration reform in the United States, and the increasingly transnational nature of political, economic, and social institutions. The concluding chapter comments on the realities that immigration law is likely to address in the future. The book demonstrates that far from being marginal or segregated social processes, the practices that define individuals' legal statuses are central to determining and contesting what it means to be an American.

Chapter 2

Illegality and the Spaces of Nonexistence

Examining the complex ways that undocumented Central Americans are situated within and outside of both the United States and their countries of origin reveals that existence itself has multiple dimensions. Individuals who are physically present and socially active in the United States can nonetheless lack legal status in this country. Conversely, individuals who are legally present in El Salvador and who have Salvadoran citizenship can be persecuted in ways that negate both their citizenship and their humanity. I refer to the domains occupied by such legal nonsubjects as spaces of nonexistence. Individuals enter such spaces not only when they cross international borders without authorization but also when they are involved in clandestine activities, when they are abducted and secretly assassinated by death squads, and when they hide to avoid being captured and tortured. Nonexistence, like existence, therefore takes multiple forms, ranging from social isolation to physical destruction to legal and political removal. It would not be inaccurate to view certain migrants' entire sojourn in the United States as an attempt to escape persecution by making themselves not exist in their homelands. Nonexistence, however, is often incomplete in that migrants, refugees, dissidents, and death-squad targets continue to live, work, eat, play, visit, and so forth. In fact, there are multiple nonexistences and gradations of existence. It might be most accurate to say that, like characters who experience a temporal rift in a Star Trek episode, such individuals come in and out of existence and exist simultaneously in multiple ways, depending on the frame of reality being used (see also Stoler and Cooper 1997:6–7).

Although spaces of nonexistence share certain features of domains that have been characterized as subversive, they are largely sites of subjugation. Spaces and persons that transcend or transgress borders of various sorts have recently been celebrated for the challenges that they pose to established structures and categories (Featherstone 1995; Malkki 1995b). Borderlands, for example, have been seen as sites of resistance where a modus vivendi that redefines the social order can be devised (Anzaldua 1987; Gupta and Ferguson 1997; Rosaldo 1989). Similarly subjugated discourses have been used to expose the structures of power that render these discourses dangerous or illegitimate (Abu-Lughod 1986; Peteet 1991). My focus on nonexistence shares certain features of these projects. For example, by examining the practices and discourses that make nonexistence both necessary and real, I seek to expose and decenter boundaries between the legal and the illegal, the legitimate and the illegitimate, and the overt and the clandestine. While such decentering could have political and even counterhegemonic implications, spaces of nonexistence themselves are largely loci of repression. Nonexistence is produced through excluding people, limiting rights, restricting services, and erasing personhood. Although there are sometimes advantages to not existing, as when a political activist enters clandestinity to challenge repressive practices, I cannot celebrate this space. I can, however, attempt to make both it and its occupants visible.

This chapter attempts an ethnography of the multiple borders between existence and nonexistence. I begin by detailing the practices that render undocumented immigrants legally absent. I then situate such legal absences within Central Americans' narratives of persecution and exile. This relocation reveals that, for at least certain migrants, legal clandestinity is a continuation rather than an initiation of nonexistence. I next examine the impossibility of complete nonexistence and the limited relevance of law. To do so, I recount the various ways in which undocumented immigrants assert their social, physical, and thus potentially legal presences. Finally, I note ways that immigrants sometimes turn nonexistence to their advantage and thereby subvert the power of immigration law.

Spaces of Nonexistence

The spaces of nonexistence occupied by the undocumented derive from the conflation of and disjuncture between physical and legal presence. Physical and legal presence are conflated in that citizens are assumed to be located within particular national territories (Gupta and Ferguson 1997), physical presence confers certain legal rights (J. Bhabha 1996; Churgin 1996), and periods of continuous residence are often prerequisites for legalization and naturalization. A disjuncture between physical and legal presence arises when individuals cross or remain within borders without legal authorization. This disjuncture renders unauthorized immigrants legally absent, as one activist who was involved in Salvadoran immigrants' struggle for legal status in the United States explained: "We need to be here legally or its like we're not here." Another activist who had worked clandestinely with a Salvadoran political organization recalled his days as an undocumented immigrant: "Everything we did was illegal! We had no recognition from the Salvadoran government! We had no recognition from the U.S. government! We didn't exist!" Similarly, a formerly undocumented Salvadoran community college student noted that without a work permit, "you don't exist. Well, they know you are there, but they ignore you. They don't see you as like you exist. And this is the people who raise children, and you know, whenever they come, 'Well, they're illegals.'" These comments indicate that those who do not exist legally are imagined to be "outside," in an "underground" (Harwood 1986), or "not there" (see Chavez 1991, 1992; Coombe 1997; Coutin 1993). The undocumented therefore exist in a nondomain, a space of illegality (see L. Sanchez 1998). Often conflated with criminals (Malkki 1992), unauthorized immigrants are officially outside both the law and the social body (Hull 1985; Fuchs 1985).

Like its residents, the space of nonexistence both is and is not there. This space is imagined in that like other social spaces, it is culturally constructed and demarcated (B. Anderson 1991; Caldeira 1996; Clifford 1997; Gupta and Ferguson 1997; Malkki 1992; Shapiro 1988; Sorkin 1992). At the same time, this space is real in that the practices that make people not exist have material effects, ranging from hunger (Ellis 1998) to unemployment to death (American Friends Service Committee 1992; Americas Watch 1993; EBSC

1997; Ellingwood 1998). The materiality of imagined nonexistences is conveyed vividly by a graphic that accompanied a Tucson newspaper's series on the 1986 amnesty program. This graphic depicts a Hispanic-looking man standing behind a wire mesh fence with the caption, "They overcame their fears, came out of the shadows and walked into legalization offices" (*Tucson Citizen* 1987). Given that most amnesty applicants were not actually in detention centers, the fence that locates the applicant in the shadows is a legal rather than physical barrier. In both visual and verbal depictions of the undocumented, this barrier appears as shadow, fence, underground, separation, and exclusion, indicating that the illegality of the undocumented materializes around them wherever they go, like a force field that sets them apart from the legally privileged.

To describe the features of nonexistence, I detail the practices that locate the undocumented on the other side of this imagined fence—assuming for the moment that people can be confined to this space. One such practice is limiting reality to that which can be documented. Because many undocumented immigrants live with relatives, employers, or coworkers, their physical presence is not always documented. Recent arrivals reduce their expenses by sharing apartments with other individuals. Their names may not appear on utility accounts, leases, or rent receipts. Women who work as live-in domestics reside in homes that are not their own (Maher 1997). These women's employers—many of whom are violating tax and labor codes—are rarely eager to officially acknowledge their employees' presence (Hagan 1994). If the undocumented attempt to prove that they have been continuously present in the United States since a particular date, which is a prerequisite for certain means of legalization, these immigrants find that unregistered presences are deemed absences. Consider the following example. Suppose that a woman enters the United States in 1987 and works as a live-in domestic for two years. In 1989, she moves into her own apartment, obtains a California identification card, and gets a job in the garment industry, where she is officially on the payroll. In 1997, she applies for asylum, loses, and is placed in removal proceedings. If she can prove that she has been in the United States for ten years, she may be eligible for cancellation of removal. She has no documentation of her first two years in the United States, however, as all residential records were in her employer's name, her employer will not sign an affidavit certifying that she was here, and she has no medical, school, or other records of her presence during this period. A judge could deny her application on the grounds that she can only prove continuous residence for eight years. So, where was she during the first two years? She was not in her country of origin, but she was not here either. She was in a space of nonexistence.

Another practice that situates the undocumented in a nonlocation is the temporalization of presence. Because accumulating years of continuous presence can help to qualify the undocumented for legalization, attorneys and immigration officials speak as though an invisible immigration timepiece is measuring the temporal presence of illegal aliens. For example, ten years of continuous presence are required to qualify for cancellation of removal. As a result, an undocumented immigrant who has only been in the United States for seven years must manage to remain in this country for another three years so that the clock will strike ten. Yet, as noted earlier, presences that are completely unregistered cannot count toward completing required periods of continuous residence for legalization purposes. Moreover, temporal presences that fall short of the requirements do not confer equity on the undocumented. Additionally, the clock can be stopped on the accumulation of time, propelling the undocumented into a temporal void. According to the 1996 Illegal Immigration Reform and Immigrant Responsibility Act (IIRIRA), the issuance of a notice to appear in court stops the immigration timepiece, so that, for example, an immigrant who has only been in the United States for five years when summoned to court cannot accumulate more time. IIRIRA also created a new temporality: illegal time.[1] Individuals who are in the United States without authorization after April 1, 1997, accumulate illegal time. If these individuals accumulate 180 days of illegal time and then leave the United States, they are barred from reentering for a period of three years. A full year of illegal time activates a ten-year bar on reentry. Like a financial account, a surfeit of illegal time must be balanced by a period of nonresidency.

The undocumented are also denied existence by policies that define wage labor—a key marker of presence, personhood, and citizenship (Engel and Munger 1996; Thomas 1985)—as a privilege that states can either grant or deny to particular categories of persons (see Bosniak 1991). Because the undocumented lack authorization, they cannot officially work. Some try to define their labor as something other than work.[2] For example, the undocumented can provide gardening and other services as independent contractors or can participate in the informal economy as self-employed street vendors. Others work under false pretenses, with fake IDs and invented social security numbers. Through such practices, the undocumented pretend to exist. Unofficial workers are often paid in cash, leaving no record of their supposed employment. When asked to recount their work history for the past five years, as is required on many immigration forms, such unofficial workers hesitate, saying, "I was only paid in cash." Prohibited work that is unreported, unregistered, and untaxed cannot always be proven to have occurred. Low wages problematize unofficial workers' material existence, while lack of employment records impedes legal recognition of their physical and temporal presences.[3]

The undocumented are further rendered nonexistent by policies that make their kin ties legally inert for immigration purposes. Lacking legal status themselves, the undocumented cannot petition for the legalization of their parents or other relatives, and they also lack the right to leave and reenter the United States so that they can visit relatives abroad. Worse yet, the undocumented can be arbitrarily separated from their relatives. For example, suppose that a woman who is undocumented marries a man who is a legal permanent resident, and they have two children who are U.S. citizens by birth. Although her husband can petition for her, this woman will be undocumented until a visa becomes available. If she is apprehended by the INS and is found ineligible for legal relief, she can be removed to her country of origin, even though her husband and children have legal status in the United States. The recent controversy over a section of immigration law known as 245(i) exposes the legal aconsanguinity of the undocumented. Section 245(i) permitted undocumented immigrants to adjust their status in the United States instead of having to return to their countries of origin (see *La Opinión* 1998). When IIRIRA created illegal time with its consequent bars on reentry, 245(i) assumed new significance. If immigrants who accumulated illegal time had to leave the United States to obtain family visas, then the bars on reentry would be triggered. Because 245(i) was slated to expire (and did so in January 1998), families had to choose between splitting up so that they could preserve rights to green cards or forgoing the possibility of legalization. The unauthorized discovered that they could not reverse the laws of descent so that having U.S. citizen children conferred legal rights on undocumented parents. In the space of nonexistence, they could not be full social persons.

Undocumented immigrants are also positioned outside the law in that many of their daily practices must be clandestine. To pretend to exist, the undocumented purchase false identification cards. Those whose income is not reported find it difficult to pay their income taxes. The undocumented perform unauthorized work. They labor in sweatshops, fields, homes, and elsewhere, often in conditions that violate federal and state labor codes. Denied driver's licenses (in California, at least), they drive without authorization. Without driver's licenses, they cannot obtain car insurance as required by law. Lacking travel documents, their entries and exits are clandestine. Instead of petitioning for relatives, they smuggle them into the country. The field of illegality that surrounds the undocumented renders such commonplace actions as working, traveling, and driving illicit.

Finally, the unauthorized are confined to illegality through practices that limit their mobility. Subjected to detention and deportation if apprehended, the undocumented sometimes limit their travel, staying home, avoiding areas where immigration officials conduct raids, staying away from checkpoints, and moving about only as necessary. One Guatemalan migrant characterized this situation as "democracy with a stick." He explained, "You are free to move about to whatever place within the United States as long as you have the required papers. A visa or green card is required to leave the Los Angeles area.⁴ . . . If you are illegal, you don't have freedom of movement. You go from your workplace to your house and as much as possible you avoid contact with the authorities." A Salvadoran immigrant expressed a similar sense of confinement, noting that he and his wife could not take their daughter to Sea World until his wife received a new work permit. Without the work permit, the family would not be able to pass through the San Clemente checkpoint on their way between their home in Los Angeles and Sea World in San Diego. Ironically, or perhaps logically, the unauthorized movement of the undocumented renders them immobile. Sometimes defined by their mobility as "boat people," "feet people," or a "flood" (see Coutin 1993), when they enter a space of nonexistence, the undocumented are confined to social and territorial nonlocations. Immobility, which in medical practice could be a sign of death, prevents full social personhood. Because the undocumented are denied public assistance, financial aid, college admission, and work authorization, they find that their social mobility is as limited as their physical mobility (J. Craig Jenkins 1978; Portes 1978).

Having identified the practices that produce legal nonexistence, it remains to delimit the boundaries of this otherworld. The space of legal nonexistence is often referred to as another place, elsewhere, distant from the reality inhabited by those who are legal. For example, a recent *Los Angeles Times* article about the legalization quest of a Salvadoran man who had lived in the United States for years was entitled, "Hunting a Way In" (McDonnell 1997a). Where are those who, like animals, "hunt" a way "in"? Terms like *underground* suggest that this place is frequented by shady characters, perhaps the sort of place that mobsters hung out in the 1930s or where drug dealers do business. Where is this forbidden place? Consider for a moment the actual places where the undocumented can be found: shopping centers; apartment buildings; restaurants; buses; factories; businesses; grocery stores; homes. These places only become an underground when the undocumented are present, and these places are forbidden only to the undocumented.[5] In short, the physical dimensions of the space of nonexistence coincide with the territorial boundaries of the United States. Because undocumented people's bases for social membership are negated—blood ties, labor, presence, humanity—they are forbidden to be in the United States. The undocumented are therefore situated "outside" of U.S. territory, in a realm of nonexistence. They only have to be legally outside the United States because they are physically in the United States. The space of legal nonexistence is therefore a hidden dimension of the space of social and physical existence. The potential congruity of these dimensions can make it difficult to determine the location of particular individuals.

There are multiple senses in which migrants can be said to not exist. In the case of Salvadorans, among whom I have been doing research since the mid-1980s, becoming an unauthorized immigrant is often a continuation rather than an initiation of nonexistence.

Disappearing

Central Americans' narratives about civil war, political persecution, and immigration to the United States reveal multiple sorts of nonexistence. To these immigrants, the legal nonexistence conferred by entering the United States without authorization is merely the latest in a series of violent erasures of personhood. Death-squad activity in El Salvador and Guatemala not only killed people but annihilated them, ripping them from their homes, tearing them limb from limb, destroying houses and property, massacring communities, and discarding limbs and bodies in trash dumps or in the streets. Those who feared that they would be subjected to such violence often sought to save themselves by disappearing before authorities could destroy them. Potential death-squad targets cut off their social ties, avoided family and friends, stopped working, gave up their studies, abandoned their homes, moved from place to place, slept in fields instead of houses, went into hiding, and sometimes left the country. Emigrating to the United States can therefore be understood as an attempt to make oneself not exist in one's country of origin. Central Americans sometimes drew parallels between their experiences as fugitives from political repression and as fugitives from U.S. immigration authorities. Some emigrants, for example, compared the INS to death squads, deportation to exile, and U.S. immigration policy to repressive policies in their homelands. Such comparisons reveal that nonexistence in the United States has political as well as legal, social, and physical dimensions.

Whether recounted to legal workers, INS officials, or visiting anthropologists, Central Americans' narratives of persecution and flight often describe an earlier, happier time, prior to the onset of civil conflict, when the subjects of these narratives existed socially, physically, and legally in their countries of origin. Such accounts implicitly or explicitly contrast this happier time with tellers' subsequent difficulties. Maria Bonilla, a Salvadoran woman who had been targeted by the military due to a nephew's involvement with the guerrillas, recalled her life in El Salvador: "Why did I have to leave my mother and my father and everything that I had and come to this country? There we had a business. And we had a house. We were building onto the house. . . . And we were poor, but we had beds for all of us." Maria's description of her earlier life mentions family, a home, a business, plans for the future, and residential belonging—the beds for every family member.[6] These are precisely the elements of existence that are denied to unauthorized immigrants in the United States. Similarly, a former Salvadoran political prisoner told me of the indignation he felt when an asylum official suggested that he had come to the United States for economic reasons. He said that he told the official, "Do you know what I was doing in El Salvador? I was going to school. I worked. I had my own office. I had three secretaries. I dressed in a suit. And my wife—she was a doctor. She was very respected." Though as a professional, this man may have been better off than many migrants, his description of the completeness of his life—family, friends, studies, a home, a profession, respect—is typical. In retrospect, the normalcy of the emigrants' former lives seems a sharp contrast to their current illicitness. Angela Reyes, who was detained in Texas shortly after entering the United States, described her reaction to being imprisoned: "This was so different from my earlier experience. In El Salvador, I'd been studying, I'd been going to school, I was living with my family. It was terrible." Before civil war jeopardized their futures, migrants were forming families, pursuing careers, participating in social networks. They existed.

The outbreak of armed conflict in El Salvador at the end of the 1970s created new forms of nonexistence. Repression was nothing new to El Salvador, where some twenty-five thousand people were killed in 1932 following a peasant uprising (Byrne 1996). Prolonged civil war, however, created a polarization that left no room for neutrality. As a former political prisoner explained, "For the [Salvadoran] government, political struggle is stronger [than armed struggle]. . . . And this is the reason for the huge repression and the huge massacres, because [the authorities] abducted people. Upon suspecting someone, they captured him and killed his family." According to victims and observers, such suspects were abducted from their homes, their workplaces, or the street by heavily armed men wearing civilian clothing and driving vehicles that witnesses identified as being of government issue. Homes were ransacked in search of weapons, women were raped, and residents were lined up and massacred. Victims who were abducted were often interrogated under torture, killed, dismembered, and discarded. A survivor described her experience to me during an interview:

They abducted my father and me . . . [and] four other men, including my cousin, other cousins, and an uncle of mine. . . . They wanted to take us to an isolated place, where there was nothing. . . . And they took us, but little by little they were letting people go, and I spoke to them, "My uncle is in the civil patrols." But they didn't listen. But thus we walked and walked. By then it was about midnight, maybe, when they released my two cousins, they released my uncle, and they only had my cousin, my father, and me. They took us because to them I was the leader of the guerrillas, about which they were very mistaken. But I begged to God and said, "My God! It isn't possible, they are going to kill us unjustly! But I'm going to die together with my father." . . .

[After walking about three kilometers, the commander] said, "We are going to let you go, but you're going to run!" But my cousin wasn't released. They only released my father and me. . . . And yes, they got into a group and told us, "Go! Run! Go away! Run!" And I put my father in front, I covered my father with my back. "Papá!" I said to him, "Papaíto, run Papaíto! Run Papá! Run!" I could feel the bullets! I could feel the bullets! But I wanted to cover myself. If they fell on me, let them fall, but not on my father. But no, they didn't shoot at us, and we arrived home. . . .

But my cousin—there, when they released us in the middle of the night, there, in that place where they released us, there they just took my cousin to a coffee field and my cousin, they killed my cousin there, that same night. They broke his arms behind him, alive. Because there was a family that heard the cries. The family lived on that ranch, and . . . they heard my cousin cry like a child. Crying, calling for my uncle, my aunt, like a child! They broke his arms behind him, they put out his eyes, they broke his fingers, finger by finger. Because when they found him, that's how they found him. They skinned his head. . . . The last thing that they did was slit his throat. That was the end. Afterward they cut out his tongue. They tortured him completely.

Such accounts reveal that authorities treated a suspected subversive or guerrilla as someone who had betrayed the social order; someone who was dirty, dangerous, an animal; someone who deserved to be tortured, stamped out of existence, the body discarded as an example to others; someone who had neither legal nor human rights. Death-squad members seemingly did not differentiate among guerrillas, guerrilla supporters, and the uninvolved. Instead, the entire population was suspect (Green 1994; Stephen 1995). Torturers twisted, pulled, stamped, kicked, and cut suspected guerrillas, exposing their interiors. Like trash, victims were then thrown away. But as they were destroyed, alleged subversives were interrogated, a process that simultaneously defined and erased victims. Victims were defined in that they were named as subversives, guerrillas, the unwanted, illegals (see Coutin and Hirsch 1998). They were erased in that they were defaced, killed, or forced into exile. As they were defined and erased, pulled in and out of existence, victims were torn apart. Spaces of nonexistence are spaces of violence (Taylor 1997).

Central Americans who feared that persecution was imminent placed themselves in a space of nonexistence, saving authorities the trouble. Signs of having been targeted by death squads included anonymous threatening phone calls, warning letters left under doors, unidentified individuals asking one's whereabouts, knocks on doors in the middle of the night, shots fired into houses, threatening visits by armed men, and the abduction of relatives or colleagues. Confronted with such signs, potential victims often went into hiding, ceasing to work, abandoning their studies, moving from place to place, distancing themselves from family and friends.[7] They hid their existence, trying to be "not there." Sonya Hernandez, a Salvadoran woman whose family had experienced political difficulties when the government business where she worked had become unionized, recalled fleeing her hometown when she was nineteen: "We had to leave and move to the city. We can't go back to our *canton,* to where we're from, because there, they know us, so we're afraid. In the city, we weren't so afraid, because no one knew who we were. But we had to leave without anything. We left behind our money, our clothes, our land, everything." Fearing that they would fall victim to death squads, Sonya and her family became socially nonexistent. When two of Sonya's brothers were killed, the family dispersed even further, with her parents moving to the Guatemalan border and the rest of the family coming to the United States. The places where they were known became forever forbidden, as Sonya explained: "There, we have houses and we have lands, but it isn't safe for us. There, in the town that we're from, we're known, and the people who killed my brothers are still there and their hatred is deep. There's a lot of desire for vengeance. We can't go back there."

In such narratives of persecution and flight, illegal sojourn in the United States is a more extreme version of earlier efforts to hide. The space of legal nonexistence occupied by unauthorized immigrants is therefore another dimension of a previously entered space of social and political nonexistence. Like the undocumented, individuals who go into hiding within their countries of origin cannot work, be with their families, have residences, move about freely, or fulfill their plans for the future. Like legal nonexistence, social and political nonexistence is a spatial and temporal void. It is an asocial space, the *monte* (wild) where people sleep to avoid being captured by death squads (see Anker 1992). Like undocumented immigrants, those hiding from death squads engage in clandestine, illicit practices. They assume false identities, hire smugglers, pay bribes, travel through mountains and deserts, and enter a land where they continue to not exist. Clandestinity, not migration, marks many Central Americans' entry into nonexistence.

It is not unusual for Central Americans to draw connections between experiencing political persecution abroad and experiencing illegality in the United States. For example, Rodolfo Nuñez, a Salvadoran student activist who narrowly escaped assassination, commented that in the United States,

> it seems like we are living through the same anxiety that we lived through there in El Salvador, right? That is, sometimes when they say, "Here comes immigration." [It is] exactly like when they said there, "Here comes the [National] Guard," see. Everyone looks for a way of surviving at that moment, at that instant. There, to save one's life, here to save one's life too, to not have to return to one's country.

Like Rodolfo, Roberto and Alicia Mendez, Guatemalan migrants who fled to the United States after Roberto was detained and tortured, connected their need for legal existence in the United States to their fear of physical nonexistence in Guatemala. After a judge denied their asylum petition, Alicia told me, "The judge was making our tomb." Jorge Lima, a Salvadoran who had been active in opposition

groups in both the United States and El Salvador, attributed such
judicial decisions to the United States' lack of responsibility regarding the consequences of U.S. policies that destroyed lives in El Salvador. Jorge told me that the situation of Central American immigrants "is like when a woman has been raped and is pregnant, see?
Then there's a reality! Understand? She has conceived, and however
you try to exterminate that fact, it's a reality! You can't keep it a
secret. You may not register it in your structures, as though it never
existed. But yes, it did exist!" In this graphic image, El Salvador is a
raped woman, the United States is the rapist, Central American
immigrants are the illegitimate child, and U.S. immigration law is a
means of denying the child's existence. By failing to legalize its own
children/refugees, this activist asserts, the United States refused to
acknowledge its complicity in the violence that led Central Americans to flee their countries.[8] Yet though its existence is denied,
unregistered, even exterminated, the child continues to reassert
itself. Nonexistence cannot be sustained.

Being Here

The undocumented are not, of course, confined to spaces of nonexistence. Like the illegitimate child referred to by Jorge Lima, they are
a reality. Though they are not legally present, the undocumented get
jobs, rent apartments, buy property, go to school, get married, have
children, join churches, found organizations, and develop friend-
ships. On a day-to-day basis, their illegality may be irrelevant to most
of their activities, only becoming an issue in certain contexts, such as
when changing jobs, applying for college, or encountering an immigration official. The undocumented thus move in and out of existence. Much of the time they are undifferentiated from those around
them, but suddenly, when legal reality is superimposed on daily life,
they are once more in a space of nonexistence. The borders between
existence and nonexistence remain blurred and permeable.

Legal nonexistence does not prevent physical presence and
social participation because illegal immigration has long been
officially prohibited but unofficially tolerated (Calavita 1992; Chavez
1992; Delgado 1993; Harwood 1985). In a recent essay, Kitty Calavita
(1994) attributes this contradiction to three underlying tensions

within U.S. policy: (1) employers want cheap, immigrant labor, but native workers want immigration controls to prevent wages from declining; (2) policies that are in the interests of the native labor force and that could prevent illegal immigration, such as enforcing U.S. labor laws, are politically unpalatable; and (3) liberal democratic ideals conflict with the policing that would be required to bar illegal immigration. As a result, the legal sanctions that do exist can be easily flouted. Those who are deported can reenter the country (Heyman 1995), false identity documents are readily available to those who need them, employer sanctions are not fully enforced (Bean, Edmonston, and Passel 1990; Calavita 1990), and most INS enforcement efforts are directed toward the U.S.-Mexico border, creating a de facto tolerance for those who make it to the interior (Chavez 1992; Delgado 1993). Though they are barred from working, obtaining valid driver's licenses, or receiving certain social services, the undocumented are not legally prohibited from engaging in other sorts of transactions, such as renting homes. As a result, many who are officially illegal manage to live in the United States for years. Immigration law does affect the undocumented in profound, even life-threatening ways, but there are also many contexts in which it is simply irrelevant.

Because the legally nonexistent exist socially and physically, records of their presences can be generated. Attending classes produces school records, seeking medical assistance produces medical records, working can produce check stubs, and renting or purchasing a home produces deeds, leases, rent receipts, and utility bills. As the undocumented venture out of spaces of nonexistence, their presence becomes documented. If it is powerful enough, the social existence of the undocumented can confer legal status on them and thus pull them completely out of the space of legal nonexistence. Some scholars have recently argued that there is an implicit contract between migrant workers and the states in which their labor is employed (Bosniak 1991; Hammar 1994; Holston and Appadurai 1996). According to this implicit contract, when migrants contribute to a society through their labor, the society incurs certain obligations to migrants, such as the obligation to recognize them as full social and legal persons. Through various forms of social participation (going to school, forming a family, obtaining an address, working), migrants "imitate citizens" and thus act on the rights that this implied contract promises (see Singer 1988).[9] The principle that social citizenship and territorial presence confer legality has been recognized to some degree in U.S. immigration law as well. The rationale for creating an amnesty for immigrants who had been continually and illegally present in the United States since January 1, 1982 (see Hing 1986), was that individuals who were already de facto members of society ought to be allowed to regularize their stay. Suspension of deportation and cancellation of removal—two defenses available to aliens who are in deportation or removal proceedings—also allocate residency on the basis of social ties in the United States and periods of physical presence. Those who manage to make legal nonexistence irrelevant for long periods of time may eventually make it permanently irrelevant.

For Central Americans who came to the United States fearing that they would cease to exist physically in their countries of origin, extensive social existence and lengthy physical presence have become the strongest claim to legalization. This claim was articulated repeatedly during the rallies and vigils that led to the passage of NACARA in November 1997. At a weeklong vigil in front of the Los Angeles Federal Building, for example, two hundred fasting people and their supporters marched in a circle, chanting, "¡Aqui estamos! ¡Y no nos vamos!" "We are here! And we're not leaving!" As I listened to this slogan, I was suddenly reminded of the Dr. Seuss story *Horton Hears a Who!* To prevent the destruction of their world by those who doubted its existence, all the Whos in Whoville had to shout "We are here! We are here!" The assertion "¡Aqui estamos!" began to seem more important than the defiant "¡Y no nos vamos!" By asserting their presences—their ties to U.S. citizen children, their work, their tax payments, their time spent in the United States, their contributions to society—formerly undocumented Salvadorans and Guatemalans secured the collective right to apply for suspension of deportation in court, where they will individually reiterate these claims. Physical presence and social participation have proven stronger rationales for legalization than was the need to escape physical destruction.

Though legal nonexistence is a form of subjugation that most would like to escape, there are sometimes advantages to not existing, as those who do not exist have discovered.

FIG. 3.   Fasters and their supporters chant "¡Aquí estamos!
¡Y no nos vamos!" during vigil at the federal building in Los
Angeles. Photo by author.

The Art of Not Existing

Because they are placed outside the law, those who do not exist
legally are strangely liberated. Theirs may be the nebulous and
oppressive "freedom" experienced by the homeless and the unemployed, but it is nonetheless worthwhile to consider for a moment
the subversions that are made possible by nonexistence. If the
undocumented are not party to the social contract, they evade certain legal obligations. Though they are legally accountable for their
actions, their illicit presence is, in and of itself, a challenge to the
legal order, as advocates of immigration reform have noted (Fuchs
1985; Hull 1985). Illegal aliens' movements can avoid detection
and regulation, their income can be untaxed (Morales n.d.),[10] and
their actions can be clandestine.[11] The space of nonexistence
intrinsically defies a discipline that, according to Foucault
(1977:143), seeks to

eliminate the effects of imprecise distributions, the uncontrolled disappearance of individuals, their diffuse circulation, their unusable and dangerous coagulation; [discipline] was a tactic of anti-desertion, anti-vagabondage, anti-concentration. Its aim was to establish presences and absences, to know where and how to locate individuals, to set up useful communications, to interrupt others, to be able at each moment to supervise the conduct of each individual, to assess it, to judge it, to calculate its qualities or merits.

Unknowable, unquantifiable,[12] and illicit, the legally nonexistent seem potentially subversive to authorities. It is not a coincidence that the 1996 Antiterrorism and Effective Death Penalty Act (AEDPA) addressed immigration issues.[13]

The potential utility of nonexistence was not lost on Salvadoran activists who perfected the art of clandestinity. Just as death-squad targets hid their social existence in El Salvador, hoping to avoid being assassinated, political activists who deliberately engaged in politically risky activities sometimes cut off their social ties, assumed false identities, and distanced themselves from homes and relatives. These measures were taken to protect themselves, their families, and their organizations. A former member of one of the organizations that made up the FMLN explained that joining the political struggle meant that "you have to sacrifice many things—your family, your studies, your children, what you love—so that you can dedicate yourself to [the struggle]." Activists who emigrated to the United States both to save their lives and as emissaries for their political movements also experienced such denial of self, as one participant related: "We were denying ourselves everything. There were lots of divorces among my *compañeros.* Your life was at risk all the time! [It was at risk] physically, emotionally, mentally." The clandestinity of their political work securing funding, supplies, legitimacy, and even arms for their organizations in El Salvador was matched by their legal clandestinity as undocumented immigrants. A man who was involved in such work in Los Angeles in the 1980s recalled, "For us, being illegal was like a form of civil disobedience. It was part of the radicalism that we were practicing."

Even undocumented individuals who are politically inactive occasionally exploit their nonexistence. The undocumented can be paid under the table, and, depending on their relationship with their employers, can sometimes choose how much, if any, of their income to disclose to the government. The undocumented thus have some flexibility regarding what to make official and what to keep unofficial and therefore nonexistent. Clandestinity may be comforting to those who are trying to escape human rights abuses in their countries of origin. The undocumented also have some ability to create realities, for example, by using false documents to create a presence that was really an absence. Such fabrications were apparently quite common during the 1986 amnesty program. According to Hagan (1994:98), the INS's willingness to accept affidavits as proof of presence transformed the problem of not having been present in the United States since January 1, 1982—the cutoff date to be eligible for legalization—into "a short-term technical consideration, one that could be overcome (for at least some groups in the [undocumented Mayan] community)." Finally, clandestine absences do not officially interrupt one's continuous presence in the United States. At a public presentation on immigration law that I attended in January 1996, an immigrant asked the speaker—a paralegal who worked for a Central American community organization—whether the fact that he left the United States to visit relatives and thus interrupted his continuous presence disqualified him for the benefits of the ABC settlement agreement. The staff member asked how he traveled. "Pues, mojado" (illegally), the man answered. Choosing his words carefully, the speaker explained, "You don't qualify. You don't qualify because you went to El Salvador without permission. But you are the only one who knows you went."

Finally, like borderlands, the space of illegality produces innovative strategies and practices. Instead of being a "natural resource" of a given nation (see Chock 1995), migrants participate in multiple and globalized economies (Sassen 1989; Schiller, Basch, and Blanc 1995). In the case of El Salvador, remittances from Salvadoran migrants are a major source of national income (Darling 1996; Menjívar et al. 1998). In the United States, unauthorized Central American immigrants have also fueled local economies through the development of courier services and ethnic businesses (Lopez, Popkin, and Telles 1996; Hagan 1994; Mahler 1995). In contrast to the idea that one can only belong to one place (Malkki 1992; Gupta and Ferguson 1997), undocumented migrants, who live on the legal if not geographic boundary of nations, devise new concepts of citizenship and belonging (Basch, Schiller, and Blanc 1994; Hammar 1990). With families that span borders (Hondagneu-Sotelo 1994), transnational community relations (Hagan 1994; Kearney 1995a) and claims on multiple states, unauthorized immigrants can become constituencies in more than one locality. During a recent visit to Salvadorans in Los Angeles, the mayor of San Salvador told his audience that he and the mayor of Los Angeles "are the only two people in this world who are mayors of a city that has more than 250,000 Salvadorans." The same activists who greeted the mayor of San Salvador as "our mayor" have been campaigning for residency for Salvadorans in the United States. Multiple nonexistences give rise to multiple existences as an underestimated consequence of that which is politically, economically, and legally clandestine.

Conclusion

I cannot celebrate spaces of nonexistence. Even if these spaces are in some ways subversive, even if their boundaries are permeable, and even if they are sometimes irrelevant to individuals' everyday lives, nonexistence can be deadly. Legal nonexistence can mean being detained and deported, perhaps to life-threatening conditions. It can mean working for low wages in a sweatshop or being unemployed. It can mean the denial of medical care, food, social services, education, and public housing. And it can mean an erasure of rights and personhood thus making violence not only legitimate but even required. Legal, social, and physical nonexistences coalesce and separate. The violence that destroys lives also demands an erasure of legal personhood (see L. Sanchez 1998). Placing subversives or guerrillas outside of the legal order in a "lawless" realm justifies extreme actions and exempts authorities from their legal obligations to their citizenries. Likewise, the rights of those who do not exist legally in the United States are ambiguous (Hull 1985; Neuman 1996). Legal ideas of agency, causation, and individual culpability (Shapiro 1988; Wagner-Pacifici 1994) make it difficult to ascertain responsibility for illegal immigrants who drown in the Rio Grande, perish in the mountains when the INS militarizes easier routes, or are injured in confrontations with border patrol officers (see Kearney 1995a; L. Sanchez

1998). Moreover, social nonexistence is connected to physical and legal nonexistence in that hiding one's social existence is a means of preventing physical execution, and those who do not exist legally are made to not exist socially as well. Nonetheless, physical, legal, and social nonexistence are not the same thing, as demonstrated by the physical and social presence of the legally nonexistent. Identifying the relationships between yet incommensurability of multiple nonexistences is critical to understanding the power relations intrinsic to U.S. immigration law.

To definitively leave the space of legal nonexistence, unauthorized immigrants must obtain legal status. Doing so, however, is no easy task. Not only have U.S. immigration laws become more stringent in recent years, not only do the features of nonexistence (such as unregistered presences) pose particular obstacles to the undocumented, but also immigration law itself gives rise to a plethora of illicit legalities. When unauthorized immigrants act as these illicit legal subjects, they create divergent but not necessarily counterhegemonic immigration systems.

Chapter 3
Papeles, Permisos, and Permanence

In the domain of illegality occupied by unauthorized immigrants, immigration law assumes unique forms. The practices that render the unauthorized illicit produce legal subjectivities, strategies, and discourses that differ from those that are operative in formal legal proceedings such as deportation hearings. Official proceedings determine legality by assessing individuals' immigration records and legal histories. The practice of immigration law is not, however, limited to official proceedings, given that the enforcement of immigration law has been increasingly displaced from INS officials to employers and others who are required to verify individuals' identity documents. During such extrajudicial adjudications, status is assessed not according to individuals' life histories but rather by whether individuals possess the right papers. Potential and actual requests for identity documents therefore equate status with papers, define some individuals as undocumented, and give rise to a variety of enterprises—document forgery, immigration consulting, unlicensed legal practice, applications for legal status, duly licensed legal offices, and even formal court hearings—through which the undocumented attempt to obtain papers. These practices derive from, produce, and yet differ from official immigration law. They *derive from* law in that without the distinctions that immigration law creates, it would not be necessary to issue immigration-related identity documents, base rights on immigration status, or apply for papers. These practices *produce law* in that applying for papers results in hearings, which in turn clarify and refine both the boundary between legality and illegality and the criteria that permit one to cross. These practices *differ from*

official law in that they follow a dynamic that is created by enforcement more than by adjudication. In other words, unauthorized
immigrants strive more to define themselves as legal than to legalize.

Both unofficial and official forms of immigration law are authoritative in their own ways. Unofficial versions of immigration law
derive from social realities, albeit extralegal ones. To the degree that
they enable immigrants to obtain papers, unofficial legal strategies
are successful. Conversely, given that unofficial versions of law define
both legal status and legalization differently than does official law,
strategies that are grounded in unofficial versions of the law are likely
to unravel during formal court proceedings. As both official and
unofficial versions of immigration law have some but not complete
authority, I view the relationship between these forms of law not as a
contest to see which version will triumph but rather as mutually productive and reinforcing (Foucault 1977; Fitzpatrick 1992, 1993).
Official law produces illegality by demarcating the legal. Illegality in
turn justifies the continued elaboration and revision of official law.
These acts of demarcation and elaboration create the interstices
through which unofficial law emerges. The practices that distinguish
legal from illegal beings identify criteria that can be used to claim
deservingness. Thus, permitting the legalization of individuals who
have lived in the United States since a certain date suggests that time
spent in the country is a basis for legal status. Likewise, the elaboration of immigration law raises the possibility that extralegal strategies
will be legitimized. Official and unofficial law are therefore mutually
interdependent and in multiple ways. James Holston's (1991:722)
conclusion regarding land law in Brazil applies equally well to U.S.
immigration law: "illegal practices produce law, extralegal solutions
are incorporated into the judicial process, and law is confirmed as a
channel of strategic disorder" (see also Gonos 1997).

This chapter examines how unofficial versions of immigration
law are created, reproduced, delegitimized, and rendered authoritative. To begin, I explicate the understandings of legal status and legalization that inhere in official immigration proceedings, such as asylum interviews or deportation proceedings. Second, I examine how
enforcing the distinctions created by these official proceedings produces legal subjectivities that differ from those that operate in the
formal legal domain. Third, I turn to the legalization strategies and
practices authorized by these subjectivities. Finally, I discuss the limi-

tations and authority of both official and unofficial versions of immigration law.

Official Law and Legal Personhood

Immigration officials, judges, and attorneys who specialize in immigration law depict everyone as having an immigration status of one sort or another—as a citizen, an illegal alien, a legal permanent resident, and so forth. This depiction derives from the nation-state model of citizenship, according to which an individual's relationship to a state confers rights and responsibilities (J. Bhabha 1996). This form of legal personhood is so critical to securing individual rights, including the right to be present within a national territory, that the United Nations Universal Declaration of Human Rights asserts, "Everyone has the right to a nationality" (Ishay 1997:409; see also Marrus 1985). The same model that grants citizens the right to territorial presence also reserves for states the right to determine which nonnationals can enter states' territories (Sassen 1996). As a result, noncitizens present within a given national territory can be there either legally or illegally—that is, with or without state authorization.[1] To address the ambiguous status of legally present nonnationals, states have created a range of temporary or permanent interim statuses (student, tourist, guest worker, legal permanent resident) that permit differing degrees of inclusion and exclusion. Theoretically at least, everyone who is present within a given national territory ought to be classifiable as a citizen, an illegal alien, a legal resident, or a temporarily legal visitor of some sort.[2] In this sense, legal status is (again, theoretically at least) like marital status: everyone is presumed to have one.[3] Immigration status can sometimes be difficult to determine, as when individuals have two birth certificates, do not know the circumstances of their birth, are missing immigration files, do not know their parents' citizenship, and so forth. However, even when unclear, immigration status officially exists as an external and verifiable truth, if only the appropriate records could be found or reconstructed.[4]

As something that "everyone has," immigration status is treated as an intrinsic but not immutable aspect of personhood. For example, when approving immigrants' applications for suspension of deportation, judges sometimes announce applicants' change of status, saying, "You are now a legal permanent resident." Similarly, at the beginning of many political asylum hearings, applicants concede deportability, thus admitting their status as illegal aliens.[5] According to such statements, immigration status is a characteristic that an individual possesses, temporarily at least. It thus joins a long litany of other characteristics—race, class, age, gender, marital status, ethnicity, sexual orientation, occupation—that can describe an individual. Immigration status can be lost if individuals violate the terms of their status, as one attorney related to me during an interview:

> Someone [who is a legal permanent resident] will be hiking and they won't realize quite where the border is and before they know it, they're on the other side [and then they attempt to enter without inspection]. Or they get lost, or they've been drinking. Stupid things. But these nonetheless bring life as you know it crashing down. Because if you're an alien, and you enter the country without inspection, that makes you deportable. There's nothing you can do about it or nothing you can say. That's just how it is. And no waiver exists.

Barring changes or violations, immigration status remains constant during—though not necessarily pertinent to—a variety of social contexts and in this sense is like other aspects of personhood.

According to attorneys and INS officials, individuals' immigration status is determined by their legal histories. Individuals become illegal aliens, for example, by entering the United States without authorization, entering with authorization but overstaying their visas, or having a status revoked. Likewise, individuals become citizens by being born on U.S. soil, having U.S. citizen parents, or undergoing naturalization (see Levy 1995). Legalization is available only to those who meet relatively restrictive eligibility requirements. Thus one El Rescate attorney regularly instructed his clients that there were only four means of legalizing: suspension of deportation, political asylum, family visa petitions, and labor certification. Similarly, one judge whose court I observed attempted to dispense with a troublesome asylum/suspension case by encouraging the applicant to marry his U.S. citizen girlfriend and thus become eligible for a spousal petition. Attorneys want to know *how* people legalized, not simply whether they have or lack papers, because this information tells attorneys people's status. Officials and attorneys who discuss legalization frequently suggest that only those with "strong cases" (see chapter 4) or who meet the requirements of a particular program (such as the 1986 amnesty program or TPS for Salvadorans) will be eligible. For instance, a judge instructed an asylum applicant who wanted to represent herself, "It's not easy to be granted asylum. You have to prove that you're entitled." Such references to "proving entitlement" and "meeting requirements" do permit some room for maneuverability, as when judges advise aliens that they will be able to present their cases better if they hire attorneys, but within this framework maneuverability is always limited by individuals' abilities to meet basic eligibility requirements.

Attorneys and INS officials depict legalization as depending not only on applicants' merit but also on applicants' abilities to comply with the rules that govern the application process. Forms must be submitted by particular deadlines, documents must be translated into English, fingerprint checks must be obtained, the proper number of copies of all documentation must be submitted, documentation packets must be numbered and paginated according to local rules. One El Rescate paralegal, for example, warned a client that to present his suspension case in court, he had to have three copies of all supporting documentation, hole-punched and tabulated, in chronological order. Regardless of applicants' merit, judges sometimes refuse to accept applications that have not been properly prepared.[6] The fact that in asylum and suspension cases, applicants rather than the government have the burden of proving eligibility places the onus for adequate preparation and for complying with deadlines on applicants. When an attorney attempted to fix a poorly prepared application packet that had been submitted by her client's prior counsel, a judge warned, "Your client has the burden [of proof], and I should never have accepted this application." Winning a case therefore requires not only meeting eligibility requirements but also being able to *demonstrate* that one meets these requirements.

According to officials and attorneys, individuals who do succeed in acquiring or changing their immigration statuses are transformed. Naturalization ceremonies emphasize this transformation by depicting the conferral of citizenship on an alien as a mystical experience. As one judge who was himself a naturalized citizen told the naturalizing citizens, "I felt from the outset, as I believe you feel, the unique sensation of freedom upon the taking of the oath." Similarly, an attorney advised a client who had just been awarded suspension of deportation, "From now on, if anyone asks you what your immigration status is, tell them that you are a legal permanent resident." As a result of their transformation, individuals enjoy the rights and privileges that pertain to their new status. Naturalization ceremonies, for example, inform new citizens of their rights to vote and to serve on juries. Immigration attorneys often advise individuals who are eligible for naturalization that once they take the oath of citizenship, any family visa petitions that they have submitted will be processed more quickly. Legal permanent residents also acquire particular rights with this status, such as the right to work, to petition for certain categories of relatives, and to remain in the United States indefinitely as long as they do not violate the terms of their status.

To enable individuals to demonstrate their immigration status and to thus avail themselves of their rights, INS and other state authorities issue identity documents, such as green cards, work permits, social security cards, passports, and driver's licenses. In immigration court, when individuals are granted political asylum or suspension of deportation, the first thing that their attorneys do is ask how to get a copy of the decision. This written decision is needed to obtain other documents. The official relationship between status, rights, and documents is that a status confers rights (Barbalet 1988) and entitles individuals to documents that provide evidence of their eligibility for these rights. Thus, for example, attorneys tell ABC class members that they are entitled to work permits as long as their asylum applications are pending. Similarly, an INS news release instructs readers regarding the "documents that employers may accept when verifying the employment eligibility of new hires" (INS 1998). Documents verify eligibility, which is a product of status.

The need to present various papers to claim rights or obtain services creates a dynamic that contradicts this official legal theory. As Robert Cover (1992a:112), notes, law acquires meaning not only from official proceedings but also from "social activity that is not subject to the strictures of provenance that characterize what we call formal lawmaking. Even when authoritative institutions try to create meaning for the precepts they articulate, they act, in that respect, in an unprivileged fashion." To understand how formal legal concepts become unprivileged, I turn to the everyday practice of immigration law within the spaces of nonexistence occupied by unauthorized immigrants.

Illegal Subjectivities

Although it might seem that U.S. immigration law exists at least in part to combat illegal immigration, it is also true that illegal immigrants are produced through the laws that criminalize their presence (Coutin 1996). As Robert L. Bach (1978:548) notes, "The liberal, political intervention at the [U.S.-Mexico] border also created illegal immigration. The National Acts placing restrictions on the number and type of immigrants and the 'closing' of the U.S.-Mexican border through administrative action rendered the exchange of labor illegal." The enforcement practices that distinguish between "legal" and "illegal" residents follow a different logic than those that permit legalization. Because documents are required to demonstrate eligibility for rights and services, and because those who can demonstrate eligibility are materially situated in particular subject positions (as citizens, legal permanent residents, and so on), enforcing immigration law makes it appear that *status inheres in papers, not persons.* For this reason, unauthorized immigrants are simultaneously constituted as paperless and as illegal. Their explications of immigration law constitute what Donna Haraway (1991) terms "situated knowledge," an account that is narrated from a particular subject position (see also Rosaldo 1989). These accounts are particularly valuable because, as beings who are created and delegitimized through law, unauthorized immigrants can expose law's mythic character—that is, the idea that law operates within a reality that is "unitary, exclusive, and objectively knowable" (Fitzpatrick 1993:464; see also Fitzpatrick 1992; Bruner 1986:25; Hunt 1993). Attending to the legal expertise of immigration law's "illegal subjects" is thus a means of explicating unofficial versions of immigration law and demonstrating how law produces its own alterities.

Most of the Central American immigrants among whom I have been doing research first became legally illicit by sneaking across the U.S.-Mexico border, usually with the assistance of an alien smuggler.[7] This illicit entry was necessitated by the fact that they lacked travel documents that would have permitted them to enter through an official checkpoint. Angela Reyes, a twenty-five-year-old Salvadoran woman who came to the United States in 1990, described her experiences to me during an interview:

> When we left [Mexico], it was in the afternoon. And we had to cross the river, which came up [chest] high. The women went first. We had to take off all of our clothes so that they wouldn't get wet, because if we emerged on the other side wearing wet clothes, they'd suspect that we'd crossed the river. So I entered the country naked. And when I got to the other side, we saw a patrol passing. He shouted at us and chased us, so we ran. We grabbed a taxi and got out of there. . . . After this, we were taken to Brownsville. And that's when I ran into problems. We had to stay in an apartment for fifteen days. And the *coyote's* [smuggler's] wife was angry that we were there. We were hungry, because she didn't bring us any food. I gave her money, some of the little money that I had, to buy some shoes for me. But do you know what she did? She bought shoes that were a children's size, so they didn't fit at all. I needed shoes, clothes, and food, and she wouldn't buy any of these things.

Angela's narrative of clandestine entry is strangely reminiscent of the rites of passage described by Victor Turner (1969; see also Chavez 1991, 1992; Kearney 1991). To go from Mexico to the United States, existence to nonexistence, Salvadoran citizen to U.S. illegal alien, Angela had to become naked, wade through water, fast, and be treated like a child. This "rite" became increasingly nightmarish, however, as Angela faced exhaustion, extortion, deception, fear, and the threat of rape:

> Again, we left the apartment in the afternoon. We had to pay another $250 just to get from Brownsville to L.A. And [the smuggler] lied to us. He told us that he was taking us to where our relatives would be waiting to meet us. And it turned out to be lies, pure lies, because there was no one there. We started walking, and we walked day and night, through the mountains and through the desert. . . . My friend fainted from exhaustion, and the guy had to carry her. And at night we heard the coyotes, and

we were very frightened. . . . There were only five of us traveling at this point, because those who didn't have the six hundred dollars to pay the *coyote* had had to stay behind until they raised the money. And the women and the men traveled together, and thankfully, we didn't have any problems in that regard. There were no rapes.

Angela's status as illegal fugitive who cannot share the space occupied by the citizenry is actualized at the end of her narrative, when she is incarcerated:

So we spent two days and night walking through the desert. And when we got across the mountains, our relatives weren't waiting. Instead, we saw a man on a horse ride past, and he saw us. Shortly afterward, the helicopters came. Everyone ran. Can you imagine? I had no shoes, and my shirt was torn from walking through the desert, and from the cactuses.

So we were caught. And we were taken to the prison in Brownsville.

Like Angela's story, other Central Americans' accounts of clandestine border crossings are replete with references to becoming illicit, to getting dirty, to their torn or missing clothing, to their exposure to the elements. For example, Luis Alfaro, a Salvadoran union activist, related that after three attempts to cross the border between Mexico and Guatemala, he was "dirty, almost without shoes, and ruined." Maria Bonilla, another Salvadoran woman, told me that when the border patrol chased her, she hid in some trash barrels, only to find herself covered with feces and thorns. Immigrants' references to the sullying nature of border crossings express their discomfort with their newfound illicitness (Kearney 1991). Angela's description of being imprisoned in Texas in "El Corralón" (the corral) made her sense of violation explicit:

They took our fingerprints and our pictures and gave us orange suits to wear.[8] We became carrot women. And the men and the women were separated. I'd left in June and I was captured on the first of August. I'll never forget that date. It's engraved in my mind. I'd arrived without shoes, and it was very ugly there. There

were beds everywhere. I never thought I'd be in a place like that.
They called us gang members.

As unauthorized immigrants are materially constituted as illicit,
they simultaneously experience themselves as lacking the right
papers. Martin Padilla, a Salvadoran man who returned to the United
States in 1985 only a few months after having been deported, lost his
job in 1987 when his employer began to require papers of all employees. Carlos Perez, a young Salvadoran who fled forced recruitment,
was unable to find work in the United States until he obtained a work
permit. Ana Sanchez, who came to the United States in 1985,
avoided going to public places, such as church, parks, or the beach,
so that she would not be apprehended by INS authorities. Knowing
that they do not have the papers that employers, INS officials, and
others might request, unauthorized immigrants describe themselves
as defenseless when their rights to work, public assistance, medical
care, or movement are challenged. Paradoxically, the undocumented
are "spatially incarcerated" (Gupta and Ferguson 1992:17) because
of their illicit mobility.[9] Having entered or remained in the United
States without authorization, these individuals are reconstituted as
illegal and, through the denial of rights and services, are situated outside the citizenry.

The solution that unauthorized Central Americans propose for
the problem of being illegal sheds light on their understanding of
their illicit subjectivity. To overcome their undocumented status,
these immigrants assert, they have to *arreglar papeles*. The term *arreglar*
can be translated as "to fix, arrange, or put in order," and in an immigration context, it means "to legalize." Other things that people can
arreglar include a time and place to meet, a calendar that has fallen
apart, a television set that does not work properly, or a filing system
that has become unworkable. What the undocumented need to fix,
arrange, or put in order is revealed by the object of this phrase: *papeles* (papers). *Arreglar* can be used with or without an object, however,
as in the statements, "Yo quiero arreglar" (I want to fix, arrange, put
in order, or I want to legalize) or "Mi esposo me está arreglando" (my
husband is fixing me, arranging me, putting me in order, or my husband is legalizing me). Such phrasings suggest that not only papers
but also unauthorized immigrants themselves are broken, in disarray,
or out of order. In fact, the term for false papers is *papeles chuecos*,

which can be roughly translated as "papers that have something wrong with them." When I asked informants for examples of other things that can be *chueco,* I received the following responses: a road that is uneven and covered with rocks, a car that does not run, a stomach that hurts, a paper that is in error. Referring to legalization as "fixing" or "arranging" rather than as "obtaining" papers implies that unauthorized immigrants do have papers but that their papers are *chuecos*—they have something wrong with them. When I asked a Guatemalan ABC applicant why undocumented individuals need to "fix" rather than "get" papers, she explained, "Immigration does have a record of us, but perhaps it's without our intention." In other words, people who are legally nonexistent possess potential or imaginary documents that materialize as an Order to Show Cause or a Notice to Appear (documents that charge individuals with having violated immigration law) in the event that they are apprehended.

Many of the Central Americans whom I met in the course of my research had obtained papers—specifically work permits—through TPS, DED, and ABC. TPS and DED recipients were entitled to work permits while their status was in effect, and the ABC agreement allowed these individuals to remain eligible for work permits by applying for political asylum. In addition, the passage of IRCA in 1986 led individuals who might otherwise have remained undocumented to apply for asylum as a means of obtaining a work permit. When they obtained valid work permits, these unauthorized immigrants were repositioned vis-à-vis both immigration law and the INS. When asked for papers, they could present their EADs and could, in most contexts, define themselves as legal. In addition, because their work permits were valid for only one year, work-permit holders had to continually reapply for work authorization. In contrast to the days when they sought to avoid INS officials, they began to have annual contact with the INS, albeit through the mail.

Although, officially speaking, asylum applicants were not permanent residents and were permitted to remain in the United States only until a decision was reached in their cases, the immigrants served by the Central American community organizations where I did fieldwork often described the *permiso* (work permit) as a form of legal status. In so doing, they defined ABC class members and others who were in interstitial categories as documented residents.[10] For example, when asked if any of their relatives had legal status, community organizations' clients often listed three categories of legal relatives: U.S. citizens, legal permanent residents, and relatives with work permits. Asylum applicants also sometimes viewed the receipt of a work permit as a sign that their applications had been approved. One El Rescate client who had applied for asylum in 1989 told me that the asylum official who had interviewed him had said, "I can't give you asylum. All I can give you is a work permit." This client, who had asked me when he could exchange his work permit—which always had to be renewed—for something more permanent, was surprised to be advised that his case was still pending and that if he were to be denied asylum, he would lose even the work permit. The fact that immigrants often refer to work permits simply as *permisos* (permits) rather than as *permisos de trabajo* (work permits) creates ambiguity regarding what the permit is for and suggests that *permisos* entitle their holders not only to work but to remain in the United States. Ana Sanchez, for example, who had been afraid to frequent public places when she lacked papers, described TPS as "a way to go from anonymity to something more dignified. I could raise my head in public. I would be able to get any job, even working in a factory. It was a way to not be illegal anymore. If I was asked for my papers, I would be able to show them my [work permit] card."[11] Ana's comment indicates that regarding work permits as a form of legal status redefines unauthorized immigrants as "economic citizens" who are entitled to compete in the U.S. labor market (Thomas 1985) rather than as disenfranchised laborers who are objectified and dehumanized as a natural and therefore unregulated labor force (Chock 1995; Heyman 1991).

Claiming work permits as a form of legal status suggests that documents confer, rather than derive from, statuses—a view of papers not unlike that found in civil law. An expression that encapsulates this notion of documentation is "¡No tiene ni un papel!" (She does not have a single paper!) This expression initially puzzled me, because, drawing on the idea that documentation reflects status, it seemed to me that an individual either is or is not authorized to be in the United States and therefore either does or does not have "papers." Partial documentation—having one paper or three papers—is precluded within this framework, since, while different statuses can entitle individuals to different sorts of documents, assessing an individual's "legality" is a dichotomous determination. However, as I heard immigrants describe their own experiences obtaining papers, I realized that partial documentation is unofficially possible. For example, Luis Alfaro, a Salvadoran immigrant, described obtaining a series of documents via a pending asylum application: "I needed my driver's license. And now I have it. [And] now I have a social security number and I'm able to pay my income taxes." There are unauthorized immigrants who lack work permits and social security cards but who obtained driver's licenses or California identification cards before proof of legal residence was a prerequisite. Moreover, there are individuals who used to have legal status in the United States and who obtained both driver's licenses and valid social security numbers but who are no longer eligible for work permits. Such individuals' documentation is partial in that they can defend themselves in certain contexts (e.g., when getting a traffic ticket) but not in others (e.g., when questioned by an INS agent at a bus stop). Moreover, to be documentless is to be vulnerable, as shown by one new citizen who had sent her naturalization certificate to the passport office along with her passport application and who joked, "Now I'm illegal."

In depicting themselves as documented, Central Americans with pending asylum applications drew on but redefined the criteria through which legal status is allocated. Like INS officials, who reserved legalization for the meritorious, Central Americans with pending asylum applications reasoned that those who demonstrated good behavior would (or should) be granted residency. Beatriz Sandoval, who came to the United States from El Salvador in 1993, explained why she had, as she put it, applied for papers: "I thought, 'Why can't I get a work permit, if everyone else has done it? So why not? Especially if I behave better than other people, and do things better than other people.'" Similarly, another asylum applicant told me why she thought her case would be approved: "I've heard that the government wants to throw out the people who aren't working, but I'm working and I've always worked and so has my husband. So we fit the requirements." Such comments imbue immigration criteria with a morality that differs from the notions of merit and meeting requirements that are used to decide immigration cases. Officially, to be meritorious, individuals first have to be minimally eligible for a particular status, occupy the appropriate procedural position, meet narrowly defined legal criteria, have proof of their claims, and so forth.

In partial contrast to these official notions of merit, the immigrants I interviewed overwhelmingly linked deservingness to work, self-sufficiency, and law-abidingness. In other words, as public rhetoric about immigration denounces welfare recipients as "undesirable" (Calavita 1996; see also Thomas 1985), those who see themselves as deserving claim the legitimacy that they believe derives from their labor.[12] These notions are recognized in immigration court in that employment history is relevant to certain forms of legalization; however, other factors are also important, and work history is of only limited relevance to political asylum claims.

Another means by which unauthorized Central Americans claim deservingness is by citing the amount of time they have lived in the United States. The stated basis for this claim is the law regarding suspension of deportation, which is known in Spanish as *la ley de los siete años* (the law of seven years). The immigrants whom I met generally emphasized the temporal component of suspension over the good moral character and extreme hardship requirements, saying, "I can legalize through time" ("Puedo arreglar por el tiempo"). One Salvadoran woman who had received public assistance and who in my estimation would therefore have a difficult time winning suspension optimistically based her chances of legalizing solely on time, telling me, "In a few months, I'll complete eleven years here, so I have a lot more than seven years." The notion that time (like documents) confers legality is delegitimized, however, by authorities who are concerned not only with *amounts* of time but also with how time is *spent* (see Thompson 1967) and whether suspension applicants have progressed during their seven-plus years in this country. Moreover, strong evidence of poor moral character can outweigh any amount of time, as a legal permanent resident who had been placed in deportation proceedings after being convicted of an aggravated felony discovered. When this man asked an attorney, "Even with twenty years here, you can't defend yourself [against deportation]?" and was told that he could not, the man commented bitterly, "So, time doesn't count if you're not a citizen."[13] And yet the unofficial notion that time improves individuals' chances of legalizing is sometimes confirmed by legal practitioners and immigration officials alike. Before IIRIRA recalibrated time, one attorney frequently advised El Rescate legal staff that "time is beneficial where immigration is concerned," and one judge whose court I observed remarked of a suspension applicant, "Thirteen years in the United States creates an equity that the court has to take into account in deciding this case." Official and unofficial versions of law are sometimes inextricable. The unofficial versions of immigration law that are produced through enforcement practices and articulated by law's illegal subjects also suggest particular legalization strategies. By acting on these strategies, unauthorized immigrants, notary publics, immigration consultants, and others seize and elaborate on the illegalities that are set in motion by issuing and requiring identity documents. These illicit and quasi-legal practices in turn shape official law.

Bargaining Law in the Shadows

Unauthorized immigrants' efforts to negotiate their subject positions focus on obtaining papers, through both legal and quasi-legal endeavors (Hagan 1994; Hagan and Baker 1993; Mahler 1995). To borrow and rephrase Mnookin and Kornhauser's (1979) formulation, unauthorized immigrants "bargain law in the shadows" (see also Jacob 1992), with the "shadows" referring to the fringes of formal law, an area that is peopled by notary publics posing as attorneys, pastors who handle their congregants' immigration matters, attorneys who are in cahoots with notary publics, employers who tell undocumented job applicants to get false papers, counterfeiters who forge documents, and illegal immigrants who are desperate for work permits. Forgery, fraud, and misguided legalization efforts emerge in the cracks between law and illegality as a means of at least temporarily documenting those whose existence is denied. Papers are made critical to both existence and legality by practices that enforce distinctions between authorized and unauthorized residents. Those who lack papers that "work" strive to get them, putting their understanding of law and legalization into practice. Thus, for example, unauthorized immigrants who perceive work permits as a form of legal status and who see that other immigrants have obtained these documents may conclude that they too are capable of obtaining work permits. In fact, the U.S. government can appear to be part of a quasi-legitimate, quasi-corrupt paper-fixing scheme. These understandings, however, derive from realities that are rendered illicit by immigration law itself. When documents are redefined as a product of status, and status is reconstituted as a product of legal history, then the legal strategies of undocumented immigrants suddenly appear to be riddled with legal misconceptions.

One of the most common and straightforward ways for undocumented individuals to obtain papers is to purchase fraudulent identity documents. One Salvadoran man told me that even in El Salvador, people know how to get false documents in the United States. This man reported that when he arrived in the United States in 1989, he purchased a false social security card on the street and used it to work. When he later obtained a valid social security number, he simply notified his employer and the Internal Revenue Service of the new number. The use of false documents has been both necessitated by and to a degree tolerated within immigration law itself. According to Kitty Calavita (1990), the U.S. business community's support for IRCA was secured by making it possible for employers to avoid legal responsibility for hiring job applicants who presented false identity documents. This was accomplished by building a loophole into IRCA's employer-sanctions provisions: employers were considered to be acting in good faith as long as the documents that they accepted "appear[ed] on their face to be genuine." One official interviewed by Calavita stated that documents could be assumed to be genuine as long as they did not contain "five tons of white-out" (1990:1063). Many of the immigrants whom I interviewed reported having worked without documents or with false documents. Beatriz Sandoval, a Salvadoran woman who worked in the garment industry, told me how her employer handled the problem of hiring undocumented workers: "They'll tell you, 'I'm sure you know where to buy papers,' and the person will come back with papers the next day and be hired." Recounting the situation of a coworker, who had worked under a false social security number, filed income tax returns, and received refunds from the U.S. government, Beatriz marveled that a country with "so much technology" accepted false documents. According to Beatriz, the social security department had eventually notified this coworker that her number was being used by two people and then had assigned the coworker a new number. "So," Beatriz concluded, "there are laws that favor the illegal. How is it that [the coworker and her husband] got a true number when others can't get one? And they got it for using a false number? And what does the government gain by sending money [tax refunds] to them?" These questions depicted the U.S. government as complicit in the production and use of fraudulent documents.

In addition to purchasing false papers, unauthorized immigrants attempt to obtain papers by applying for them, a practice that is almost as mired in illegality as is document forgery. The experiences of Mario Rodrigues, a twenty-two-year-old Mexican immigrant who approached El Rescate for legal assistance in 1996, demonstrate the shadiness of legalization strategies that are formulated on the margins of legality. When I first met Mario, he was anxiously preparing for a deportation hearing and was hoping that El Rescate would represent him without change. I was present at his intake interview with an El Rescate legal worker, the meeting at which El Rescate accepted his case, and his court hearing. I also interviewed Mario after he was awarded suspension of deportation. Mario, who had immigrated to the United States without legal status in 1988 at age fourteen, told me that he "had always wanted to *arreglar,* ever since coming to this country. But due to lack of information, I never did it." Mario's parents and siblings had been more fortunate. Several siblings had either married U.S. citizens or qualified for legalization through the 1986 amnesty program. These siblings had then petitioned for Mario's parents, who, along with his youngest siblings, were able to become legal permanent residents. Mistakenly believing that a legal permanent resident had to wait five years before petitioning for a relative, Mario's father did not petition for him, as Mario explained: "We were blind. It was a case of someone leading you to school, and they're blind, so you get stepped on all the way as you go."

Because his relatives had legal status, Mario believed it would be easy for him to obtain a green card. Therefore, when a friend told him about a woman in Huntington Park who had connections with the INS and who could help him get his papers, he sought her assistance. Following his friend's directions, he arrived at her office, which was in a restaurant: "You go in and they ask, 'What can we offer you?' and you say, 'I'm here to see so-and-so.' And they take you into a back room, and there she tells you what she can do." In Mario's case she promised to use her connections to accelerate a family visa petition filed by Mario's sister, a process that would normally take nine years. Mario explained,

This *señora* promised to give me my *permiso* within six months for five hundred dollars. So I gave her the money and I waited and after six months, I called and asked, "What happened? You said that I would *arreglar* in six months, and it's more than six months, and nothing has happened." She said that she needed more money. So I paid her another $250, or $850[14] altogether. . . . But I waited and waited and nothing ever happened. I realized that I was just losing my money. So I went back and asked for a refund, and she withdrew the petition and gave me my money back, except for fifty dollars, which she said she needed to keep "for expenses."

Despite the disappointing outcome of his first attempt, Mario still wanted to legalize, so when his sister recommended a particular notary as being "a good person" and "very helpful," he again sought assistance. According to Mario, this notary promised to get him a *permiso* in six weeks: "He said that it would be fifteen hundred dollars altogether, and that it would be five hundred dollars to start. So I paid him the five hundred dollars. And he committed himself to working on my case. 'Yo te arreglo en seis semanas' [I'll legalize you in six weeks], he told me. Those were his exact words." This time, the plan was different. Instead of filing for a family visa petition, the notary suggested applying through political asylum. The notary filled out the forms and gave Mario a declaration that he was to study in preparation for his asylum interview. This declaration, which Mario later showed to me and to the El Rescate legal staff, described the political and legal situation in Mexico but said nothing about Mario's individual situation. The notary promised that one of his associates would accompany Mario to the asylum interview and would choose the official who would conduct the interview. When the actual appointment arrived, however, this "associate" demanded more money, which Mario was unable to pay, forcing him to attend the interview alone: "And the official interviewed me regarding what had been written on my application, . . . that I was afraid to go back to Mexico because of all of the killings, because of the PRI official being killed, because of the uprising in Chiapas, and that I was afraid because of these things." Instead of receiving a work permit, Mario's asylum application was denied, and he was placed in deportation proceedings.

The fact that immigrants like Mario fall prey to notary fraud can be attributed at least in part to their understandings of the workings of law in their home countries. Central Americans have told me of bribing Salvadoran officials to issue Salvadoran birth certificates for their U.S.-born children, just in case their children need to obtain Salvadoran documents. One Salvadoran man told me that to get his first driver's license, he simply bribed an official in San Salvador. It is common for Mexican officials who encounter Central Americans en route to the United States to demand bribes, as one Salvadoran woman who successfully defied these demands recounted:

They took me off [the bus], and the man told me, "You have to pay." I don't remember how many dollars. And I told him, "But I'm not going to the United States. I don't have dollars, I have pesos. Supposedly, we are in Mexico!" And I also told him, "I don't know why I have to pay you if I have a visa and I'm traveling legally." And he said, "No, it's that all those who come from Central America go to the United States." I said, "Maybe everyone but me. I'm not going to the United States. I'm going to visit my sister who is married here." "Where?" he asked. "In Guanajuato. . . . And moreover," I told him, "I'm going on a visit to the Virgin of Guadalupe." . . . "Oh, okay," he told me, "then you don't pay anything, and when you reach the next booth, just put ten dollars in your passport, and they won't say anything to you." I said, "Okay," and at the next booth, I gave [the official] the ten dollars . . . and he said to me, "No, it isn't ten dollars that you have to pay, it's more!" I said, "Well, I don't think that I have to pay anything because I'm traveling legally." I told him the same thing that I'd said to the other one. . . . I said, "I don't know why I have to give this to you, if this money is for you. It's not money that you are going to give to someone, to your boss, this is money that you are stealing. So I'm not giving you anything, because I have my visa, I have my passport, everything in order, and I'm not going to give you anything. . . . Moreover, I'm visiting the Virgin of Guadalupe, and I don't think that there's any crime in that." He just stood there looking at me and said, "Okay, go on, go on."

Given such experiences, it is not surprising that unauthorized immigrants find plausible notaries' offers to manipulate legal outcomes in exchange for money. Moreover, by advertising themselves as notaries, these pseudoattorneys take advantage of the fact that in many Latin American countries *notarios* are authorized to perform certain legal transactions and are in some respects equivalent to attorneys (Hagan 1994; Mahler 1995).[15] Spanish-speaking immigrants who approached El Rescate, ASOSAL, and CARECEN often could not tell legal workers whether the person who had filled out their immigration paperwork was an attorney or a notary public. Finally, notaries who pose as INS consultants are often skilled in depicting themselves as legal authorities. According to Mario, the notary who filed his asylum application seemed knowledgeable and trustworthy and spoke "like a snake—very smart, very sharp."

Informants' accounts of their efforts to legalize indicate that their legalization strategies derive not only from their prior legal cultures but also from their experiences of U.S. immigration law. Consider, for example, Mario Rodrigues's own explanation for his having been taken in by a *notario:* "I had illusions of *arreglando,* and that's why he was able to take advantage of me in that way." Undocumented immigrants' illusion that they can legalize stems in part from comparisons between themselves and those who have obtained papers, just as Mario believed that because his relatives had obtained green cards, he too could do so. Beatriz Sandoval, quoted previously, also based her decision to seek papers on the fact that other individuals whom she considered to be less deserving had obtained work permits. Individuals' accounts of their interaction with notaries often began by describing the experience of a friend or relative who successfully obtained papers through this individual. For example, Ricardo Mejía, a Salvadoran who applied for asylum through a notary, told me, "Some neighbors in my apartment building gave me the name of an attorney [probably a notary], and I went, and I asked, and they told me that yes, work permits were being given out. But they didn't tell me that what I was applying for was political asylum. . . . But I don't regret it. Because that was nine years ago, and Immigration has not deported me." In fact, prior to January 1995, applying for asylum often did generate a work permit, given that individuals with pending asylum applications were entitled to work authorization.[16] Because other similarly situated individuals are able to obtain papers, law appears manipulable, and legal status seems to be within the grasp of the enterprising. For example, at a CARECEN *charla* (public presentation), a man who had been told that there was no way that he could qualify for legal status asked disbelievingly, "You mean there really isn't any way? What if I get the right attorney? Or spend more money?" Such comments echoed the claims of notaries posing as attorneys and were debunked as misconceptions by immigration attorneys associated with Central American community organizations.

The legal subjectivities formed in the space of illegality also shape unauthorized immigrants' legal goals: to obtain papers and thus legal status. The notaries who assisted Mario Rodrigues promised him a *permiso*, which, as noted earlier, is sometimes deemed *a form of* legal status but officially is *the product of* a temporary or permanent status that confers the right to work. When I began volunteering with community organizations in Los Angeles, I was surprised to discover that ABC class members often submitted work permit applications for children who were as young as five or six years old. In so doing, parents hoped to define their children as legal. Student interns who were not yet versed in immigration law sometimes echoed clients' claims that work permits conferred legality. In response, one attorney frequently advised students to make legal status rather than work permits central to their analysis of clients' legalization options: "Something that you need to learn is that the expiration date of the work permit means something to the client, but it's irrelevant to an immigration analysis."[17] In contrast, notaries who were willing to exchange the short-term goal of obtaining a work permit for the long-term goal of legalization played on immigrants' desires to *arreglar papeles*,[18] but, as occurred in the case of Mario Rodrigues, often simply informed the INS of their clients' presence. Such strategies obscure the official distinction between papers and status by promoting the idea that work permits are available to those who pursue them correctly. A CARECEN attorney told me that at presentations about the ABC program, she was frequently approached by immigrants who insisted that they had applied for work permits but who did not have copies of asylum applications that would have made them eligible for these permits.

Instead of distinguishing "illegitimate" notary publics from "legitimate" legal authorities, the legalization strategies that are constructed in the interstices of legality depict the INS, along with document forgers and unlicensed immigration consultants, as part of an only quasi-legitimate paper-producing scheme.[19] One ABC class member, for example, attributed INS practices to the desire for financial gain, pointing out, "If everyone has to apply for work permits, Immigration gets more money [from the application fees]." A Mayan immigrant in Jacqueline Maria Hagan's (1994:105) study characterized the INS as "the biggest *coyote* [alien smuggler] around." Similarly, immigrant advocates whom I interviewed referred to the fees that the INS charges for work permits as a rent that immigrants have to pay for the right to work and therefore as unjustified.[20] One activist estimated that since 1991, ABC class members have paid the INS seventy million dollars in work authorization fees. Like the belief that notaries might indeed have connections with INS officials, the idea that the INS is seeking to profit from illegal immigration suggests that the systems that deny papers to some and award them to others are themselves of questionable legitimacy. Official law is thus inextricably entangled with the illegalities that it creates. Not only do the practices that enforce immigration law give rise to alternative legalities, such as the idea that papers confer status, but in addition, these alternative legalities are sometimes incorporated into official law. Such, at least, has been the experience of Salvadoran and Guatemalan asylum seekers.

Entangled Legalities

If official law gives rise to alternative legalities, and if these alternatives are sometimes officially recognized, then the authority of both official and unofficial versions of immigration law is contingent and incomplete.[21] The formal and the unofficial are interdependent in that defining one simultaneously demarcates the other (Fitzpatrick 1992; Foucault 1977; Holston 1991). As Foucault (1977:280) notes, "[T]he existence of a legal prohibition creates around it a field of illegal practices." Prohibiting unauthorized entry gives rise to such illegalities as entry without inspection, illegal transportation, alien smuggling, the use of fraudulent documents, and so forth. The persons engaged in these practices exist in a space of illegality whose boundaries must continually be examined, refined, and specified to determine who has left and who remains behind. As both official and unofficial versions of immigration law are produced through these determinations, each has some authority. Just as undocumented immigrants come in and out of existence (see chapter 2), the authority and illegitimacy of official and unofficial versions of law depend on the frame of reality being used to interpret an event, and multiple frames of reality can be used simultaneously.[22] For example, when individuals present identity documents to employers, they are simultaneously establishing their employment eligibility and using a document to define themselves as legal. The fact that official and unofficial legalities are entangled does not depoliticize their relationship. On the contrary, the authority of "official law" depends on denying law's dependence on the unofficial and the illegal (Greenhouse 1996; Fitzpatrick 1992). It is not a given, however, that official law rules. Because formal law depends on the informal, unofficial law cannot be completely delegitimized. Rather, alternative legalities remain operative in the realm of illegality and are sometimes subsumed by official law.

The ways that formal legal proceedings depend on yet deny their relationships to unofficial law are illustrated by the deportation hearing of Roberto Mendez, a Guatemalan asylum applicant. Roberto came to the United States in 1993, after having been detained, tortured, and forced to sign an incriminating document. Nine months after his arrival, Roberto applied for asylum through a notary agency that his sister-in-law had recommended. Roberto's wife, Alicia, told me about the application process during an interview: "We had just arrived from Guatemala. We didn't speak English. . . . They just gave us the form and said, 'Sign here.' We didn't understand exactly what the form said. But we believed in the [agency]." Unfortunately, Roberto and Alicia's trust turned out to be misplaced, as the agency that prepared their application wrote a narrative in English that did not reflect their experiences, gave them no copies of their paperwork, and charged extra for translating their application into Spanish. Out of work and with a baby on the way, Roberto and Alicia declined the translation. Roberto and Alicia received an appointment for an asylum interview in Anaheim, but their application was denied on the grounds that they lacked proof of their claim. They then were placed in deportation proceedings. At Roberto's court hearing, which I attended, the INS attorney questioned him about the accuracy of the asylum application that the notary had prepared:

> *INS Attorney:* Were there specific parts in the application that aren't correct?

> *Roberto:* Most aren't. I don't recognize the story in the application, because they didn't read it to me in Spanish and I don't understand English.

> *INS Attorney:* So why did you sign it if you didn't understand it?

> *Roberto:* My wife's family said that the [notary office] would help me. I didn't understand the application because it was in English.

> *INS Attorney:* So you signed the application without reading it.

> *Roberto:* Exactly.

> *INS Attorney:* You signed this knowing that you were applying for asylum from the United States government?

> *Roberto:* I thought that I was going to get good help from them and—

> *INS Attorney:* I'm not talking about the [notary office], I'm talking about you. You signed the application not knowing what was in it?

> *Roberto:* Yes.

The INS attorney's questions divorced Roberto's act of signing an application that he had not read from the circumstances under which he applied for asylum. Roberto's limited English skills, his confidence in the legal expertise of the agency that prepared his application, and the fact that trusted family members had recommended this agency were deemed irrelevant to his decision to sign what was to him an unintelligible statement. The illegitimacy of the legal office that prepared Roberto's application was transferred to Roberto, making both him and his account not credible. Although this hearing might not have occurred had Roberto not acted in the unofficial legal realm, the judge's decision to deny Roberto's application denied the existence of this realm. The judge, for example, stated that it was not plausible that Roberto had paid a notary hundreds of dollars to submit paperwork that he had not even understood. For Roberto's actions to be plausible, illegitimate legal notions and practices would have to be recognized.

The experiences of Roberto and Alicia Mendez also shed light on how the idea of papers that informs undocumented immigrants' legalization strategies is formally delegitimized. The idea that documents confer status suggests that documents themselves, not the external realities to which documents supposedly refer, are intrinsically authoritative. Moreover, if documents are imbued with authority by legal practitioners—ranging from *notarios* to attorneys to U.S. officials—as agents/experts, then it makes sense for asylum applicants to sign blank forms or to submit untranslated English documents to the U.S. government. Conversely, if, as the INS attorney suggests in the testimony quoted earlier, documents are validated through authorship, then the denial of authorship invalidates both the process and products of documentation. When Roberto denied authorship of his signed account, the judge who heard his case defined Roberto as someone who was attempting to manipulate law and to fake a legal claim instead of as really being a victim of political persecution. Because unlicensed legal practice, document forgery, and unofficial forms of immigration law untether validity from authorship, each of these practices can be deemed fraudulent. On the rare occasions when individuals have official documents but not status, it becomes clear that papers that confer rather than reflect status are unauthorized and therefore illegitimate. For instance, one Mexican man who attended El Rescate's legal clinic had received a letter from the INS stating that his amnesty application had been denied. The man still had an unexpired work permit and had traveled to Mexico thinking that this document would enable him to reenter the country. Upon returning, however, INS authorities placed the man in exclusion proceedings on the grounds that he was not eligible to be admitted to the United States.[23] Like Roberto Mendez, who denied his own authorship of the paperwork that he submitted to the INS, this man had erred in locating authority in a document that did not reflect his official identity.

Another way that formal legal proceedings delegitimize unofficial versions of law is by linking seemingly arbitrary distinctions—such as arrival dates—to determinations of deservingness. Individuals with pending asylum applications, for example, have not all received the same treatment from U.S. officials. Mario Rodrigues, who applied for asylum after the INS had adopted a last-in/first-out policy, was quickly placed in deportation proceedings. Roberto and Alicia Mendez applied for asylum shortly before this policy went into effect and therefore received work permits but were interviewed soon after the INS began to work through the backlog of pending asylum applications. Ricardo Mejía applied for asylum in 1985 and nine years later had not been called before a judge. Would-be applicants who missed the deadlines for particular programs have fared worse, as the following quotation from my field notes indicates:

> While I was hanging around the reception area of El Rescate yesterday, a woman came in who was trying to find out how to apply for a work permit. The receptionist told her that she couldn't simply apply for a work permit, that she could only get a permit as the result of obtaining a status. She was surprised, and she said that she knew other people who were apply[ing] for work permits and getting them. He explained that these people probably had been part of the TPS program and were now eligible to apply for ABC. He asked her when she came into the country, and I believe that she said 1990. He then explained that she should have applied for TPS, [and he warned her not to go to a notary.] "So there's nothing I can do?" she asked. "Nothing," he said. "And I can't work?" she asked. "You can, but only illegally," he said. "Yes," she said, "that's the problem."

Though comparing herself to her peers suggested that she could apply for a work permit, this woman's assumption that she was eligible for work authorization underestimated the degree to which arbitrary distinctions are made real by law itself. Cutoff dates create discrete groups and thus counter fears that amnesty, TPS, and other such programs open the floodgates to illegal immigrants (J. Bhabha 1996). Because the criteria that define these groups are not necessarily meaningful, however, the "deserving" are mythic beings, individuals who are assumed to demonstrate particular characteristics (e.g., working hard, paying taxes, contributing to society) and who are made real by being defined within particular categories of citizenship (Coutin and Chock 1995; Fitzpatrick 1992; Mertz 1994). As a result, the "deserving" can work legally, whereas the almost identical "undeserving"—such as this woman—cannot.

Although official law often denies and thus delegitimizes its connections to the unofficial, alternative legalities are sometimes officially recognized. During the 1980s, the numbers of asylum applications filed in the United States skyrocketed as Central Americans sought to avoid being deported after being apprehended by INS officials.[24] The passage of IRCA in 1986 also gave asylum applications a boost, as notaries and immigration practitioners figured out that it was possible to obtain a work permit by applying for political asylum.[25] Like Mario Rodrigues, these immigrants acted on the notions that to get a work permit, one simply has to apply and that it is possible to *arreglar papeles*. Because of the extensive delay in hearing these cases, many applicants did receive an asylum of sorts—that is, work permits and permission to remain in the United States while their applications were pending.[26] Although the INS eventually closed this loophole by adopting a last-in/first-out policy and instituting a six-month delay in issuing work permits to asylum applicants, the legal system temporarily tolerated this unofficial means of "legalization."

Central Americans' struggle for legal residency has resulted in the legitimization of this strategy for at least certain asylum applicants. The sanctuary movement, the Central American solidarity movement, and class-action lawsuits on behalf of Central American asylum seekers denounced the illegitimacy of official asylum proceedings that denied the claims of individuals who had experienced torture, massacres, bombings, and political violence (Anker 1992; Blum 1991; Coutin forthcoming; Fiederlein 1991; MacEoin 1985; Pirie 1990). The legal remedies that resulted from these mobilizations—TPS, DED, ABC, and NACARA—legitimized the unofficial legal strategy that many undocumented immigrants had been pursuing. TPS, DED, and ABC permitted Salvadorans and Guatemalans to live and work in the United States while civil strife continued in El Salvador and Guatemala and while their asylum applications were pending. NACARA recognized that these asylum applicants had been living in the country in a somewhat documented status for a long period of time and made them eligible to apply for the equivalent of suspension of deportation. Thus, an alternative legality was incorporated into official law.

The authority of unofficial law is not limited to the ABC case. For example, the idea that documents confer legal status correctly notes that holding individuals legally accountable for the immigration status of those with whom they interact gives private citizens some control over determination of legality. Thus, when employers check job applicants' work authorization, when school officials require students' social security numbers, and when Department of Motor Vehicles clerks demand proof of legal presence before issuing driver's licenses, those who possess *permisos* can define themselves as legal, as Ana Sanchez noted when she commented that the *permiso* that she obtained through TPS made her "not be illegal anymore." In this sense, a work permit *is* a legal status: *permisos* enable those who have them to define their presence as legitimate.[27] In addition, when immigrants conclude that time alone is a basis for legalization or that there must be some way of "fixing" their papers, they are recognizing that the distinctions between those who do and do not obtain papers are often socially meaningless, that in contrast to current rhetoric distinguishing "good" legal immigrants from "bad" illegal immigrants, these are often the same individuals. Immigrants' emphasis on time as a basis for legalization may accurately suggest that if they remain in the United States long enough, the law may arbitrarily select a characteristic that they can demonstrate as a basis for legalization. This, in essence, is what occurred when the 1986 amnesty program selected January 1, 1982, as the date by which immigrants had to be continuously and illegally present to legalize. Moreover, immigrants' efforts to claim deservingness may seek to counter their imagined detrimental documents with an imagined contract that allocates status to the deserving. Such strategies are sometimes rewarded with grants of suspension of deportation or cancellation of removal. Official and unofficial law remain entangled.

Conclusion

The multiplicity of legal forms calls into question law's claim to speak with a unitary voice (Fitzpatrick 1992; Greenhouse 1996; Sierra

1995) and thus challenges the authority of law itself. If the interdependence of official and unofficial law were to be openly acknowledged, then the bases for assessing truth, credibility, and legality would have to be revised so that the sorts of legal strategies pursued by Roberto Mendez would be rendered plausible. To characterize alternative legalities simply as a form of resistance, however, would negate the ways that these practices make official law possible. Often, immigrants' efforts to obtain work permits subject them to the scrutiny of legal authorities, who then bring official law to bear on these cases (see also Yngvesson 1993b). Moreover, because resistance is not limited to negating or opposing (Foucault 1978), both official and unofficial versions of immigration law suggest strategies that unauthorized immigrants can pursue. Applying for a *permiso* through a notary public under the assumption that it is possible to "fix" one's papers did at one time enable applicants to obtain work permits and thus become temporarily legal. Similarly, official law also gives rise to particular legalization strategies in which immigration attorneys are well versed. Under pre-IIRIRA immigration law, these strategies included delaying deportation hearings long enough for immigrants to become eligible for suspension, appealing denials of asylum so that immigrants could remain in the United States with work authorization while waiting for a family petition to become current, and so forth. Both official and unofficial versions of immigration law have complex and contradictory political implications. These contradictory implications make advocacy on behalf of the undocumented a complicated endeavor.

Chapter 4
"Law Is One Thing, Justice Is Another"

Organizations that provide free or low-cost legal services to the undocumented are situated in complex ways vis-à-vis their clients, government authorities, and immigration law itself. To resituate their (undocumented) clients in a domain of legality, advocates act as brokers of immigration law, negotiating the authoritativeness of both official and unofficial legal discourses. Advocacy does not consist of simply trying to legitimize unofficial versions of immigration law. Such an approach would be futile, given that advocacy occurs largely in an "official" realm where law's dependence on the unofficial is denied. Rather, to advocate for clients, legal-services providers must manipulate both official legal discourse and clients' accounts to redefine clients' actions and experiences as grounds for legalization. Such manipulation entails both negotiating the meaning of legal categories to argue that their clients fit and attempting to make clients' life narratives conform to predefined prototypes of the deserving (see McKinley 1997). In that advocacy enforces and reproduces legal notions that derive from the state, advocates become, in an odd way, agents of the state. At the same time, advocates' political perspectives, participation in immigrants'-rights movements, and organizational links to popular movements in Central America make them critical of some of the official legal notions that they must deploy on clients' behalf. Moreover, to work effectively with clients, advocates must in some way acknowledge the multiplicity of law and the at least partial validity of clients' legal realities. Advocacy is therefore a multifaceted and contradictory project (Merry 1995), as advocates simultaneously challenge and reinforce both official and unofficial legal notions.

I focus my discussion of legal advocacy on community organizations not because they handle the majority of immigration cases—they do not—but rather because these organizations are positioned simultaneously at the center and on the fringes of law. Community organizations are at the center of law in that they try to make law work for their clients, they are vigilant to see that clients' legal rights are respected, and they define law through legal arguments and class actions that establish precedents and force policy changes. They are on the fringes of law in that they are marginalized economically, they stand outside of dominant legal institutions and call for them to act justly, and they critique and seek to get around certain aspects of immigration law (see McBarnet 1984; Holston 1991). Community organizations' legal advocacy thus explores and exposes the limits of law as an oppressive force and a means of pursuing justice. Analyzing advocacy therefore provides insight into the contradictory workings of law itself.

I begin my account of legal advocacy by situating the organizations where I did fieldwork, their staff, and their clients within the panoply of actors who negotiate the meaning of immigration law in Los Angeles. I then turn to a microanalysis of the interpretive processes through which advocates construct and evaluate clients' cases. I next examine how working on cases produces narratives that claim (and at times redefine) legal categories. Finally, I delineate the sort of "legal consciousness" (Engel and Munger 1996; Merry 1990; Sarat 1990) promoted by community organizations' legal advocacy as well as the ways that this consciousness deconstructs "official law." This analysis of advocacy demonstrates the political complexity of negotiating legal identities, even with people who are very sympathetic to immigrants.

Community Organizations

The term *community organization* (*organización comunitaria* in Spanish) is difficult to define. Most of the Los Angeles–based immigration-related organizations that claim this designation are nonprofits that work with low-income people and whose mission includes not only providing services but also some form of political advocacy concerning immigrants' rights. *Community* is a legitimizing term within both

U.S. and Central American legal and political activism. In the United States, there is a long tradition of trying to make institutions serve the community, as evidenced by community-based policing, the alternative-dispute-resolution movement, and so forth (Merry and Milner 1993; see also William Fisher 1997). Political activism in Central America has also been performed on behalf of *las masas* (the masses), *la base* (the base), and *la comunidad* (as in the base Christian community movement; see Berryman 1984; Cardenal 1976; Gutierrez 1973; Lernoux 1982). The term *community* confers a certain representational authority on an organization by implying that the organization is made up of members of a community, works on behalf of a community, or is supported by a particular community. The relationship between an organization and "its community" may, however, be more complex than this designation suggests (William Fisher 1997). For example, organizations may have to devise procedures to "manage" the clients who seek services. Organizations may also struggle to mobilize their constituencies to support organizations' goals and activities. Moreover, the term *community* can idealize the people it represents in that this term glosses over divisions and implies homogeneity and boundedness (Yngvesson 1993a). Despite these limitations, I will use the term *community organization* to mark a group's self-designated vision and structural position.

In Los Angeles, community organizations are only one element in a spectrum of individuals and entities that provide immigration services. At one end of this spectrum are law firms that handle immigration cases along with many other legal matters. Only corporations and affluent individuals can afford their services, which are typically of high quality. At the other end of this spectrum are notary publics who advertise themselves as immigration specialists and who probably handle the majority of immigration cases. As discussed in chapter 3, notaries charge high fees, submit fraudulent applications, mislead clients, refuse to give clients copies of their paperwork, and disappear into the woodwork overnight. To be fair, there are probably some notaries who provide decent immigration services for low cost, but I have encountered few, if any, accounts of such individuals. Private attorneys who practice immigration law range across the spectrum. There are highly skilled, conscientious attorneys (some of whom formerly worked for community organizations) who specialize in immigration law as well as shadier, what some might call incompetent, attorneys who work with notaries (see Hagan 1994). Both types of attorneys are relatively expensive, but the latter advertise more aggressively. The final component of this spectrum is made up of nonprofit organizations that handle immigration cases. Nonprofits include advocacy groups such as Legal Aid as well as organizations that serve particular immigrant communities, such as Armenians, Russians, Asians, and Central Americans. Clients of community organizations are typically indigent or low-income individuals, sometimes of a particular ethnic or national origin, who have legally compelling immigration cases.

The three Central American community organizations with which I worked have complex and interconnected histories. Two of these groups—El Rescate and CARECEN—were founded during the early 1980s by activists who were members of political movements in Central America. The Frente Farabundo Martí para la Liberación Nacional (FMLN, Farabundo Martí National Liberation Front), the force that opposed the Salvadoran government during the civil war, was made up of five organizations, each of which had its own history and membership.[1] When members of these organizations went into exile in the late 1970s and early 1980s, they did so not only to escape persecution by government authorities but also to launch a movement in solidarity with political struggles in Central America. In Los Angeles, which was a common destination for these early migrants, activists founded political committees devoted to raising funds for their parent organizations in El Salvador, publicizing human rights abuses and other injustices, organizing the burgeoning Salvadoran refugee population, and so forth. Activism initially was directed primarily toward the struggle in Central America, because activists believed that the war would be over in a couple of years, enabling Salvadorans living in exile to return home. By 1982 or 1983, however, activists realized that the war would be prolonged and therefore began to direct their efforts not only toward El Salvador but also toward the refugee community living in the United States. To address this community's legal and social needs, political committees around the United States founded refugee centers, including El Rescate and CARECEN. Though the political committees that founded them have either dissolved or regrouped since the signing of peace accords in 1992, El Rescate and CARECEN have continued to advocate on behalf of Central American immigrants in Los Angeles.[2]

ASOSAL, the third community organization whose activities I observed, was founded more recently, in the 1990s, as part of the effort to extend the eighteen months of TPS that was awarded to Salvadorans through the 1990 Immigration Act (see Coutin 1998b). Originally a subcommittee of CARECEN, ASOSAL became an independent organization in 1991 so that its members could focus exclusively on the legal, civic, and cultural needs of Salvadorans rather than on the broader range of issues addressed by CARECEN. One of its members described ASOSAL's founding: "We began to have activities, such as fund-raisers, to try to motivate people, to educate the people who were within the [TPS] program . . . so that the people who were applicants would feel that they had to fight for their own program." ASOSAL members note that ASOSAL differs from CARECEN and El Rescate in that ASOSAL focuses primarily on Salvadorans instead of attempting serve the Central American community more generally. In addition, ASOSAL strives to be apolitical within Salvadoran party politics. A staff member told me, "We don't have a defined political position referring to this type of *tendencia* [political movement]. We work here as Salvadorans with Salvadorans and for Salvadorans, without giving any importance to what [political] color someone is, what band someone was involved in, or anything." Notwithstanding its official stance, some of the individuals who are active within ASOSAL do have political connections and prior organizational experience.

The relationship among El Rescate, CARECEN, and ASOSAL has occasionally been contentious, sometimes making it a delicate task to work closely with all three organizations. Rivalry among these groups is in part a product of factionalism within Salvadoran political movements (see Byrne 1996; Montgomery 1995). In addition, each of these groups competes with the others for prestige, funding, and members. One activist noted that the organizations "fought for the same community, funds, and every organization supposedly was supposed to generate political and economic support. . . . So it was going to be difficult. So everyone ran around trying to bring water to their own mill. . . . Always, there was division. It wasn't a monolithic matter." Central American community organizations have worked together on particular projects over the years, such as the recent campaign for residency for ABC class members, but have maintained their institutional distinctiveness.[3] Each of these organizations welcomed me as a volunteer, a researcher, and a supporter, and no one attempted to restrict my access to other groups. I was, however, asked by one group not to discuss its policies and procedures with one of the other groups. Personally, I found the staff at each of the organizations to be professional and dedicated, and I came to respect each group and its work.

Central American immigrants' legal needs changed over the course of these organizations' histories. Both El Rescate and CARE-CEN were founded at a time when Central Americans' primary legal need was to avoid being deported to life-threatening conditions. Their legal programs therefore initially focused on preparing asylum applications for individuals who were at risk of persecution and who had been apprehended by the INS and placed in deportation proceedings.[4] An attorney who worked at El Rescate during this period recalled, "There was just an overwhelming need [for clients] to avoid deportation. And we knew that those who were deported could be killed, so that gave an urgency to our work. This was a cause!" By 1995, when I began to work with community organizations in Los Angeles, a sizable segment of the Central American immigrant population had obtained bona fide but precarious legal status through TPS, DED, and ABC.[5] The 1986 amnesty program also enabled Central Americans who immigrated before January 1, 1982, to become legal permanent residents and even citizens.

The legal services that El Rescate, CARECEN, and ASOSAL provided in the mid-1990s reflected these changed circumstances. In addition to trying to save the lives of desperate asylum seekers, staff filled out family visa petition forms, completed naturalization applications, represented individuals applying for suspension of deportation, defended aliens being deported due to criminal convictions, assisted victims of domestic violence in applying for residency, filled out work-permit renewal application forms, filed requests for immigration files through the Freedom of Information Act, and so forth. The urgency of this work—which one El Rescate attorney characterized as "trying to keep a family together or to help someone keep what they've acquired here in the U.S."—came less from a sense that refugees would be killed if they were to be deported and more from an awareness of the devastating effects that U.S. immigration policies could have on individuals, families, and communities.

In designing their legal-services programs,[6] community organizations had to devise workable means of managing the potentially overwhelming numbers of clients who sought their services. The need to manage clients arose out of organizations' short staffing and limited resources. Though their size and structure changed several times during my fieldwork,[7] CARECEN and El Rescate usually had two staff attorneys, several paralegals, and a fluctuating number of volunteers and student interns. As both CARECEN and El Rescate charged only minimal fees for services and did not charge for legal representation, organizational resources were not sufficient to represent large numbers of clients. Staff members at both El Rescate and CARECEN therefore set unofficial limits on the numbers of clients that could request their services.[8] At El Rescate, for example, clients seeking legal representation and other relatively time-consuming services were required to first attend a public presentation—known as a *charla*—on immigration law. At charlas, El Rescate staff gave out a limited number of appointments to individuals who seemed to have compelling cases. These appointments were used to dispense legal advice and also to obtain information that would allow El Rescate staff to decide whether to accept individuals' cases. Of the hundred or more people who attended charlas during a given week, ten to twelve might receive appointments, and at most only one or two of these people's cases would be accepted. At CARECEN, legal staff gave out a limited number of appointments (ten to fifteen) per week for consultations on a first-come, first served basis. In most instances, consultations were used to advise clients and provide brief services, but clients with particularly compelling cases were sometimes accepted for pro bono legal representation. Although they limited the number of clients to whom they provided direct services, staff members at CARECEN and El Rescate did strive to be accessible by giving charlas and scheduling consultations. ASOSAL had less need to limit the numbers of clients that it served, because the group had no staff attorney and therefore could not provide legal representation. ASOSAL staff members did, however, manage clients by reminding them to renew their work permits, urging them to support ASOSAL activities, and inviting them to join in campaigns for permanent residency.

Although legal staff limited their most expensive and time-consuming services, these workers also sought to advocate on behalf of the Central American community as a whole. Unlike legal services, which generally aided only individuals,[9] such advocacy work was intended to change the conditions in which individuals operated. All three organizations held regular charlas that sought to educate immigrants about their legal rights, their chances of legalizing, the workings of the INS, immigration law, and so forth. Legal staff hoped that through charlas, the immigrants whom they could not serve would be able to devise legalization strategies that were more viable than those created in the space of nonexistence. In addition to charlas, organizations' community-advocacy work included participating in class-action suits, lobbying Congress regarding immigration legislation, issuing human-rights reports, holding press conferences about changes in immigration law, negotiating with INS officials regarding asylum and other procedures, and joining in political campaigns to shape immigration policies. Organizations nonetheless faced continual dilemmas regarding whether to prioritize political advocacy or services to individuals (see Coutin 1993).

Though the details of their legal-services programs differed, staff members at all three of these organizations attempted to assist undocumented immigrants who sought legal status. Such assistance required "diagnosing" individuals' immigration cases.

Diagnosing a Case

Legal-services providers sometimes resorted to medical metaphors to describe their work.[10] One private attorney who allowed me to sit in while he met with clients claimed that he could "diagnose" clients' cases in a matter of minutes. Attorneys and paralegals at community organizations advised clients that, like patients who have been told that they need to have an operation, they should get a second opinion about their legalization options. During a press conference regarding proposals to grant residency to ABC class members, a minister commented, "Distinguishing between victims of communism and victims of other forms of oppressive government is like saying that victims of cancer deserve our compassion and research funding but victims of AIDS or tuberculosis do not." Though advocates probably do not actually mean to imply that those they serve are ill, such metaphors exemplify both the idea that the undocumented and their papers are in need of "fixing" and the more general pathologizing of refugees (Malkki 1992).[11] The diagnosis referred to in these metaphors consisted of assessing clients' current legal situation, their potential for legalization, and their legalization options. To diagnose cases, service providers had to elicit accounts of clients' legal histories and personal circumstances. Service providers could then determine the match between clients' own circumstances and the prototype for a particular form of legalization. Because they were conducted with an eye to how clients' cases would fare in court, such assessments required advocates to view clients' cases from the standpoint of immigration officials. Though these diagnoses lacked the official character of court decisions and other legal determinations, advocates' assessments determined whether clients would receive free legal representation from the organization and were therefore a critical moment in clients' efforts to negotiate their legal statuses in the United States.

Diagnosing clients' cases required advocates to develop a sort of triple vision that saw a case from the perspective of the client, the advocate, and the officials who would eventually render a judgment. During an interview, a student intern used the metaphor of translation to describe this triple vision: "You get to translate these two dictionaries. From the English to the Spanish and then the legal to the English to the Spanish. You're interface." Of course, cases were themselves constructed through this process of translation and did not exist as independent or transparent realities (Mather and Yngvesson 1980–81; Merry 1990; Yngvesson 1993b). They had to be continually read, worked on, and judged, as another student intern explained: "On one side, you have a story that this person needs to tell . . . and on the other side you have legal criteria that needs [sic] to be met. Okay? And so you have to take that story and somehow fit it into the legal criteria." Diagnosis read clients' stories in anticipation of how they would eventually be judged and assessed whether working on a case could lead to a favorable outcome. As a result, diagnosis in some ways anticipated and rehearsed the future hearing in immigration court. If the client could convince the service provider—who acted simultaneously as legal advocate, sympathetic ear, and judge[12]—of his or her deservingness, then there was some chance that the organization might accept the client's case (or, in the case of ASOSAL, assist the client in locating pro bono legal representation).

In addition to the multiple positionings required by diagnosis, advocates were also positioned in multiple ways by their legal status, nationality, gender, and political and legal expertise (see Bogoch 1997). Some paralegals were themselves Salvadoran immigrants who had pending asylum applications through the ABC settlement agreement. This situation enabled them to emphasize their commonality with clients, as an ASOSAL member told clients who had assembled for an ABC update: "I too am an applicant. What happens in this campaign [for permanent residency for ABC class members] will affect me." When diagnosing clients' cases, Anglo legal workers sometimes deferred to Salvadoran workers regarding the credibility of clients' claimed political histories or the possibility that a client might have abused someone's human rights. When working on ABC asylum applications, for example, I was told to refer clients who had held positions in the police or the military to Central American staff members. Female clients who either stated or hinted that they had experienced sexual violence were sometimes referred to female advocates under the assumption that such clients would feel more comfortable with or speak more freely to another woman. In such instances, assumed gender commonalities were thought to supersede national or ethnic differences. Legal workers were also differentiated by their degree of legal expertise. Attorneys ultimately had authority over assessing the legal viability of clients' cases, though other legal staff members could influence decisions to accept or reject a client's case. Legal advocates' "identities" were thus as constructed and contingent as those of the clients they served.

The first step in diagnosing a case was to decipher clients' prior legal histories. This step was crucial because clients' options and immediate legal needs were determined by the procedural statuses of their cases as well as the legal record that had already been generated. For example, an individual who was in proceedings was at risk of being deported, someone who had a pending asylum application but had never received an appointment for an asylum interview did not have a pressing need for legal representation, and a person who had never applied for any form of legal status and had not been detained could decide whether to reveal his or her presence to immigration officials. Deciphering this history was not easy, however, given that clients and advocates did not share the same legal vocabulary. If copies of clients' legal records were unavailable, service providers had to translate between their own and their clients' legal categories.[13] For example, if clients said that they appeared in court, advocates often asked where the court was. If clients answered that the court was in Anaheim, advocates concluded that clients had not yet been in immigration court (which was in Los Angeles) but rather had had an asylum interview at the INS asylum unit in Anaheim. Analyzing the past and future trajectories of clients' cases required advocates to distinguish between individuals as social beings and as legal constructs—a distinction that clients did not always make. One client whose hearing was scheduled for the day after he first sought El Rescate's legal assistance was eager to present his case instead of seeking an extension as a legal worker advised. The legal worker cautioned him, "No, don't do that. You have a good case. If you do that, it's not in your interests. You'll lose. What you need to do is get all this documentation in order, prepare it, and then when you're ready, then present your case." From the client's perspective, the date of his hearing was irrelevant to his intrinsic deservingness, but from the legal worker's point of view, his intrinsic deservingness mattered less than the presentable and documented narrative of this deservingness that could be constructed with a bit more time.[14]

Once the procedural status of a case was clear, advocates explored clients' legal histories to determine the statuses they could confer. Legal histories included not only clients' prior interaction with the INS but also those aspects of clients' lives that had legal meanings. Family relationships were a central element of clients' legal histories, as certain kin ties could transmit legality. U.S. citizens, for example, had the right to immigrate their spouses, children, parents, and siblings, while legal permanent residents could petition for their spouses, minor children, and unmarried children over the age of twenty-one.[15] Although family petitions officially were intended to enable citizens and legal immigrants to reunify their families, they actually had become a means of legalizing undocumented relatives in the United States.[16] Clients, however, did not always see their kin primarily in terms of legal status. For example, on being advised that his U.S. citizen sister could petition for him, one client told a paralegal, "I can't ask her to do that, because we aren't on good terms." Another discrepancy between legal and social relationships arose from the fact that only those (largely nuclear) family relationships that were recognized within immigration law counted as a means of transmitting legality. For example, individuals could not petition for their unmarried partners (particularly problematic for gay or lesbian couples), and an aunt could not petition for a niece or nephew for whom she had cared since birth, but a father could immigrate a child from whom he was estranged. Despite the constraints of legal definitions of family, there was some room for manipulating one's relationships. A legal permanent resident relative could naturalize and thus accelerate a visa petition, a heterosexual couple could marry and thus make the undocumented partner eligible for a petition, and an unmarried child of a legal permanent resident could remain single to preserve his or her visa eligibility.[17]

Legal advocates explored clients' eligibility not only for family visa petitions but also for the forms of relief that (at the time of my research) could be awarded in court: political asylum and suspension of deportation. The triple vision through which they read clients' cases situated advocates both as sympathetic listeners who understood the effects of state terrorism and the predicament of the undocumented and as adjudicators or even trial attorneys on the lookout for plot holes, weaknesses, or untruths within clients' accounts. To differentiate what ASOSAL staff termed a "real" asylum case from asylum applications that were filed as a means of obtaining a work permit, advocates asked clients the following sorts of questions: Why did you leave your country? Are you afraid to go back? What do you think would happen to you if you had to return? Like INS officials, advocates sought to distinguish victims of generalized violence (who were ineligible for asylum) from individuals who had been singled out by their persecutors. This distinction was implied by an ASOSAL staff member's question of a Salvadoran man who had been wounded by the Salvadoran National Guard: "Were they shooting at you in particular, or did you just happen to get shot?" Similarly, legal staff assessed clients' eligibility for suspension of deportation according to the same criteria used by immigration judges. These criteria included the applicant's degree of acculturation and roots (including legalized kin) in the United States; financial considerations, such as loss of property, employment, or opportunities for advancement; the need to provide financial support to aging parents or young children; the emotional cost of uprooting U.S. citizen children who were unaccustomed to life in their parents' homelands; and medical problems that could only be treated in the United States. Just as courts require some evidence of applicants' claims, so too did legal workers ask to see proof that clients had lived in the U.S.

for seven years or had belonged to a dissident group as claimed. Such requests for proof were justified on the grounds that, to later win in court, clients would need to either obtain this documentation or explain why they could not do so. Legal workers also sought to fill any plot holes in clients' accounts. For instance, one El Rescate paralegal asked her client, "How was it that when [the security forces] blindfolded you, they didn't tie the blindfold tight enough so that you couldn't see? They were going to kill you. Wouldn't they be careful about this?"

To the degree that they adopted the perspective of a judge, legal staff members viewed clients' accounts of persecution with some skepticism. When training interns, attorneys at both CARECEN and El Rescate advised students to look out for clients who were not telling the truth. Tests of credibility used by legal workers included the details of clients' accounts, the emotional state of the speaker, and the extent of clients' knowledge. One paralegal told me that she had declined to accept the case of a woman who claimed to have been raped in the course of a recruitment effort because the woman had recounted the rape unemotionally, in front of her young child, despite the paralegal's offers to allow the child to leave the room. "In all my experience with rape victims, I've never seen a woman do that," the paralegal related. Too much emotion could also be a sign of deception. For instance, after a client had buried his face in his hands, seemingly in tears, while recounting an occasion when a gun was put to his head, a paralegal told me, "He was faking it. I could see him. There were no tears." A student intern questioned the account of a Guatemalan man who claimed to have run for mayor of his town but who could provide no details about his campaign or his party's ideology. Similarly, workers viewed skeptically individuals who claimed to have belonged to the FMLN but could not name the subgroup to which they had belonged. I sometimes found myself adopting the skeptical attitude of other legal workers. For example, when an ABC applicant dictated a succinct but coherent account of her recruitment by the Salvadoran guerrilla forces and her activities as a guerrilla fighter, I found myself wondering whether she had memorized this narrative.

As diagnosis positioned workers in multiple ways, service providers listened not only skeptically but also sympathetically. One student intern, for example, distinguished his role from that of a judge:

> Say someone was tortured, okay? . . . I have a person in front of
> me who's in tears, who's shaking, who's trembling. Okay? The
> court never has to deal with that. The court doesn't want to know
> he or she was in tears, was shaking, was trembling, was pouring
> their heart out to me. All they want to know is, was this person
> tortured, in this analytical framework, right? And there are
> times, young as I am in my career, when I want to go to the judge
> and say, "Don't you understand how this person feels?"

As sympathetic and politically conscious listeners, legal staff members
often expressed sympathy with clients whose cases were morally or
politically but not legally compelling. For example, when a Salvadoran woman began sobbing as she described being separated from
family members by a military roadblock and then having to leave
behind her worldly possessions to flee to the United States, a legal
worker (who later told me that the woman had a weak asylum case)
commented sympathetically, "INS doesn't understand what it is to
flee a country." Advocates were also sympathetic to the hardship theories volunteered by some suspension applicants whose cases they
could not accept. One client explained such a theory to me during
an interview: "If I don't get papers here, then that will affect not only
me but also people in El Salvador who depend on me economically.
They will go hungry. But Immigration doesn't think about this when
they decide whether or not to give someone a work permit." Though
it is difficult to base a suspension case on the economic difficulties of
family members in El Salvador, advocates who sought permanent residency for ABC class members often cited the economic impact of
remittances in their campaigns to legalize this group (see chapter 6).

Though they sympathized with clients' need to legalize, advocates, like judges, ultimately had to assess the merit of clients' cases.
Assessments were rendered in two ways. Sometimes advocates communicated their assessments to clients directly, usually displacing the
authority for their conclusions from themselves to the INS and the
law. For example, one El Rescate paralegal told her client, "I understand why you are afraid to return to El Salvador, but it is very hard to
win asylum in the United States. Only two or three out of every hundred cases wins. So most likely, you will have a hard time winning. But
you should still try." Similarly, another paralegal told a client, "I
understand that when someone knocked on your door in the middle

of the night, you were afraid that you were going to be assassinated. I'm from El Salvador, and I know these things. But to the Immigration officials, that isn't proof. They will think that it could have been anyone knocking on the door. So to them this won't be a strong case in comparison to someone who was tortured." A second means of rendering an assessment was to simply decline to accept a case and to refer a client elsewhere. Though the reasons for such a decision were not always explained to clients, referrals indirectly rendered a "judgment" of a case. Such judgments were, however, mitigated by advocates' advice to clients. Even if they could not represent clients, advocates sought to improve clients' chances of winning by instructing them in immigration law, revising their asylum declarations, and recommending lifestyle changes that would strengthen their suspension cases. For example, clients were advised to do volunteer work, go to school, learn English, get jobs, pay taxes, get off welfare, reimburse the government for any assistance received, and so forth. Even such advice was politically contradictory, however, given that it emphasized categories and practices that were important to INS officials rather than to advocates.

Diagnosing cases positioned advocates as agents of the state in that advocates used the state's criteria to assess the merit of clients' cases and encouraged clients to comply with state law. It is true that advocates sometimes accepted cases that had the potential to establish precedents that would further legal justice. Examples of such cases included HIV-positive asylum seekers, sexual orientation asylum cases, domestic-violence suspension cases, and emotionally based past persecution cases. One attorney told me that he was on the lookout for a case that would allow him to argue that gang members faced persecution at the hands of government vigilantes if they were deported to El Salvador. In such cases, advocacy sought to stretch or redefine the legal meanings of "hardship," "persecution," "refugee," "social group," and so forth. Yet the bulk of community organizations' legal services were designed to address a dilemma posed by organizations' continual shortages of resources: Is it better to ignore the realities of the courts and to accept morally compelling cases that have little chance of winning, or is it more effective to limit legal representation to cases that may win? Adopting the latter course was more practical but required advocates to prioritize official ways of seeing.

Like diagnosing cases, preparing clients' cases entailed matching clients to legal prototypes. Like the assessment required by diagnosis, case preparation produced narratives that were designed to qualify clients for particular forms of legalization.

Preparing a Case

Although legal staff at El Rescate, ASOSAL, and CARECEN worked on suspension, adjustment, and naturalization cases, family visa petitions, and other sorts of claims, my discussion of case preparation focuses on procedures in which the politics of producing legal narratives were particularly visible: the ABC application process.[18] While all legal narratives are, in a sense, constructed (Mertz 1994), the process of diagnosing clients' cases would normally limit community organizations' legal advocacy to asylum applicants whose narratives of persecution largely matched that of the prototypical refugee. In the case of ABC clients, however, the fact that class members had special protections under the settlement agreement and had already revealed their presence to the INS by soliciting TPS meant that preparing an asylum application for a client with a "weak" but nonfrivolous case did not expose the client to legal risks. As a result, legal staff had greater rein to apply their own (rather than INS officials') eligibility criteria during the ABC application process than when deciding whether to accept regular asylum cases. As their organizations had spent the 1980s denouncing the severity, pervasiveness, and arbitrariness of political violence in El Salvador, legal workers contended that almost anyone who fled El Salvador during the civil war had a nonfrivolous asylum claim and was eligible to apply. By suggesting that ABC class members as a group merited legal status in the United States, these criteria challenged the more restrictive definitions of *refugee* used during diagnosis. At the same time, the prototypical idea of a refugee influenced the ABC application process in that advocates narrated clients' asylum claims in terms of this prototype. In so doing, advocates sought both to make clients' cases legally compelling and to demonstrate that they were not preparing frivolous asylum claims. Advocates—who sharply distinguished themselves from notary publics—did *not* invent narratives but did recount them in the most legally compelling way possible.

Though legal workers at El Rescate, ASOSAL, and CARECEN were committed to preparing asylum applications for ABC class members, these staff members faced the same dilemma that they encountered in the rest of their legal work: How can organizational resources be most effectively allocated when only a small percentage of immigrants are likely to qualify for relief? This dilemma arose because, despite the fact that many had experienced life-threatening and emotionally devastating political violence, few ABC class members could prove that they had been singled out for persecution and that in postwar El Salvador they were still at risk. As one ASOSAL staff member explained while training me to prepare ABC class members' asylum applications, "Some people practically don't have a case." To prepare the extensive, detailed, and well-documented application packets that were typical of organizations' regular asylum cases would be a misuse of resources, because, even with such attention, few applicants would be likely to win. Organizations therefore decided to prepare accurate but brief asylum applications in all but the most compelling cases, thus registering applicants for the benefits of the ABC settlement agreement and securing them work permits while their cases were pending. One legal worker drew attention to this strategy by commenting, "I don't understand why we have to bother to explain what happened to them in El Salvador when all we are doing is registering them for a status." Legal staff also hoped that, as a group, ABC applicants would eventually be granted residency or permitted to apply for suspension of deportation. Indeed, in retrospect, ABC class members' asylum claims may be less important to their hopes of legalization than the lives they have established in the United States. NACARA, which was passed in November 1997, allows ABC class members to apply for suspension of deportation, and streamlined procedures may make it possible for INS officials to consider their asylum and suspension claims simultaneously.

The decision to prepare skeletal asylum applications for most ABC class members led legal staff members to use highly inclusive criteria when screening clients for eligibility. Though all three organizations required class members to attend an ABC charla before requesting services, it was not necessary for organizations to limit the number of ABC clients they served, since the cost of preparing applications was covered by the minimal processing fees charged to ABC applicants. All charla attendees who, after being instructed regarding

political asylum, wished to apply for benefits of the settlement agreement were screened through intake forms that asked them why they
had left El Salvador, whether they feared returning, and whether they
or a family member had belonged to any one of a number of groups
known to have been persecuted. If clients indicated that they feared
returning, and if this fear could be traced to their (imputed or
expressed) political opinion, membership in a social group, or
another of the five recognized grounds for seeking asylum, clients
were minimally eligible.[19] Clients' answers to the questions on the
intake forms were sometimes ambiguous. For example, clients sometimes wrote that they fled to find work or because a spouse or parent
had sent for them but that they feared returning. Whereas an asylum
official might desist at this point, deeming the client's responses evidence of an unfounded claim (see Anker 1992), legal workers per-
sisted in exploring the basis for clients' fear. It was necessary, I was
told, to dig for information, as many Salvadorans took experiences
like being forced off buses by soldiers for granted and did not see
themselves as victims of persecution. A legal worker at one organization told me that if clients failed to check off any of the forms of persecution listed on the intake form, he categorized them as either
unemployed by the war or as residents of a conflictive zone because
"these are general categories that almost everyone fits into." In addition to seeking an articulable fear of persecution, legal workers also
screened out individuals—such as military officers, members of the
Salvadoran National Guard, soldiers who served more than the two
obligatory years of service, or members of special forces—who might
themselves have violated human rights. Also, though organizations'
definitions of eligibility were broad, they did refuse to submit applications for individuals who insisted that they had immigrated solely
for economic reasons.

After determining that a client was eligible to apply for asylum as
an ABC class member, legal workers completed an asylum application form, which entailed constructing a narrative of persecution. In
some cases this narrative was written in pieces as answers to different
questions on the form itself, and in other cases the narrative was
appended to the form as a separate asylum declaration. Whether
choppy or uninterrupted, this narrative recounted individuals' political (or imputedly political) actions, experiences of persecution, and
flight to the United States. To construct this narrative, legal workers

asked clients to describe instances of persecution. Only rarely did a client's response take the form of an immediately coherent and logical narrative. Rather, clients recounted one bad experience after another, seemingly connecting these experiences by the suffering they entailed more than through temporal cause and effect. To create the logical coherence required to demonstrate a rational and well-founded fear of persecution, legal workers reordered this narrative, recounting events chronologically. For instance, my field notes regarding one ABC asylum application read, "As I tried to construct a narrative, I found it very important to get down some dates and to put things in the right order. I wanted to know, for instance, what had happened to [the client] before her father had been elected mayor, what had happened afterwards, etc. She wasn't as concerned about chronology, and seemed to me to just be pouring out her story." Putting events in chronological order situated events in linear time— the temporality favored by U.S. law—and thus created coherence by implying agency and intentionality (see also Greenhouse 1996:180). The rationality of accounts was enhanced by questioning clients regarding potential plot holes, such as temporal discontinuities within their accounts. For example, if individuals were abducted and beaten and then remained in El Salvador for two years before coming to the United States, the discontinuity between their persecution and flight implied that these were two separate instances rather than interconnected events. To reconnect the persecution and flight, legal workers asked clients what measures they took to protect themselves during the intervening years and what had finally led the individuals to abandon their country.

In addition to reordering clients' accounts chronologically, legal workers edited clients' narratives of persecution. Statements that legal workers considered damaging or irrelevant were omitted. For example, a staff member crossed out references to economic difficulties in an ABC client's written draft of her asylum declaration, another staff member advised me not to include a client's comments about the United States being a great and generous country, and in another case, I was told to omit a client's statement that "through begging and pleading and a small bribe" she had been able to secure her son's release from the army. In addition to eliminating statements, legal workers added details that they felt would enhance the coherence and credibility of clients' accounts. For example, when clients recounted instances of persecution, legal staff members asked for the dates and locations of incidents, the names of those involved, and so forth. During an interview, a legal worker explained that such details were important because they "make the story more solid. You have so many more details because Immigration would say, 'This is like a mold letter.' . . . It's to individualize it and to let them know that we didn't just copy it and stamp it and send it." This comment demonstrates the dilemma that both legal workers and clients faced in preparing asylum narratives: to win, narratives had to conform to a predefined prototype, but to be credible, accounts had to deviate from this prototype lest they be taken as invented or canned. Finally, legal workers reworded clients' accounts to make them more compelling. At one organization, I was told to change statements such as "I decided to leave El Salvador" to "I was forced to leave El Salvador," because the former wording implied that the client could have chosen to remain in the country.[20] Such nuanced attention to the wording of asylum narratives suggests that although their main goal may have been to register class members for the benefits of the ABC settlement agreement, legal workers had at least some faith in narratives' power to confer legality (in this case, asylum) on narratives' subjects.

The ABC application process demonstrates that the political implications of case preparation are complex. On the one hand, constructing asylum narratives imposes legal categories on the complexity of individuals' lives, rendering them as yet another instance of an already written story. Carol Greenhouse (1996:209) notes that in institutional contexts, "A life story . . . is constructed out of forms and circumstances that are already legible, even before they acquire their particulars. A life story in linear form can never be personal" (see also Ewick and Silbey 1995). ABC clients sometimes resisted becoming the subjects created by asylum narratives.[21] For example, one client insisted that not he but rather his mother feared that he would be persecuted if he returned to El Salvador. In another case, a client asserted that he did not fear the individuals who had killed his brother; rather, he feared what he would do to these individuals if he were to encounter them in the future. Such clients sought to alter the asylum narrative itself, in the first case by ascribing agency and intention to a relative rather than to the applicant and in the second by proposing an alternative ending—the vengeance of the wronged brother rather than the further persecution of the already fearful asylum seeker. Yet despite the seeming cultural and political hegemony involved in producing asylum narratives, to not render clients' life stories as instances of a prototype would be to do clients a disservice, because it is only as "prototypes" that these people can obtain political asylum. Moreover, as noted earlier, the ABC asylum application process was part of a larger strategy to obtain recognition of the suffering caused by the Salvadoran civil war, of the U.S. government's involvement in the conflict, and of the justice of Salvadorans' petitions for legal status in the United States. As such, the content of asylum applications may be less significant than the act of registration and organizations' political advocacy on behalf of ABC class members as a group.

Because community organizations accepted only a handful of cases, their services to most of the immigrants who walked into their offices were limited to providing information about immigration law, the INS, and legal proceedings. The political dynamics of such public education differed from those of diagnosing and preparing cases.

Deconstructing Law

Although diagnosing and preparing clients' cases in some ways enforced and applied official legal concepts, advocates' efforts to explain U.S. immigration law to unauthorized immigrants deconstructed law in ways that challenged these notions. Advocates explained immigration law to clients during public charlas on immigration law and during the private consultations discussed earlier. Both of these contexts were a type of "free space" (Evans and Boyte 1986; see also Benmayor, Torruellas, and Juarbe 1997) in which the multiplicity of legal concepts could be acknowledged and addressed. During both consultations and charlas, clients owned up to their own illicit status as well as to shady practices in which they had engaged and did not suffer negative consequences as a result of such revelations. In fact, revealing that which would normally be hidden or denied was necessary to both charlas and consultations, given that the purpose of these meetings was to aid clients in resolving their legal difficulties.[22] Advocates' authority in such contexts derived from their ability to simultaneously acknowledge the validity of unofficial versions of law and enable clients to assess their cases from the point of view of INS officials. This moving between legal realities deconstructed immigration law by exposing the assumptions and procedures that authorize both law and legality.

One of the ways that advocates de- (and re)authorized immigration law was by exposing law's role in perpetuating systems of power and inequality. In liberal democracies, law is supposed to reflect generally accepted social norms and ideas of justice. Indeed, a justification for law's existence is that law facilitates the pursuit of justice (Thompson 1975). Yet, much like the scholars who formed the Critical Legal Studies movement during the 1970s (see Kairys 1990; Lazarus-Black and Hirsch 1994; Starr and Collier 1989), legal advocates at Central American community organizations—whose thinking was far from uniform—linked U.S. immigration law to racism, xenophobia, discrimination, exploitation, injustice, and inequality. One attorney drew immigrants' attention to rising nativist sentiment by asking charla attendees, "Who is the governor of California? And why is it that everyone here knows his name?"[23] This attorney also made a point of distinguishing between what is right and what is legal, telling his audience, "Law is one thing, justice is another." Similarly, attorneys who gave charlas at CARECEN noted that the new deeming requirements established by IIRIRA discriminated against low-income families and that AEDPA's distinction between visa overstays and people who entered without inspection discriminated against immigrants from Latin America. ASOSAL staff were equally vocal in their criticisms of US immigration policy. During an informational meeting, an ASOSAL staff member asked the hundred or so ABC applicants in attendance, "[California Governor] Mr. [Pete] Wilson says that he has nothing against Latinos, but then why does enforcement focus on the border when there are people who are here illegally from other countries, even from Canada, but they enter in other ways?" Such criticisms of U.S. immigration law echo unauthorized immigrants' idea that law is arbitrary (see chapter 3) but suggest that as far as the manipulability of law, the odds are stacked against immigrants.

Advocates not only questioned the justification for U.S. immigration law but also warned immigrants that the INS was somewhat inefficient and disorganized. One ASOSAL staff member who had toured an INS processing unit told me, "The officers work in cubicles, surrounded by piles and piles of forms." Advocates told immigrants that overworked INS agents sometimes lost files, failed to read information included in immigrants' application packets, substituted one person's photo for another when issuing work permits, generated multiple files and multiple alien numbers for the same individual, and so forth. These depictions of the INS contrasted sharply with a view I sometimes heard from organizations' clients: the idea that the INS operated efficiently, like a computer or a machine. For example, one man told me that he assumed that the INS had some record of the fact that he had used two social security numbers "in its computer," while another remarked that all the computers were "becoming connected," so that giving an employer a false identification card would lead to being picked up by the INS. Advocates' depiction of the INS as an overloaded bureaucracy has numerous practical implications for immigrants who are devising legalization strategies. This image suggests that immigrants ought to keep copies of their paperwork in case the INS loses it, that submitting a form to one branch of the INS will not necessarily mean that the information on the form reaches another branch, that proceedings are likely to be time-consuming, and that it is more effective to resubmit or reconstruct lost forms than it is to attempt to get at the root of a problem.

In addition to noting that law is not always just and that the INS is a bureaucracy, advocates distinguished between law in the abstract and law as carried out by individuals. For example, when he informed charla attendees of their right to remain silent when questioned by INS agents, one attorney acknowledged that though they were not legally entitled to do so, agents might respond to silence by beating or otherwise abusing those they were questioning. Service providers also told their clients that the outcomes of their cases might depend on which judge they got. In the words of one ASOSAL member, "There are good judges and bad judges." Such depictions of justice as at least in part a matter of luck suggest that law is arbitrary, that there is some room for play within the system, but that the conditions that determine this play (namely, the assignation of cases to particular officials or courts) are beyond immigrants' control. This message was explicit in one attorney's immigration charla:

> [In your countries] you know that sweet-talking an official can sometimes calm things. And you know what? Here it isn't that

way. I don't want to say that there is no corruption here; there *is* corruption here. But it is not at your reach. So never try to offer a bribe to an Immigration official here. It won't work. Okay, yes, there is corruption here, but at a much higher level, like the drug traffickers. They can buy their entry there in San Ysidro easily, no? . . . But not you. It isn't within your reach. . . . It's like the game of *fútbol* [soccer or football]. The whole world plays *fútbol* with the feet, right? And suddenly you come to the United States and they are playing *fútbol* with their hands! Okay, it's the same regarding the legal system. If you are in your country, there is a legal game, and if you suddenly are in the United States, you have to learn new rules if you want to play in the legal system of the United States.

Like attorneys' acknowledgment of differences in judges' and officials' rulings on similar cases, characterizing law as a game that can be played challenged the notion of transcendent justice that is created by the more typical equation of office and officeholder (Greenhouse 1996). Tellingly, this attorney's recommendation against bribing INS officials did not characterize bribery as illegitimate and the U.S. system as above such corruption. Rather, the attorney depicted offering bribes and going through official channels as appropriate responses to particular sets of legal conditions. Legality and extralegality were thus placed on a par.

Advocates also attempted to demystify legalization by teaching immigrants how to diagnose cases. At charlas and when advising clients, legal-service providers typically reviewed the definitions of and criteria for obtaining family-based visas, political asylum, suspension of deportation/cancellation of removal, and labor certification. These explanations enabled immigrants to not only assess the strength of their cases and the viability of different legalization options but also to act in ways that improved their chances of legalization. For example, immigrants who were eligible for suspension might file tax returns on previously unreported earnings, set up payment plans to reimburse the U.S. government for public assistance, seek to expunge a criminal conviction, or begin to volunteer at their children's schools. Advocates hoped that at the very least, teaching clients to assess their own cases would help them to avoid falling prey to unscrupulous immigration consultants or turning themselves in to the INS when they were not yet eligible for relief from deportation.

As one paralegal admonished his audience during a charla, "Even if you are undocumented, isn't it better to not be in proceedings than to be in the process of being deported?"

Finally, advocates advised clients to create paper trails that documented legalization claims. Clients had to not only do volunteer work but also get letters stating that they did so; they had to not only live in the United States but also produce check stubs, utility bills, and other documents confirming their residence; they had to not only work but also obtain letters verifying their employment. When clients' documentary records proved problematic, advocates urged them to get their papers in order. For example, during an informational meeting at one organization, an ABC applicant asked a legal worker how he could include his wife in his asylum petition. The applicant explained that he and his wife had married in Mexico and that his marriage certificate erroneously stated that he was Mexican instead of Salvadoran. To include his wife, he would have to submit a copy of his marriage certificate, which could raise questions about his status as an ABC class member (because Mexicans are not included in the suit) as well as his credibility (because he apparently lied on his marriage certificate). In response, the speaker suggested holding another wedding in the United States, which would produce a new certificate on which his nationality could be reported as Salvadoran. This certificate could be used to include his wife in his application, thus avoiding the problems posed by the other marriage certificate. In other words, advocates suggested that producing the correct evidentiary record is more important than some external but undocumented truth. This solution to the problems posed by the requirement that reality be documented attempted neither to confer status through papers nor to claim papers on the basis of status but rather to bring papers and status into conformity.

Advocates' efforts to deconstruct immigration law for clients did not delegitimize unofficial law but did add to the legal discourses available to clients. Some of the legal concepts operative in the realm of illegality—such as the idea that law is manipulable and arbitrary—emerged in attorneys' accounts as well, though the implications of these ideas differed in attorneys' and immigrants' discourse. Service providers' accounts of law sought to distill their legal expertise into a form that would better equip immigrants to operate in the formal legal arena. These accounts even acknowledged the mutually constitutive relationship between law and illegality (see chapter 3), that immigrants' efforts to legalize and legal readings of actions taken "in the shadow of the law" (Mnookin and Kornhauser 1979) produced both law and determinations of illegality. It is beyond the scope of my research to assess the effectiveness of legal education as a means of improving clients' legalization strategies. How well these strategies fared in court, however, is the subject of the next chapter.

Conclusion

Legal advocacy is politically complex. Advocates at Central American community organizations were situated simultaneously as agents and critics of law. Acknowledging that law is not the same thing as justice, they nonetheless sought to wrest whatever justice they could from law. This was the goal of accepting strong cases for free legal representation, pushing the limits of law through potentially precedent-setting cases, adopting broad eligibility criteria when preparing asylum applications for ABC class members, and advocating on behalf of immigrants as a group. Some of this work required advocates to adopt and apply "official" versions of law—distinguishing between strong and weak cases, narrating asylum applicants' stories as yet another instance of a prototype, and engaging political opponents in terms that pervaded popular debate (e.g., arguing that immigrants do not receive welfare instead of questioning the assumptions that make welfare use relevant to assessments of deservingness). This work also required managing clients by requiring charla attendance before rendering service, limiting the number of appointments available to clients, and so forth. Though such practices were in part an inevitable consequence of short staffing, these tactics also helped attorneys and paralegals manage their caseloads in the face of an overwhelming need for their services. At the same time, because law is not always just, advocates critiqued law, pursued political change, and advised certain clients not to seek legalization—yet. Charlas, political advocacy, and litigation were meant to aid the many clients who could not benefit directly from organizations' services.

Understanding advocates' strategies as well as the relationship between law and illegality requires turning to the formal legal arena, where immigrants' legal status is ultimately determined and the limits of law's authority are reached.

Chapter 5

"In the Wolf's Mouth"

Authoritative determinations of the merit of immigrants' claims to legality are produced during formal immigration proceedings such as asylum interviews, citizenship examinations, deportation hearings, and so forth. In this chapter, I analyze the relationship between the procedures through which legalization is allocated and the content of immigrants' legal claims. For example, officials who conduct proceedings are concerned with managing time. Proceedings need to be run efficiently, witnesses are urged to get to the point, and heavy caseloads and overcrowded calendars make advocates compete for officials' time and attention. Similarly, the outcomes of individuals' legalization cases sometimes hinge on how immigrants have spent their time, whether they have been productive, and the temporal coherence of their narratives. Official proceedings are thus designed to identify individuals who can depict themselves as disciplined subjects, as instances of a prototype, and as credible. Identifying such individuals entails constructing and erasing personhood (see Conklin 1997; Coutin and Chock 1995; White 1985). Proceedings construct personhood in that they produce narratives of being and render determinations of status and identity. Proceedings erase personhood in that deportation and removal deny immigrants' social legitimacy but also in that to win, immigrants must erase other, alternative, illegitimate accounts of their experiences.

Official determinations of legality are not, however, fully final in that those who are designated as illegitimate can continue to pursue and even seek to legitimize the modes of being that courts and officials disallow (Coutin 1995).[1] Individuals who agree to depart voluntarily can remain in the country, those who are ordered deported in absentia can try to hide their presence from INS officials, and even those who are actually excluded, deported, or removed can reenter the United States clandestinely (Harwood 1984, 1985). Each of these strategies bears costs—living with fear, coming up with the money to pay a *coyote,* risking the dangers of a border crossing—but, as should be clear by now, denials of legal status do not necessarily prevent unauthorized presence and entry. Such denials do, however, confine immigrants to a domain of illegality (Bach 1978; Portes 1981; Sassen 1989), especially given that the avenues leading out of this domain are increasingly being blocked. Law therefore continually produces illegality, just as illegality gives rise to continual refinements and elaborations of law (Holston 1991).

When law's role in producing illegality is taken into account, legal proceedings are exposed as somewhat bizarre rituals that, though powerful, cannot completely govern a reality that remains unruly. Legal proceedings thus reveal two seemingly conflicting facets of subjugation to which I refer as the "trappings of power": first, the ways that officials and formal proceedings catch or entrap individuals within preexisting webs of signification (Bennett and Feldman 1981; Bumiller 1991; Clifford 1988; Mather and Yngvesson 1980–81; Matoesian 1997; McKinley 1997; Yngvesson 1993b); and second, the fact that many of the accouterments of legal power— black robes, formal decisions, official notices—have only a limited ability to create the reality that they authorize. The hierarchy between immigrants and officials, the illicit and the legal, and aliens and citizens is nonetheless real. By seeking to establish the boundaries between these groups, by subjecting the unauthorized to the judgment of the empowered, and by producing records that instantiate legal reality, proceedings reveal both their materiality and irrelevance. Formal proceedings constitute individuals as legal permanent residents, citizens, asylees, deportable aliens, and so forth, but these designations cannot fully shape social reality. For example, illegal aliens who are deported can reenter the country and can perhaps become eligible for legalization in the future. Likewise, racism, sexism, and other oppressions can prevent the full citizenship of the juridically included.

The procedural construction of legality and illegitimacy is accomplished through the instantiation of prototypes and the denial of structural agency. By the instantiation of prototypes, I mean the paradoxical processes through which legal subjects become prototypes of the deserving and the undeserving. To prevail in immigration court or during an asylum interview, applicants must render their lives as instances of a legal prototype such as political refugee. At the same time, to be credible, applicants must avoid seeming too much like prototypes lest their stories be deemed canned or invented. This narrative project is further complicated by the fact that immigration hearings require applicants to simultaneously tell good stories and construct good arguments.[2] These two ways of thinking are in tension, as "arguments convince one of their truth, stories of their lifelikeness" (Bruner 1986:11). Stories, for example, create characters through subjectification: "the depiction of reality not through an omniscient eye that views a timeless reality, but through the filter of the consciousness of protagonists in the story" (Bruner 1986:25). Yet law's claim to the universal and the transcendent relies precisely on adopting the perspective of an "omniscient eye that views a timeless reality." As a result, the contexts in which characters' consciousnesses have meaning are erased in legal analyses of narratives as arguments. The realities of political repression, life as an undocumented immigrant, and shady legal practices cannot be granted explanatory power in narrative depictions of characters' actions and decisions. Agency is thus linked to individual capacities, and illicit conditions are treated as aspects of personhood.

My analysis of immigration proceedings begins with a discussion of what Mindie Lazarus-Black (1997) has called "the rites of domination": namely, the ways that legal personnel and legal proceedings discipline their subjects—in this case, immigrants who are applying for various forms of legalization. The first section of this chapter discusses the relationships between these disciplinary practices and individuals' legalization claims. The second section focuses on the narrative process through which asylum and suspension applicants instantiate prototypes of deservingness. The third section discusses how legal proceedings ignore the structures that produce both lives and legal histories. The final section explores the limits of legal proceedings as a means of shaping immigrants' lives. The simultaneous centrality yet futility of legal proceedings is at issue throughout the chapter.

Going to Court

Legal proceedings are hierarchical and power-laden processes (Kairys 1990; Lazarus-Black and Hirsch 1994; Starr and Collier 1989), despite immigration reformers' contention that by permitting illegal aliens to defend themselves against deportation and to appeal adverse decisions, the United States has been too lenient on the undocumented (FAIR 1997). The legalization strategies that immigrants devise in the space of nonexistence "catch them up" (to paraphrase Abu-Lughod 1990:53) when they enter the formal legal arena. My analysis of procedural subjugation is based on my observations of 129 immigration proceedings between June 1995 and January 1998. By "proceeding," I mean an official hearing or interview at which an INS official takes some sort of action on an alien's immigration case. The action can range from simply rescheduling the hearing to rendering a decision in the case. In certain instances, following an individual's case meant attending several proceedings, such as a hearing at which the case was rescheduled, another at which the individual's testimony was taken, another at which cross-examination occurred, another at which an expert witness testified, and so forth. Of the proceedings that I observed, twenty-nine were hearings on the merits of individuals' asylum claims (fifteen proceedings), suspension claims (eleven) or both (three); twelve concerned petitions for adjustment; nine were requests for voluntary departure; five involved aliens with criminal convictions; eight were in-absentia deportations; and six were interviews by asylum officials in Anaheim. In sixty proceedings, or 47 percent of the hearings that I observed, nothing was done to assess the merit of individuals' cases, and the hearing was simply rescheduled for another date. Such rescheduling was sometimes planned in that hearings are held specifically to calendar cases, accept filings, or set the date of the hearing on the merits of the case. In other instances, rescheduling resulted from overbooking of hearings, applicants being unprepared to present their cases, or scheduling conflicts on the part of attorneys. Rescheduling also resulted from the fact that with the passage of AEDPA and IIRIRA in 1996, the law itself was in flux, making it necessary to postpone certain cases until regulations were issued or higher courts ruled on competing legal theories.

My goal in attending proceedings was to observe the outcomes of the cases that were prepared by El Rescate and CARECEN. (ASOSAL did not represent individuals in court.) Therefore, I did not attempt to systematically observe or analyze immigration hearings in general. I attended court to hear particular cases, and, while I was there waiting for a case to begin, I also observed preceding cases. Like immigrants who seek to legalize, I had the experience of going to court for a hearing only to find that the hearing was postponed because of overscheduling. On such occasions, I sometimes wandered into another courtroom to observe a different hearing. I also followed several cases being handled by an attorney whose organization provides pro bono legal assistance to indigent clients. In roughly one-third of the hearings that I observed, I knew the applicant and/or the applicant's attorney; in two-thirds, I did not. The immigrants whose hearings I observed included not only Central Americans but also Mexicans, Ethiopians, Armenians, and others. Though the proceedings that I observed are probably not statistically representative, I did see a good cross section of what occurs in immigration court.

Outcomes in the hearings that I observed varied. In 61 percent of these proceedings—including some at which testimony was taken—the hearing was continued or reset. In 21 percent of the proceedings, aliens were granted the right to leave the United States voluntarily or were ordered deported. Almost all of the deportation orders were issued because the alien had failed to attend the hearing. Aliens who were granted voluntary departure sometimes had pending family petitions that were likely to become current before their departure dates and that would permit them to remain in the United States. Sixteen percent of the proceedings resulted in outcomes that were favorable to applicants, including six grants of suspension of deportation, five approvals of petitions for adjustment of status, four grants of asylum in court, three grants of asylum at the interview stage, one termination of proceedings, and one administrative resolution of an individual's case. In 2 percent of the proceedings, the outcome was unknown, either because I was unable to stay to hear the judge's decision or because the decision is still pending. These figures should not be taken as indicative of the overall rates at which cases are denied and granted.

Though I did sit in on three hearings at the detention center in San Pedro and volunteer as an interpreter in Anaheim for six asylum interviews, most of the hearings that I observed took place at the immigration court in downtown Los Angeles. The individuals whose cases are heard at this court are not in custody, either because they have posted bail and been released from detention or because they were never detained. There are several ways that individuals are placed in deportation (now called removal) proceedings. One of the most common is that, thinking it a means of obtaining a work permit, individuals apply for asylum through a notary (Mahler 1995; see also chapter 3). After asylum officials deny these cases, cases are referred to immigration court, where applicants are placed in proceedings. Criminal aliens can also be deported or removed, a practice that became increasingly common during the period of my research due to legislative changes (see Brady and Kesselbrenner 1996). Individuals are, of course, also placed in proceedings after being apprehended. If they are able to bond themselves out of detention, their cases are transferred to a court—such as the one in downtown Los Angeles—that is not located at a detention center. Finally, while I was conducting this research, it became common for undocumented immigrants who had strong suspension cases to turn themselves in to the INS so that proceedings would be initiated before IIRIRA went into effect on April 1, 1997.

Proceedings involve multiple steps.[3] In the case of individuals who are apprehended, proceedings occur only if detainees refuse to depart voluntarily (Harwood 1984; Weissinger 1996). In the case of individuals who bring themselves to the attention of INS officials by applying for political asylum, proceedings begin if asylum officials do not approve their petition. At this stage, a notice to appear (formerly an order to show cause) is issued. This document charges an individual with having violated U.S. immigration law and therefore with being deportable or excludable. The alien in question is referred to as a "respondent" rather than a "defendant." The first proceeding after the notice to appear is issued is a master calendar hearing. These are brief hearings (five to ten minutes each) at which a judge questions respondents regarding their eligibility for any form of relief from deportation or removal, the validity of the charges against them, whether they need more time to seek an attorney, and so forth. Individuals who do not present themselves for this or subsequent hearings can be deported or removed in absentia. A respondent's case usually stays with the same judge, and there can be several such preliminary hearings to allow the respondent to seek counsel, complete and file applications, pay fees, and so forth. When individuals are ineligible for relief, unaware of their rights, willing to leave the United States, or not present in court, their cases are dispensed with in these early stages. If a respondent persists in seeking a form of relief for which he or she is eligible, a hearing on the merits is scheduled. Cases that reach this stage are the exception, however, rather than the rule.

Procedural subjugation begins when an immigrant presents him- or herself at an asylum unit for an interview or in immigration court for a hearing.[4] Attending such appointments is not easy. The asylum unit in the Los Angeles area is located in Anaheim, a one-hour drive or a three-hour bus ride from Los Angeles. Interviews begin as early as 7:00 A.M., making it difficult for applicants who lack cars to arrive punctually. In contrast to courts, where interpreters are provided, interviewees are responsible for providing their own interpreters if they wish to testify in a language other than English. Would-be interpreters whose English may or may not be adequate to the task "lurk" (to quote one asylum applicant) around the asylum unit, in wait for unprepared interviewees. Though these interpreters are not monitored or certified by the U.S. government, asylum applicants are held accountable for their interpreters' ability to translate their testimony. Similarly, to arrive at the Federal Building at 300 North Los Angeles Street (the former site of the immigration court, which has now moved to 606 South Olive Street), immigrants had to pass through a gamut of notaries and pseudo-attorneys who offered their services to those in proceedings. Even entering the Federal Building was difficult. At peak times, it was necessary to wait in line for twenty to thirty minutes to pass through security and enter the building. After entering, immigrants had to find the right courtroom, which meant studying the court schedules posted on the second floor and sometimes going to yet another building and passing through another security check. Failing to allow extra time for getting in the building and finding the courtroom could mean arriving late.[5] Having arrived in the courtroom, many immigrants are unrepresented and therefore somewhat confused. Those with legal representation are not necessarily much better off. Regarding the skill of the attorneys that she usually dealt with, one judge joked with a CARECEN attorney, "What? You have expertise? Is that a requirement? Can you *read*? Can you make objections? If so, you're in the top flight!" In short, immigrants act in a particularly sleazy legal context. Made desperate by a system that denies their existence, immigrants apply for papers only to find themselves thrust into a forum that denies their realities.

The difficulty of arriving in court is particularly significant given a related feature of subjugation: officials' management of time (see Greenhouse 1996). The consequences of arriving late or failing to arrive at all are severe. When informing one respondent of the date and time of his next hearing, a judge warned, "Be on time! If you are more than fifteen minutes late, I will order you deported!" Those who fail to appear are deemed to have abandoned their cases and are deported or removed in absentia. Only if absence is due to a death in the family or a serious illness can cases be reopened. Arriving punctually, however, does not necessarily expedite matters for respondents. Multiple hearings are scheduled at the same time (generally at 8:30 A.M. for the morning hearings and 1:00 P.M. for the afternoon hearings), meaning that most people have to wait—often watching others get deported in absentia—until their cases are heard. Attending a hearing can mean expense, sacrifice, and effort on the part of respondents, who have to assemble documentation packets, bring witnesses and family members, meet repeatedly with attorneys to prepare their cases (assuming that they have good legal counsel), ask for days off from work, pull their children out of school, and obtain time-sensitive records, such as medical reports or FBI record checks, that have to be obtained no more than six months prior to a hearing date. If the hearing is rescheduled due to an overcrowded calendar, this effort has to be repeated. Only rarely is any effort made to schedule a hearing at a time and date that would be convenient to the respondent. In contrast, attorneys' and judges' vacation schedules or conflicting obligations are taken into account in scheduling hearings. Not all officials agree with these scheduling practices. One judge not only went out of his way to accommodate immigrants' needs when setting hearing dates but also criticized in-absentia deportations: "The way it is now, to quote Kafka, the alien will go away wondering, 'Who is the judge who barred me?'"

Just as they manage official time, court officials also govern legal space. The judge's sovereignty over a courtroom is analogous to the state's sovereignty over national territory, because judges decide who can officially exist within U.S. borders. One judge drew attention to this parallel during an in-absentia deportation, commenting, "The respondent has seemingly chosen to remove herself from the jurisdiction of the court. She can do so physically but not legally. We will proceed in absentia." The sovereignty of judges is reinforced through such practices as rising when the judge enters the court, referring to the judge as "your honor," clothing judges in black robes, seating judges on raised platforms, permitting judges to refer to themselves in the third person (e.g., "the court is inclined to grant"), administering oaths, and so forth (see also Clifford 1988; Lazarus-Black 1997; Merry 1994a). Such practices reinforce the transcendence of the judge's office as embodied in but nonetheless distinct from particular judges (Greenhouse 1996). Judges assume the power to govern not only hearings and outcomes but even the bodily positioning of the individuals who enter legal space. Judges tell respondents to take off their hats, not to chew gum or drink coffee in court, and to be quiet. One judge told a respondent, "Don't sit back in your chair! Don't take a *siesta!* I don't want you lounging around here. I need you to be alert and attentive." In addition to governing posture, judges govern movement and presence, telling attorneys and witnesses whether they can approach the bench, where they should sit, and on occasion expelling people—ranging from noisy children to sequestered witnesses—from the court itself.

Officials' sovereignty over time and space empowers them to berate respondents and even attorneys. For example, on learning that a suspension applicant had not submitted copies of all of his tax returns, a judge commented, "Maybe you don't care about your case. You haven't been cooperating with your attorney! Do you want me to just give you voluntary departure and send you back to El Salvador?" Not all officials avail themselves of this power. Many treat respondents and attorneys courteously and respectfully, and some express sympathy with immigrants. For example, while questioning an adjustment applicant, one judge noted, "This government doesn't like poor people, only rich people." My point is not that judges tend to be abusive, but rather that institutionally, judges and other officials are permitted to make comments that would, in other contexts, be socially unacceptable (Lazarus-Black 1997). This is a power imbalance in that examples of judicial berating (and also, I should note, of judicial courtesy) abound in my transcripts of immigration proceedings, while instances of rude or disrespectful behavior on the part of respondents or attorneys toward judges are minimal and indirect (see Scott 1990). Attorneys for respondents or, more rarely, the government are also the targets of tongue-lashings—sometimes with negative consequences for respondents. For example, an attorney whose photocopying request offended a judge was warned, "I could just deport your client!"[6] Remarks by both judges and trial attorneys sometimes suggest that aliens are intrinsically suspect. For example, when approving a man's adjustment petition, a judge remarked, "As of now, you are a permanent resident, as long as you don't commit any crimes or terrorist acts. So don't get any ideas." Similarly, when a Guatemalan asylum applicant stated that he did not know whether the person who had interpreted during his asylum interview had translated everything he had said, the trial attorney admonished, "Stop making excuses."[7]

While officials are granted some latitude in court, respondents' speech is carefully controlled (see also Ewick and Silbey 1995; O'Barr and Conley 1985; Conley and O'Barr 1990). Faced with overwhelming numbers of cases, judges strive for efficient proceedings. They therefore seek an exact correspondence between the amount of information that they need and the testimony that is elicited. When one witness gave overly detailed testimony, the judge told the witness's attorney, "Please talk to your client and tell him to answer the questions directly. He's very informative, and while it's interesting, it doesn't help his case." Judges' understandings of relevancy, however, sometimes differ from those of witnesses and even observers. For example, one judge interrupted an asylum applicant's account of being held at gunpoint to ask about the applicant's marital status. Witnesses also have to conform to judges' notions of procedural timing. During one hearing, as the judge and the attorneys were discussing the admissibility of documents, an asylum applicant attempted to explain how he received the scars depicted in the photographs that they were discussing. The judge told him, "We'll hear from you later." In court, witnesses are also compelled to stick to the procedural format of a hearing (although asylum interviews are more flexible). Court hearings cannot be conducted partly in one language and partly in another. When a multilingual detainee noticed inaccuracies in the interpreter's translation, his hearing was postponed, even though that meant that he would have to remain in detention longer.[8] Witnesses cannot speak unless a question is posed to them, as one woman discovered when she attempted to volunteer information during her hearing. Witnesses are admonished not to nod their heads, as gestures are not recorded; to answer "yes" or "no"; and to say "yes" instead of "sure." Discrepancies that sometimes arise as the result of this format can be held against a witness. During one hearing, a judge treated a discrepancy as a lie, saying. "You just told the trial attorney that you didn't have any children, and now you are saying that you have two. Why are you being less than honest?" The woman explained that she had, in fact, testified accurately: "You asked me if my husband and I had children, and I said that we do not. These are children through my former marriage."

The creation of documentary records also subjugates individuals who are in proceedings. In court, forms, paperwork and other sorts of documents are the ideal proof of respondents' claims (Clifford 1988; Coutin 1995) but are not always admissible. Documents issued by a government can only be accepted if they are officially certified, meaning that even though relatives of a respondent may have gone to great lengths to obtain a document, a court may exclude it from the record or admit it only as background information. Documents and forms must also comply with local rules regarding three-hole punches and so forth to be admissible. Of course a problem in both asylum and suspension cases is that individuals sometimes lack documentation of their claims and therefore must rely solely on their testimony. Judges also go on and off the record—a distinction that may be interpreted differently by officials and applicants. One couple whose asylum application was denied told me that they suspected that the judge went on and off the record so that what they considered to be his objectionable statements would not be recorded. Forms, such as asylum or suspension applications, must be formally certified as true by applicants during their hearings. To do so, judges present respondents with the applications and ask, "Is the information on this form true and accurate? If so, please sign the form." Though the respondent cannot, then and there, reread the entire form—which is written in English—this signatory moment establishes that the respondent is the author of the documentary narrative and is used as a benchmark of truth for the remainder of the hearing.

The creation of evidentiary records extends to respondents, who are objectified in ways that render them peripheral to proceedings (Lazarus-Black 1997). During hearings, applicants for legalization are often referred to and even sometimes addressed as the "lead respondent," the "male respondent," the "adult female respondent," and so forth. I became so accustomed to such phrasings that it struck me as unusual when one judge referred to an asylum applicant by his name and his academic title throughout the hearing. Judges and trial attorneys often address respondents as "sir" or "ma'am," terms that seem respectful but that can also be distancing and somewhat disciplinary in tone.[9] Though respondents' presence is, to a degree, required (though, as noted earlier, hearings can be conducted in absentia), they are sometimes discussed as though they are not there. For example, during one asylum hearing, the judge and an expert witness debated whether the respondent could have faked posttraumatic stress syndrome during a psychological evaluation. Indeed, the argument over individuals' legal status is conducted in relation to legal definitions with which applicants themselves may be unfamiliar (see also Merry 1990; Yngvesson 1993b). The main participants in this argument are therefore the trial attorney, counsel for the respondent, and the judge (see also Eisenstein and Jacob 1977). Even the most important part of a hearing, the decision, is dictated to a transcriber who is not present instead of to the applicant, who is present in the courtroom and who is the person most concerned with the outcome of the case. Objectification occurs even (and perhaps to the greatest degree) when the undocumented are awarded legal status. For example, during one hearing a judge summarized a legal permanent resident's immigration history: "You have been a resident of the United States since 1978, right?" The man—who was thirteen years old in 1978—corrected him, saying, "Yes, but I've been in the United States since I was six." The judge repeated, "But you immigrated with a green card in '78." What "immigrated" to the United States in 1978 was not the man, who was already present, but rather a legal construct that corresponded to this man's physical existence.

Finally, proceedings subjugate the unauthorized by delegitimizing actions taken in the domain of illegality. Well aware of the legal obstacles created by immigrants' vulnerability to those who "practice law in the shadows" (Mnookin and Kornhauser 1979), officials nonetheless must assess immigrants' own culpability in fraudulent or inadequate representations of their life stories. Such assessments create a narrative bind for immigrants who must emphasize their agency to win asylum or suspension of deportation but, as discussed in chapter 3, must depict themselves as unwitting victims of inadequate legal counsel to control damage caused by their prior efforts at legalization. For example, during the following exchange, an INS trial attorney attributes agency to the respondent instead of to the interpreter whom the respondent hired on a notary's advice:

> *Trial attorney:* [During your asylum interview,] you told the officer that the army tried to murder you?
>
> *Respondent:* I told the interpreter.
>
> *Trial attorney:* And you told the officer that you belonged to a union?
>
> *Respondent:* Yes. . . .
>
> *Trial attorney:* So your response today is that you told the whole story to the officer?
>
> *Respondent:* I said [to whom?] that I was beaten, that they tried to murder me.
>
> *Trial attorney:* Did you explain how they tried to murder you?
>
> *Respondent:* No, because the officer directed himself to the interpreter.
>
> *Judge:* The officer spoke to the interpreter, and the interpreter spoke to you?
>
> *Respondent:* They were talking among themselves.

Perplexed by the fact that the story this individual told in court was never communicated to the asylum official, this judge called the respondent's actions potentially "sinister" and summarized his own dilemma, "You never know, is the guy telling the truth or is he using the notary as an excuse?" Focusing on the veracity of immigrants' narratives and on the consistency of the narrator as protagonist leads officials to impute narrative agency to the respondent rather than to the circumstances in which applications for legal status are prepared. As a result, narrative discrepancies are attributed to fraud, perjury, and invention on the part of the applicant instead of to the multiplicity of legal processes themselves.

The subjugation that occurs during legal proceedings is closely connected to the criteria used to allocate legality during hearings. In both asylum and suspension hearings, these criteria construct prototypes that respondents must instantiate.

Instantiating Prototypes

By emphasizing efficiency and relevancy, officials who manage the procedural timing of hearings compel asylum and suspension applicants to structure their testimony around competing prototypes. At stake in asylum hearings is which prototype a narrative matches. Is the applicant a refugee in need of protection? A conniving alien who is abusing the asylum process? A sincere but paranoid individual? A victim of generalized violence? An economic immigrant? Similarly, suspension hearings classify applicants according to prototypes of deserving and undeserving subjects. Ideally, suspension applicants depict their lives as yet another instance of the American immigrant story, according to which immigrants enter the land of opportunity, overcome adversity, and achieve success (see Chock 1991; Coutin and Chock 1995). Alternatively, suspension applicants can raise compelling humanitarian concerns, such as their need for medical treatment unavailable in their countries of origin. Examples of undeserving prototypes are that of the public charge, the nonachiever, the unassimilated, and the unrooted.[10] The questions that judges and attorneys pose to witnesses are designed to select among such prototypes. Narrative elements that deviate from available prototypes are procedurally incomprehensible unless they are reinterpreted according to prototypes. For instance, complex motives for seeking asylum—fear of persecution and lack of economic opportunity in the applicant's country of origin—can be interpreted as evidence that the applicant is an economic immigrant rather than a legitimate refugee.[11]

For cases to be approved, asylum and suspension applicants must demonstrate that they somehow differ from general populations. Difference is significant to asylum law for both practical and ideological reasons. Practically, limiting grants of asylum to those who are particularly at risk avoids opening the floodgates to the masses (J. Bhabha 1996). Ideologically, asylum law derives from the liberal notion that individuals have the right to their own political, religious, ethnic, or other differences (Collier, Maurer, and Suárez-Navaz 1995; Macpherson 1962). Difference is therefore a focus of questioning during asylum hearings and interviews. One asylum official asked an indigenous Guatemalan whether his dress and speech were distinctive, and in another case a judge asked a Nicaraguan asylum applicant who testified that authorities considered him suspicious, "But why you?" Difference must be *expressed* if it is to be recognized first by a persecutor and later by an asylum official. The protagonists in narratives of persecution must therefore exhibit agency. To dispute a Salvadoran applicant's claim that his participation in political demonstrations put him at risk, a trial attorney asked, "Did you act differently than the other marchers?" who presumably had not suffered. (In response the applicant contended that other marchers were not safe either, noting, "There were many dead.") Demonstrating agency and difference is particularly difficult for asylum seekers who are at risk because of their relationship to others (e.g., spouses and children of political activists) or who are fleeing repressive tactics that were directed at entire populations.[12]

Just as asylum applicants must demonstrate that they were singled out for persecution, matching the prototype of the deserving subject in a suspension case requires distinguishing oneself from the masses of people who are in the United States and who could be deported. Though deportation would probably be a hardship for anyone, suspension applicants are required to prove that in their cases, it would be an extreme hardship. Doing so requires characterizing themselves as either uniquely deserving, uniquely needy, or both. Examples of people who are uniquely needy would include cancer patients who are receiving treatment unavailable in their countries of origin, AIDS patients who would lack access to medical care in their home countries, battered women who are undergoing counseling,[13] parents whose U.S. citizen children have health problems, and so forth. Granting residency to such individuals is rationalized less as a reward than as a humanitarian concession. Those who depict themselves as uniquely deserving—due to their educational, cultural, financial, familial or other achievements—also imply a need (the need to continue their education, avoid losing their newly acquired culture, develop their business, support aging parents, parent their children, etc.), but this need is connected to the idea that the applicant (or a relative of the applicant) is on the road to success and that it would be inhumane to take the applicant (or a relative of the applicant) off this road. Such notions of deservingness, more than claims to be uniquely needy, link individual agency to national legitimacy.

To be deemed plausible, respondents' accounts of persecution or deservingness must be temporally and logically coherent (see Ewick and Silbey 1995). The narratives elicited in court are linear, in that they recount events in chronological order (often through such questions as, "And then what happened?") and thus imply motivations, intentions, causes, and effects (see Greenhouse 1996). Specifically, asylum applicants must demonstrate that an action or statement on their part became a basis for threat or actual persecution, which led them to fear future persecution, which in turn led them to abandon their country and seek asylum in the United States. When these events are not closely connected in time, the nexus between them is in question. During one asylum interview, an applicant testified that he had fled El Salvador, spent eighteen months in Honduras, been deported, fled to Costa Rica, gotten married, and then traveled with his wife through Mexico to the United States. This applicant was able to establish that he was at risk of future persecution, but the temporal distance between his original departure from El Salvador and his arrival in the United States suggested that he might have been firmly resettled before arriving in the United States and that his trip to the United States did not result from the original persecution but rather from something else. His attorney successfully argued that because he lacked legal rights in Honduras, Costa Rica, and Mexico, his sojourn in these countries was simply part of his flight to the United States. Another asylum applicant whose narrative was temporally discontinuous was less fortunate. This applicant, a Salvadoran union activist, had narrowly survived an assassination attempt in 1980, continued to participate in union activities throughout the 1980s, suffered only harassment and one beating between 1980 and 1991, received a death threat in 1991, and left El Salvador in 1992. During cross-examination the trial attorney asked, "So for ten years, you were okay?" thus interpreting this timeline as evidence that the applicant was not, in fact, at risk of persecution. Such interpretations hold asylum seekers accountable for their persecutors' decisions about when and how to persecute. If asylum applicants cannot depict their persecutors as logical, then applicants' narratives are deemed implausible.[14]

Temporal coherence is also critical to suspension applicants' efforts to instantiate prototypes of the deserving. Suspension applicants are assessed according to whether they have progressed since entering the United States. The officials who govern the time and space of a courtroom are also concerned with how unauthorized immigrants have spent their seven or more years in this country. Through assessments of progress, the agency of deserving individuals flows into and constructs that of the nation (Greenhouse 1996). To measure progress, officials want to know whether suspension applicants have goals and what applicants are doing to achieve these goals. Suspension applicants must account for their time in the United States, explaining any periods of unemployment. Judges also look for some indication of applicants' success, such as completed courses of study, good grades, increased earnings, the accumulation of property, or founding a business. There is a doubling of time within such assessments, as officials seek an accounting not only of applicants' years of residence but also of their daily schedules. Judges and trial attorneys ask suspension applicants for their work and school schedules, the number of hours per week they spend with their children, what they do on weekends, and so forth. This doubling of time connects daily industriousness with individual progress and national productivity (see Thompson 1967).

Instantiating prototypes requires not only distinguishing oneself from general populations and constructing temporally coherent narratives but also making lived realities meet legal standards. Asylum applicants, for example, must link their experiences of persecution to one of the five grounds listed in the United Nations Protocol Relating to the Status of Refugees: race, religion, nationality, membership in a particular social group, or political opinion. Definitions of *politics* are sometimes in contention in establishing or disputing this linkage. For example, when one applicant testified that he participated in marches as a labor activist, the trial attorney immediately asked, "So you never were involved in political activities?" a question that suggested that union activities were not political. Claiming that applicants' experiences did not constitute persecution or that applicants immigrated for reasons other than fear can also attack the linkage between persecution and the definition of *refugee*. One trial attorney suggested that an asylum applicant's scars could have been caused by an accident at work rather than by an assassination attempt, a judge characterized a Mexican couple's problems as "criminal" rather than "political," and an asylum officer and an applicant debated whether being held at gunpoint in one's home constituted detention. Claiming a match between a narrative of persecution and the definition of refugee can require creativity on the part of applicants and their attorneys. One private attorney who represents asylum applicants told me that she "created a social group of victims of infantile abuse" to argue that a child-abuse victim deserved asylum, and when an asylum official seemed to think that the category of residents of a particular town was too broad to constitute a social group, an applicant's attorney suggested the group "massacre survivors."

Like asylum applicants' experiences of persecution, suspension applicants' kin relations are measured against legal standards. It is not surprising that kinship and citizenship are interconnected, given that a nation is viewed as "a grand genealogical tree, rooted in the soil that nourishes it" (Malkki 1992:28; see also Maurer 1995; Yanagisako and Delaney 1995). Invariably, the officials who judge suspension cases want to know the legal status of applicants' parents, spouses, siblings, and children. Officials assess such relations both as a sign that the applicant has set down roots in the United States and as a measure of deservingness and therefore hardship. Only legalized relatives count in this assessment. Though one young man argued that he needed to be in the United States to be near his mother, the judge deemed the mother's presence irrelevant because she was undocumented. Assessing the hardship that separation from family members would pose entails judging the relationship itself. For example, one judge praised a father who had paid child support before being ordered to do so, saying, "It is refreshing to hear a father taking responsibility for his children."[15] The meaning of relationships is sometimes debated in suspension cases. In one hearing, the judge and trial attorney questioned an applicant's claim that his out-of-wedlock child lived with him. The judge and trial attorney wanted to know how many nights the child slept at his house in a typical week, whereas the applicant insisted that seeing his son every day and sometimes staying together constituted living together. This debate partly concerned the legality of claiming the child as a dependent on the applicant's tax return, but the criteria and categories through which relationships are judged were also at issue. The validity of a complex set of relationships—to parents, siblings, a girlfriend, and a child—was being scrutinized and questioned in the process of allocating legality.[16]

Paradoxically, to claim that they meet legal prototypes, respondents must present individualized accounts (see Merry 1994a).[17] As one judge put it during an asylum hearing, "I don't want to know what happens to 'one,' I want to know what happened to 'you.'" In other words, it is not sufficient for asylum applicants to demonstrate that because of their membership in a social group, their political opinion, and so forth, they could have been persecuted; in addition, they must demonstrate that they were actually targeted (see also Baldus, Woodworth, and Pulaski 1990; Crenshaw and Peller 1993; Ewick and Silbey 1995).[18] The distinction between one's own treatment and the treatment of similarly situated individuals is sometimes difficult to draw. One attorney who represented a deaf Guatemalan asylum applicant who had been persecuted in Guatemala by both the guerrillas and the police struggled to define him as a member of a social group without making this group so broad as to be meaningless. In her closing argument, the attorney stated that she was not claiming that "*any* deaf person faces persecution in Guatemala, but rather that *this* deaf person *was* persecuted on the basis of his social group and his imputed political opinion" (emphasis original). The need to present an individualized account can decontextualize persecution. During one asylum interview at which I interpreted, the applicant, who was a student and a member of an indigenous community, attempted to explain to the asylum officer how students and indigenous Guatemalans were treated by Guatemalan authorities. The asylum official interrupted this narrative, saying, "I have information about Guatemala in my computer. I can check on that after you leave. What I need from you today is for you to tell me what happened to you." The asylum officer wanted to know why this particular indigenous student was at risk of persecution, not why all students and all indigenous Guatemalans were at risk, whereas to the applicant, these two issues were inseparable.

Suspension applicants' instantiations of deservingness are individualized through officials' assessments of applicants' characters. To make this assessment, officials assume the authority to scrutinize virtually any aspect of applicants' lives. Lazarus-Black (1997:636) refers

to this process as "legalizing: addressing parties and making arrangements as though judicial power existed when in fact no legal basis
exists for those actions." Such assumptions of judicial authority
abound in suspension cases. In one suspension hearing, the judge
not only asked an applicant whether he planned to marry the mother
of his child but also questioned his answer that he was "not yet ready"
for marriage. When this applicant's girlfriend (whose legal status was
not at issue in this case) took the stand, the judge explored her financial and living arrangements, even asking if she was entitled to
receive welfare if she was working. A judge questioned another suspension applicant's explanation of his divorce by asking whether he
was giving his wife reason to be jealous. In another hearing, when a
suspension applicant admitted that his children had been born at
public expense, the judge immediately asked, "Are you going to have
more children?" The accusatory nature of such inquiries is clear in
the following exchange between a judge and an adjustment applicant:

Judge: Have you ever received welfare?

Applicant: No.

Judge: None at all?

Applicant: No.

Judge: Do you have children?

Applicant: Yes.

Judge: How many?

Applicant: Four.

Judge: Where are they?

Applicant: Three of them are here and one is in my country.

Judge: Who paid for the birth of your children?

Applicant: They were born in my country.

Judge: Oh, I understand. I thought some of them were born
here. Have your children ever received medical assistance from
the state?

Applicant: No.

Judge: Who pays for their medical care when they get sick?

Applicant: My husband's insurance covers it.

Judge: So you've never received state assistance for your children?

Applicant: No.

Such interrogation suggests that if applicants did receive welfare or do work for employers who do not provide medical insurance, they are undeserving. Such conclusions ignore the structural realities that shape actions like seeking welfare, having children at public expense, or even applying for papers.

Denying Structural Agency

Instantiating prototypes is rendered more difficult by narrative constraints that render the agency of structures nonexistent. Individualized life histories are embedded in national narratives (Alonso 1988) that officials may or may not find plausible. If they assume that human rights abuses are rare or nonexistent in the country an asylum applicant is fleeing, officials are likely to interpret applicants' accounts of persecution as exaggerations, paranoia, or inventions. Politics and differing definitions of the "political" (Coutin and Hirsch 1998), are therefore unavoidably central to asylum determinations. Like the criteria employed to evaluate asylum applicants' claims, the notions of deservingness that inform suspension hearings focus more on applicants' characters than their circumstances. A potential character inconsistency arises from applicants' efforts to legitimize actions—such as working without authorization—that were taken in the domain of illegality. This process of legitimization requires suspension applicants to depict their lives as basically similar to those of other citizens—in other words, to deny the policies and practices that situated applicants in a realm of illegality and to suggest that applicants "always existed." But, just as the circumstances in which asylum petitions are prepared can make applications unconvincing, the institutional illegitimacy of suspension applicants' lives can be attributed to applicants' characters, thus undermining applicants' suspension claims.

Though asylum seekers and suspension applicants must present individualized accounts of persecution and deservingness, these stories are unavoidably contextualized by listeners' assumptions about the legitimacy of particular states (see Bach 1990). At issue in Salvadoran asylum hearings, for example, is whether human rights abuses continue in the post–peace accord era. During one hearing, a judge pressed a Salvadoran asylum applicant to testify whether paramilitary groups in El Salvador are now targeting gang members or political activists. The applicant, who did not seem to see the distinction that the judge wanted to make, responded that death squads justified political killings by claiming that victims were gang members. Such contrasting perspectives arise from the fact that, in most cases, asylum seekers and U.S. immigration officials have lived different realities (Schirmer 1985). The usually unremarked gap between these realities became explicit during the aforementioned hearing when the judge asked the applicant to prove that the Salvadoran death squads and the Salvadoran military were connected, a statement that the applicant characterized as common knowledge.[19] This gap is also apparent in applicants' and officials' differing assessments of the legitimacy of authorities' actions (see also Nagengast 1994). In one hearing, for example, a Guatemalan activist testified that a colleague was taken into custody by Guatemalan soldiers at a demonstration and was never heard from again. During cross-examination, the trial attorney disputed the applicant's characterization of this incident as a disappearance, asking, "But he didn't simply disappear, did he sir? Wasn't he arrested?" a distinction that may not make sense to immigrants from places where those who are arrested can be clandestinely tortured and killed. Officials also sometimes ignore the realities of political violence by focusing on applicants' failure to seek institutional redress in their home countries. For example, one trial attorney asked a Guatemalan applicant, "Did you tell the authorities of your problems with the guerrillas?" This question implies that the applicant erred in failing to avail himself of what surely would have been authorities' forthcoming protection, thus making it difficult for him to claim that his flight to the United States was necessary.

Suspension hearings construct national narratives by linking acculturation—and its counterpart, deculturation—to deservingness (see Asad 1990). Courts accept the argument that it would be an extreme hardship for acculturated individuals—especially children who were raised in the United States and know little of the country where they or their parents were born—to adjust to life abroad. Like adoption, which has traditionally sought a clean break between a child and its birth family (Yngvesson 1997), this argument depicts suspension applicants' ties to their home countries as severed. For example, one applicant testified, "I love California. I feel like—this is my life here. I can't go back to Mexico now." Officials sometimes treat applicants' language skills as a measure of their assimilation. One judge characterized a suspension applicant's inability to speak English as evidence that she had not acculturated, another judge tested a suspension applicant's English skills before rendering a decision, and a third judge asked the ten-year-old son of a suspension applicant what language he spoke at home with his two-year-old brother. In addition to assessing applicants' language skills, judges weigh applicants' years of schooling, jobs held, and relatives present in the United States against those in their home countries. Along these lines, one trial attorney asked a Salvadoran suspension applicant, "What are your hobbies in the U.S.?" while a judge quizzed a suspension applicant's ten-year-old son on U.S. popular culture, asking him what movie just came out at the theaters (*101 Dalmatians*). Officials' attention to acculturation (and deculturation) suggests that, as is the case in asylum proceedings, suspension applicants' narratives of deservingness are simultaneously individual and national stories. When one suspension applicant testified that he did not want to return to Nicaragua because "it's politically unstable," the judge asked, "What makes you think that our system is any better?" The applicant replied, "That's why I'm here," thus invoking the narrative of immigrants who vote with their feet for the United States over their countries of birth (see Bach 1990).

As immigration proceedings construct national narratives, they simultaneously deny political realities that shape immigrants' lives. Ordering asylum narratives according to linear notions of time, for example, defines persecution as an event that occurred in the past and is now over rather than an ongoing process that exceeds its spatial and temporal limits. This concept makes asylum seekers' claims to fear persecution even after long periods of absence appear fanciful or without basis. Asylum seekers are frequently asked why authorities would be interested in harming them today. Applicants' explanations that they are still suspect are incomprehensible within the temporal framework in which this question makes sense. As an asylum applicant whose claim was denied told me, "It doesn't matter how long you've been out of the country, whether it's five years or ten years. If you're against the government and they know it, then when you return to Guatemala you are killed. People disappeared there. And the ones who are responsible for this are the army. The army that is supposed to protect you actually kills you." The temporal and spatial assumptions implicit in linear accounts of persecution became explicit during one expert witness's testimony on posttraumatic stress disorder (PTSD). After the witness testified that PTSD sufferers continually "reexperience the trauma" that provoked their condition, the judge asked, "If there's a physical distance between the site of the trauma and the individual, do the symptoms decrease?" Echoing persecution victims' claims to have been permanently affected, the witness responded, "The trauma isn't in the scene anymore. . . . The trauma is in the person." In contrast to this notion of ongoing and embodied suffering (see J. H. Jenkins 1991, 1996; Jenkins and Valiente 1994), linear versions of cause and effect suggest that the impact of persecution lessens with time. For this reason, both officials and advocates assess the severity of past persecution, reasoning that those who suffered the most may still be feeling the effects. Physical persecution is deemed more severe than psychological suffering (Merry 1994b), as rape, torture, and beatings have more clearly material and therefore measurable effects. Asylum applicants are asked to describe how many times they were beaten, the extent of their injuries, the amount of time required to recuperate, and so forth.

During suspension hearings, structures are denied through ideas of progress that attribute suspension applicants' success or failure to their characters rather than to their circumstances. This tendency—which has also characterized the welfare reform movement (Delaney 1997)—is particularly evident in officials' determinations of the likelihood that applicants will become public charges, a ground for exclusion. Suspension applicants—rather than the economy, exploitative employment practices, multitiered labor markets, or gender hierarchies—are held accountable for applicants' employment histories, earnings levels, and access to health insurance. For example, an applicant who was receiving medical treatment at government expense was told to start paying back the costs if he hoped to win his case, an unemployed couple who were supported by relatives were characterized as potential public charges by a trial attorney, and a Nicaraguan suspension applicant who had used MediCal to obtain vaccinations was asked whether she now had insurance through her job. One judge lectured a suspension applicant who admitted that his children had been born at government expense: "I expect anyone who wants to come to the United States to pay for their own expenses instead of depending on the government." The structures that permit certain people to pay for their own expenses, however, are rarely in evidence during these hearings.

Such a focus on character rather than structures sometimes undermines asylum seekers' claims to match the prototype of a deserving refugee. Asylum seekers are protagonists not only in their accounts of persecution but also in their own legal cases. Like accounts of persecution, these legal histories are decontextualized such that agency is located in the individual applicant rather than in the structures and circumstances that shape the application process. Linearity demands that the character in these narratives be consistent for the narratives to be deemed credible (Walter Fisher 1987; Greenhouse 1996).[20] Yet decontextualization—ignoring the fact that people act differently in different contexts—makes narrative consistency difficult to achieve. Judges and trial attorneys' questions to applicants sometimes explicitly juxtapose the protagonist of the persecution narrative and the protagonist of the legal case. For example, consider the following exchange between a trial attorney and Roberto Mendez, a Guatemalan asylum applicant (see chapter 3):

Trial attorney: You were a leader of an active political movement in Guatemala, is that correct?

Roberto: Exactly.

Trial attorney: You're an intelligent man, right?

Roberto: Exactly.

Trial attorney: So why do you sign documents that you don't know the contents of and send them to the Immigration Service of the United States government?

In this exchange, the protagonist's agency is at issue. Constructing a viable asylum narrative requires exhibiting agency by expressing a difference—in this case, political activism—that could be the basis for persecution. Yet in his account of his legalization efforts, Roberto attributes agency to the people who prepared his application rather than to himself. This character difference is implausible to the trial attorney, who suggests that Roberto was responsible for the fraudulent application. The difficulty of depicting structures (in this case, the policies that produce illegality) as agentive renders differences in circumstances as inconsistencies in character.

Similarly, the expansive judicial authority that officials assume during suspension hearings suggests that what is at issue in these cases is the *normalcy* of applicants' lives (see Bourdieu 1984). During suspension hearings, immigrants whose existences have been denied are asked to depict themselves as essentially the same as those who do exist. By recounting the details of their lives—their hobbies, their daily schedules, their children's experiences in school—suspension applicants make their lives visible and assert their existence. Official negation of the conditions in which applicants' lives are constructed, however, makes this a difficult task. Applicants must demonstrate that they participated in legitimizing activities—paying taxes, working, going to school—at a time when they themselves were illegitimate. Samuel Garcia, a Salvadoran suspension applicant who had lived in the United States for fourteen years, had two U.S. citizen children, and started his own business, faced this difficulty. In his suspension hearing it emerged that he had not provided evidence of insurance for his cars, he had no proof that he had obtained a license for his business, and he had not filed tax returns each year that he had been in the United States. The judge placed great importance on these missing documents, stating, "No car insurance, no relief!" Yet Samuel's decisions about work, licenses, and car insurance may have been a strategy for coping with being undocumented. Work authorization is not necessary for the self-employed (hence the business), people who are paid under the table have a hard time reporting their earnings (hence the failure to file tax returns), and the unauthorized do not always have the documents or income that allow them to insure their vehicles (hence the lack of car insurance). Suspension applicants therefore are stuck in a catch-22: legalizing requires obtaining the legitimizing documentation to which only the documented have ready access.

Though immigration proceedings attempt to distinguish between legitimacy and undeservingness, such determinations do not fully create the reality that they purport to authorize.

Law's Limits

What happens to people who are deemed undeserving, denied political asylum, granted voluntary departure, or ordered deported? The answer to this question is unclear. Many deportation orders are issued in absentia and are only executed at a later date, if the recipient is apprehended.[21] When voluntary departure is granted, officials do not usually attempt to verify whether the alien has, in fact, left. Even individuals who are physically removed from U.S. territory can attempt to reenter the country. Though they are not entitled to work authorization, such individuals may find jobs, as studies of the effectiveness of employer sanctions have demonstrated (e.g., Calavita 1990). Just as individuals can "immigrate" after they are already present, so too are people referred to as having been "deported" without leaving the United States.[22] Racism, patriarchy, and other repressive systems can prevent even those who are granted legal status from obtaining complete social legitimacy. If physical and social reality cannot be made to conform to their legal representation, what is the purpose of holding lengthy hearings on the merit of individuals' legalization claims, producing copious records of legal proceedings, issuing official orders and decisions, subjugating immigrants procedurally, and giving judges robes, gavels, and other trappings of authority?

Situating immigration hearings within broader contests over citizenship suggests that these proceedings are necessary because they determine not only the legal status of the individuals involved but also the criteria that define belonging. Exclusion, deportation, and removal hearings establish a border around the legally included and decide who is to be kept out. Whether or not those who are forbidden to cross this legal boundary are actually made to leave the United States, the boundary is used to distribute rights and privileges,[23] such as access to public services, first-tier jobs, and higher education (Bosniak 1991; Brubaker 1992). As quite a bit is at stake in its demarcation, this border is hotly contested, not only by immigrants. Race, class, gender, and other criteria that are implicitly relevant to legalization cases also situate individuals and groups on one or both sides of this border, as legal citizens whose right to citizenship is questioned (see, e.g., Barbalet 1988; Flores and Benmayor 1997; Gilroy 1987; Nelson 1984; Pratt 1990; Sapiro 1984; Taylor 1997).[24] The legitimacy of law itself—as social equalizer, tool of the elite, means of governing, source of order, cause of unrest—is at stake in the creation of this border. If legitimacy and illegitimacy, the legal and the illegal, citizen and alien cannot be distinguished, then law itself—at least in a modern sense (Fitzpatrick 1992)—does not exist. Yet the legitimacy of law also inheres in law's ambiguity (Bourdieu 1987), given that legal categories that are supposed to be universal simultaneously demarcate difference (Collier, Maurer, and Suárez-Navaz 1995; Mehta 1997; Minow 1990). By suggesting that law lacks teeth and by inviting further refinements such as IIRIRA, the gap between legal and social reality both undermines and reinforces law. This gap therefore demonstrates both law's limits and its reach. The differences between social and legal realities make both law and proceedings necessary (see Fitzpatrick 1992).

The limitations of legal reality are sometimes noted during immigration hearings themselves. The impact of judges' decisions, for example, is mitigated by immediate discussion of possible appeals, as in the following exchange between a judge and an asylum applicant:

Judge: The respondent is to depart the country on July 12, 1996. Do you understand, sir?

Respondent: Is that when I have to leave the country?

Judge: Well, your attorney may appeal my decision, in which case you may get to stay longer, but that's the date I'm appointing by which you have to depart voluntarily.

During another hearing, when counsel for the respondent gave a lengthy and detailed closing argument while the judge (who looked bored) fiddled with a rubber band, I realized that the attorney's comments were directed not to the judge but rather to whomever would be deciding the eventual appeal. Voluntary departure (which is a misnomer) is also frequently exposed as a legal ritual. Individuals are only entitled to depart voluntarily (leaving their record clean) instead of being deported (which triggers bars on reentry) if they promise to comply with the departure date set by the judge. Asylum applicants often hesitate when asked to make this promise, probably because agreeing to depart voluntarily seems to contradict their request for asylum.[25] When applicants hesitate, judges explain the pro forma nature of their questions. As one judge told an applicant, "If you say that you won't leave voluntarily, then I have no choice but to order you deported." In other words, applicants who do not know their lines cannot be granted voluntary departure.

The limitations of legal trappings are further exposed by the fact that participants in legal proceedings are well aware that legal truth is finagled as well as uncovered. Though proceedings purport to apply law to a set of facts to distinguish meritorious from nonmeritorious cases (Bourdieu 1987; Weissbourd and Mertz 1985), respondents and their attorneys (I cannot speak for judges or trial attorneys) know that outcomes depend at least in part on which judge hears a case, how well witnesses perform, and the questions posed by attorneys. One attorney told me that she consciously adjusts her style to that of the judge. Attorneys and respondents can articulate the weak points in cases as well as their strategies for addressing these points. One attorney worried that her client—who continually changed the dates and places in his narrative of persecution—would be deemed not credible by asylum officials. She attributed this applicant's success to the fact that during his asylum interview, he finally followed her advice that if he did not know the answer to a question, he should simply say so. Another attorney told me that he had questioned a suspension applicant in court about his marriage plans to suggest to the judge that the applicant's relationship to his girlfriend (a U.S. citizen) was long term. In this case, the applicant and his girlfriend had agreed in advance of the hearing to say that they were not ready for marriage. Like the process of preparing clients' cases (see chapter 4), such efforts to sculpt narrative and performance acknowledge that legal truths are themselves a construction of reality. But, once constructed, legal reality does affect people's lives.

The connections between procedural subjugation and the allocation of legality demonstrate how thoroughly the domains of law and citizenship overlap. It is not surprising that those who lack even a partial claim to national membership are referred to as *illegals*. Traversing territorial borders without authorization situates individuals in a realm of illegality and constitutes these individuals as potential legal subjects in deportation hearings. To subsequently cross the internal boundary between documented and undocumented residents (Bauböck 1994; Brubaker 1992; Chavez 1991; Hammar 1990; Kearney 1991), these illegal "legal subjects" must successfully negotiate legal procedures and define themselves as deserving. The temporal logic that governs hearings also mandates temporally coherent narratives and evidence of progress in the United States. The denial of structural agency holds immigrants individually accountable for the history of their legal cases, their actions in their countries of origin, and their success in the United States. Notions of national legitimacy authorize legal proceedings, contextualize immigrants' accounts of persecution, and incorporate people who can depict themselves as proof that the American dream lives on. Yet by drawing a line between deserving and undeserving aliens, immigration law also reproduces the notions of temporality, agency, and legitimacy that operate in the space of nonexistence. The same proceedings that legalize a few delegitimize the majority and thus give rise to a continuing struggle over legality itself.

Chapter 6

From Refugees
to Immigrants

Though U.S. immigration law cannot completely prevent unauthorized entry and presence, law is critical to domestic and transnational
struggles over citizenship and belonging. The pasts, futures, legitimacy, and sovereignty of nations are at stake in demarcating the
boundaries of both citizenship and citizenries. In the case at hand,
arguments over the legal status of Salvadorans who entered the
United States during the 1980s and 1990s raise questions about the
legitimacy of the Salvadoran state, the morality of U.S. foreign policy,
the integrity of U.S. borders, and the economic and political future
of El Salvador. Immigrants' efforts to influence immigration policies
therefore have the potential to affect the conditions that cause immigration. Asylum law, for example, can be a political tool to question
the legitimacy of particular governments. During the cold war, the
United States readily granted asylum to "victims of communism" and
cited such refugees as evidence of the iniquity of socialist systems
(Bach 1990; J. Bhabha 1996; Churgin 1996; Zolberg 1990). Following the same logic, the United States has been reluctant to grant asylum to refugees from so-called friendly nations. The linkages among
political asylum, foreign policy, and national legitimacy therefore
make it possible for immigrants to claim refugee status as a means of
denouncing abuses of human rights in their countries of origin. By
the same token, liberal immigration policies in receiving states have
practical implications for sending states. Tolerating unauthorized
immigrants or permitting legalization can (theoretically, at least)
relieve social unrest in sending states, facilitate the transfer of critical
resources to family members, fuel economies, create a tax base, and

so forth (Portes 1978). Struggles over individuals' legal statuses and over the criteria that determine legality therefore have national and transnational political implications.

Contests over immigrants' legal identities provide insight into not only the transnational implications of law but also the alternative modes of being that these contests seek to legitimize. Globalization, economic restructuring, and political repression have situated unauthorized migrants in spaces of nonexistence where their relationships, practices, and realities are denied or rendered illicit. Claiming existence entails legitimizing these illicit practices and asserting these denied realities. Because the terms of political and legal contests are often predetermined, legitimizing sometimes consists of merely inverting the arguments that delegitimize. For example, if illegal immigrants are denounced as welfare cheats, then legitimizing the undocumented could take the form of demonstrating that these immigrants do not take welfare (see, e.g., Castaneda 1995). Though they may be politically persuasive, such arguments do not necessarily challenge the assumptions that make welfare use relevant to deservingness. Other means of legitimizing the illicit engage the structures and criteria that determine legitimacy. For example, Salvadorans' ongoing quest for legal status in the United States manipulates existing models of national membership, suggests alternatives to traditional forms of citizenship, and draws attention to the structures and relationships that would have to change if such alternatives were legitimized. Struggles over citizenship therefore engage not only individual and national realities but also the processes that produce a more global future.

This chapter analyzes the ways that Salvadorans' almost twenty-year struggle for legal status in the United States engaged and redefined the structures that legitimize both nations and citizens. The first section discusses how Salvadorans' efforts to obtain refugee status during the 1980s situated these immigrants vis-à-vis both the U.S. and Salvadoran states. The second section focuses on Salvadorans' struggle for residency in the 1990s. This struggle not only redefined the U.S. Salvadoran population but also created new local and transnational political alliances. The third section analyzes Salvadoran immigrants' discourse regarding belonging and locates this discourse within activists' current efforts to obtain political, social, and legal citizenship for at least some segment of this immigrant group. The final section examines how this contest over legality creates ideas of citizenship that, if legitimized, could change the social, economic, and political structures within which they are embedded.

From Refugees . . .

Salvadorans' quest for refugee status in the 1980s was simultaneously a political strategy and a legal and physical necessity. The conflict that had been building in El Salvador through the late 1970s exploded in January 1981 with the first major FMLN offensive. With the example of Nicaragua in mind (Gordon 1989), the FMLN commanders who launched this offensive pursued a quick victory (Byrne 1996; Montgomery 1995). For both activists and guerrilla members, this was a time of great idealism and high hopes. A Salvadoran activist who was in San Salvador during the January 1981 offensive recalled, "We thought, 'Well, now [the revolution] has happened!' Because we had even prepared ourselves. Different groups that we were in had told us that . . . at a certain time, we were going to be receiving weapons, which didn't actually happen." As the guerrillas sought a military victory, paramilitary death squads targeted political activists and those suspected of being guerrillas. An activist who fled to the United States in 1979, when the violence was intensifying, described the Salvadoran government's counterinsurgency strategy:

> In the early 1980s, the Salvadoran government was practicing a politics of extermination. In 1980, they decided to get rid of the political organizations, thinking that they were supporting the guerrillas. So the government attacked people who were in organizations of *campesinos* [peasants or farmers], teachers, and others. The government tried to decapitate these movements, so it went after the leaders. Sympathizers were also targeted. So the moment came when those who were in movements or who were known to be sympathizers had a choice: to either join the guerrillas or to flee. To stay there was simply to wait for the executioner.

As political space in El Salvador shrank (Gordon 1989), activists whose lives were in danger fled to Mexico, Costa Rica, Guatemala,

Nicaragua, Canada, and the United States (Aguayo and Fagen 1988), where at least some continued to support the revolutionary movement in El Salvador. Exiled activists founded committees that worked in solidarity with the organizations that made up the FMLN. An activist who fled to the United States in 1981 described the structure that one such group in Los Angeles had developed by 1982:

> There were about three hundred active people working, and around them were many collaborators, many sympathizers. . . . There were two coordinators, and these coordinators had their work groups. . . . These work groups were in charge of coordinating the members. So these members were the ones who did the street work. They gave presentations in homes, went knocking on doors, they made tamales, they were the people who collected the money, the people who sold [items]. . . . Apart from these, there were the secretaries—the secretary of publicity, . . . the secretary of finances, and the secretary of the organization, and the secretary of public relations. . . . It was well organized.

Some of the individuals who held posts in these solidarity committees also held formal positions in Salvadoran political organizations and were accountable to higher-ranking officials within these groups.[1] Transnational solidarity networks developed, stretching from El Salvador to such countries as the United States, Mexico, Uruguay, East and West Germany, India, and Japan. A participant explained, "The nexus was in El Salvador. That had to exist, because each of the solidarity movements was supporting the movement that was occurring in El Salvador. And in addition, different solidarity groups had ties to each other. There were contacts, for example, with Mexico, and they were useful when we traveled" (see also Benítez 1990). Though the FMLN engaged in formal diplomacy, sending representatives to some thirty-three countries throughout the world (Montgomery 1995:114), solidarity networks were also clandestine. Activists who told me of this work asked me not to publish such details as organizations' names, their own posts within organizations, or the precise relationship between their organizations and groups in El Salvador.

Activism was all absorbing for many exiles who engaged in solidarity work. The immediacy and violence of the war and of human rights abuses created a sense of overwhelming urgency. One activist related, "The foundation for everything that I did was this personal relationship, see? 'If I do nothing, someone will die, today, tomorrow.' I already had lost my oldest brother, and my other siblings were [in El Salvador], so they could die, too. So it was a *rush to do something*" (italicized portion originally in English). Activists were also motivated by the belief that the war would end soon and that they could return to El Salvador to help reconstruct a new society, as another participant commented: "We had grand dreams, no? That the [FMLN] would triumph militarily, that it was going to enter San Salvador armed to take over the government offices, and that then we were going to return." Exiled activists saw their work providing material assistance, denouncing abuses, opposing U.S. intervention in Central America, and justifying the revolutionary movement as critical to political struggle in El Salvador. Their solidarity work demanded what participants characterized as extraordinary sacrifices. According to one FMLN member, "When you participate in revolutionary life in El Salvador as a party member, you lose your life," not only through physical violence but also by giving up family life, postponing studies, putting a career on hold, making financial sacrifices, and dedicating free time to political activities.[2] One activist characterized this period as "the days when people thought, 'My life only has meaning to the degree that I serve El Salvador,'" while another commented, "We were living here physically, but sentimentally, we were in El Salvador." Some activists drew parallels between the national crisis and their personal lives. Like their country, they were living a revolution that disrupted normalcy and sacrificed the present to the future.

Clandestine political work situated Salvadoran activists in complex ways vis-à-vis both the U.S. and Salvadoran states. As members of a revolutionary political movement, activists acted as citizens of a state that was coming into being (see López Casanova 1995). Their political organizations performed quasi-governmental functions, such as sending emissaries overseas, establishing internal command structures, issuing communiqués, governing territory in El Salvador, and (eventually) advocating on behalf of Salvadorans in the United States. Yet the "citizenry" of this as yet unrealized state may not have been characterized by what Benedict Anderson (1991:7) terms "deep, horizontal comradeship" (though such comradeship may have existed within particular political groups). Despite its many achievements, sectarianism and internal divisions have plagued the

Salvadoran Left both in the United States and in El Salvador (Byrne 1996; Montgomery 1995), while a well-founded fear of infiltrators could make it difficult to completely trust seeming colleagues.[3] As members of opposition movements engaged in or supportive of revolutionary struggle, activists questioned the legitimacy of the Salvadoran government (Gordon 1989), which they characterized as repressive and undemocratic. Through torture, assassination, and dismemberment, the Salvadoran government in turn defined both activists and guerrillas as noncitizens and even as nonhumans (see chapter 2). Exiled activists did not, at this time, claim citizenship in the United States. Their political work was directed toward El Salvador, they viewed their sojourn in the United States as temporary, and their requests for legal status were based on the need to avoid persecution rather than on claims to belonging. Exiled activists were therefore, in a sense, clandestine citizens, serving a *patria* where they could not actually reside. One activist described his circumstances as follows, "I was undocumented, and I traveled as I wished. I left the country illegally, and I reentered illegally. We were trying to stop the war, so we were willing to do anything. And our thinking was, 'We'll stop the war by winning it.' Everything we did was illegal!"

In this political context U.S.-based Salvadoran activists began to struggle for refugee status. This struggle had multiple goals. Practically, it was a means of preventing individuals from being deported to face torture, persecution, and assassination. Legally, asylum was the only possible avenue through which to obtain residency, as most of the recent Salvadoran immigrants were ineligible for other means of legalization, such as being petitioned for by relatives who were U.S. citizens or legal permanent residents. Politically, claiming refugee status drew attention to human rights abuses by Salvadoran authorities, which in turn legitimized the struggle against the Salvadoran government and problematized U.S. Central American policy. An activist explained this strategy: "There was a propaganda campaign on the part of the U.S. government saying that there wasn't a war in El Salvador or in Central America. Saying that we weren't dying in a war. . . . So it was important to challenge the errors within this propaganda by pointing out that Salvadorans were not economic immigrants." To make this argument, political committees held demonstrations denouncing human rights abuses in Central America, arranged for refugees to speak publicly about the persecution they had experienced, and distributed information about the war and about ongoing human rights violations.

Advocating on behalf of refugees was a significant shift within the organizational structures and political thinking of activists living in exile. By the end of 1983, the FMLN recognized that an immediate military victory would not be forthcoming and shifted its military strategy to one of prolonged war (Byrne 1996:78). Similarly, activists in the United States were by this time revising their predictions of a quick victory and reassessing their political strategies. By 1982 or 1983, the political activists who had emigrated earlier were joined by many, many other Salvadorans whose lives were endangered by repression and war. One activist recalled, "The people who had been fleeing El Salvador at the beginning of the 1980s had political roots in the organizations there. . . . But as the war continued, it affected more of the population. So, the people who began leaving after this period—let's say, after '82—were people who came from all social strata." To meet the social and legal needs of the growing Central American population in the United States, political committees founded refugee committees, such as El Rescate and CARECEN (see chapter 4). In addition to continuing the political and human rights work of the political committees, these refugee committees performed what was termed "domestic work" such as establishing shelters for newly arrived refugees, distributing food and clothing, and providing legal services. This domestic work was always linked to international work. For example, refugee committees arranged for refugees to be placed in sanctuary congregations and to give public testimonials about their experiences. Such strategies were designed to acquaint the U.S. populace with conditions in Central America and to thus make continued U.S. support for the Salvadoran government politically unfeasible. Through legal advocacy, refugee committees also sought to change U.S. refugee policies so that larger numbers of Central Americans could receive political asylum.

At the time, claiming that Central Americans were refugees was a defiant act (Coutin 1993). There is something potentially radical about refugeeness, particularly when it is combined with illegality. Refugees are defined by their mobility, their uprootedness, their lack of a fixed place or location (Malkki 1992). Refugees can be characterized as the most marginal of the marginalized, a designation that exposes the illegitimacy of institutional structures of all sorts. The states that are responsible for their welfare persecute them, immigration laws criminalize their efforts to seek safe haven, foreign policies preclude recognizing their realities, and they are constituted as, in every sense of the word, illegal beings. Religious activists who gave sanctuary to Central American refugees even argued that states that failed to protect widows, orphans, and refugees would face divine retribution (Bau 1985; Coutin 1993; MacEoin 1985). The words of these people whose existence was forbidden and on whose welfare the fates of nations depended were powerful. Scholars have noted the importance of attending to those who transgress boundaries (e.g., Appadurai 1991; Gupta 1992), priests and ministers have sat at the feet of refugees to hear their words, and hearts and minds have been changed in the process (Coutin 1993). Seeking refugee status for Central Americans therefore engaged not only political arguments about Central American realities but also powerful discourses about space, boundaries, and mobility.

The argument that Central Americans deserved political asylum in the United States created a complicated claim to membership within and exclusion from multiple citizenries.[4] Salvadorans' claim to asylum was based on their relationship to the Salvadoran state. Because this state had abrogated its contract with its citizens by persecuting them, this argument held, these asylum seekers could not enjoy the rights to which they were entitled in their countries of origin. The violation of their rights rendered these immigrants stateless in the sense that their rights as Salvadoran citizens were of no practical use, given that they could not live safely in El Salvador. As unofficially stateless persons, asylum seekers became international citizens who turned to international law and the international community to obtain respect for their rights. This search for rights took the form of a request for asylum in the United States. To make this request, these asylum seekers had to distinguish themselves from economic immigrants by arguing that they did not want to be in the United States and that they intended to return to El Salvador when conditions were safe. This emphasis on return, which was also consistent with activists' work in solidarity with struggles that were occurring in El Salvador, situated Salvadorans as outsiders to remain within the United States. Yet applying for asylum also could situate applicants outside of the Salvadoran populace, as one activist noted: "To be requesting political asylum is something that is going to be reviewed in another country. And that means that you're not going to feel the same tie to your country. It's like a negation of your origin." In short, claiming refugee status positioned Salvadorans as international yet stateless beings who both were and were not part of the Salvadoran citizenry and who were simultaneously in yet outside of the United States.

Despite its political and legal necessity, the contention that Salvadorans were refugees had certain disadvantages that eventually led this argument to be revised. Seeking asylum did not assert a claim to membership within the U.S. polity but simply a need to remain outside of El Salvador. This assertion was vulnerable to changing conditions within El Salvador. If human rights and civil war ended, Central Americans would not need asylum. This argument also depicted Salvadorans as a transitory community rather than as a permanent part of local and national realities. Claiming refugee status could also be disempowering, since refugees are considered to be needy, fearful, and persecuted (Burns 1993; Malkki 1992). One Salvadoran activist told me that he associated refugees with "like if you are an Ethiopian in the field, expecting [from] the United Nation[s] help, food, and everything." In actuality, relationships between Central Americans and U.S. solidarity workers sometimes took paternalistic forms. During the 1990s, activists told me that they disliked being regarded as *pobrecito refugiado* (poor little refugee). Most significantly, perhaps, refugee is a category that negates, that defines people according to what they lack—shelter, rights, food, status, freedom, security, a home—rather than what they have.

By the 1990s, these disadvantages combined with changing social, legal, and political circumstances to produce new strategies for legalization.

. . . to Immigrants

The late 1980s and early 1990s witnessed tremendous changes in El Salvador and within the Salvadoran community in the United States. Despite the fact that activists continued to call Central Americans "refugees," by the late 1980s, Salvadorans were settling in the United States, with or without legal status. An activist described this shift:

The whole process through which this change occurred took place during the last five years of the 1980s, to arrive at the final change at the beginning of 1990. The community said, "This isn't a community that is trying to return to El Salvador," though there are always exceptions, there's always a percentage that wants to return and that's going to do it. But we're talking about the great majority. This is no longer a community that is a typical refugee community. Many had acquired material possessions here, they had children born here, they'd gotten married. A series of factors that totally changed it, converting it into an immigrant community. And people would tell you, "I'll go to El Salvador, but to visit. I now live here."

As the war in El Salvador dragged on, individuals who had originally envisioned their stay as temporary began to change their plans. Central American businesses and restaurants sprang up in urban areas such as Los Angeles, attesting to the vibrancy and permanence of this community (Rocco 1997; Waldinger and Bozorgmehr 1996). In 1986 IRCA enabled the earliest Salvadoran immigrants—including many activists—to legalize and to petition for family members who arrived after the January 1, 1982, cutoff date for amnesty. By the late 1980s and early 1990s, hometown associations dedicated to sending money and other sorts of material assistance to Salvadorans' communities of origin began to proliferate. Children who had been born in the United States or who had immigrated at an early age urged their parents to stay in the United States. As one activist commented ruefully, "We were only thinking about the question of refugees and the political question, but the people weren't going around thinking in these terms."

As Salvadorans settled in the United States and elsewhere, the military stalemate in El Salvador continued, eventually creating an impetus for a negotiated solution to the conflict. Between 1984 and 1989, FMLN forces in El Salvador continued their strategy of trying to wear away the Salvadoran Armed Forces through economic sabotage, small-scale military actions, and popular organizing. The Salvadoran military, for its part, bombed guerrilla-controlled areas to eliminate civilian supporters, attempted to discredit the guerrilla movement, and continued to receive military and political support from the United States (Byrne 1996). In November 1989, the FMLN launched its "final offensive," designed to either provoke a national insurrection or to at least demonstrate the strength of the insurgent forces. During this offensive, members of the Salvadoran Armed Forces assassinated six Jesuit priests, their housekeeper, and her daughter. The assassination provoked international condemnation, which helped to create conditions for serious peace negotiations. On January 16, 1992, peace accords were signed. The accords mandated

> demilitarization, including halving the size of the Armed Forces, eliminating the state security forces and the FMLN's guerrilla army; legalizing the FMLN as a political party; amending the constitution; reforming the electoral and judicial systems; settling the land distribution issue, one of the root causes of the war; and establishing independent commissions to identify those responsible for major human rights abuses and to purge the army of its most serious human rights violators. (Montgomery 1995:226; see also Córdova Macías 1993)

Though the agreement was implemented slowly, the war had officially ended.

The peace accords, though welcome, created a void for U.S. activists who had dedicated themselves to solidarity work. One activist related, "When the war ended, there was a moment of celebration, when the combatants marched to the capital, and the peace accords were signed, and there was a celebration in the streets. I was there, I participated. But the moment was short. And then what came?" In the postaccord era, activists in the United States found their work more rather than less difficult. The anti-interventionist movement evaporated, providers of funding turned their attention to other causes, and Central America was a less "sexy" issue. One organizer observed almost nostalgically, "The war was opening doors. . . . Without it, it's more difficult to go out there and say, 'I want to talk about El Salvador.'" Activists who had planned to return to El Salvador found themselves reluctant to do so. One man related, "People said, 'I've learned things here that I won't be able to use there. Better to stay here. And I'll continue to struggle for my people.'" Some compared their personal transitions to those of the nation. As El Salvador embarked on postwar reconstruction, former solidarity workers rethought their priorities, went back to school, and embarked on new careers. As one participant explained, "With the peace accords, people [in the U.S.] began rethinking their lives. . . . Activists began to think of themselves, to dedicate some portion of their time to their families, in contrast to dedicating ourselves 100 percent to the war." Activists' organizations also underwent transitions. The political committees that had engaged in solidarity work either disbanded or regrouped, changing their names and their missions in the process.

During this introspective moment, activists reassessed their claim that Central Americans were refugees and instead began to call themselves and their communities immigrants. According to many, this shift was necessary. When they used the term *refugees,* activists based Central Americans' claim to U.S. residency solely on conditions in Central America. In the postaccord period, this strategy was not likely to succeed and therefore ran the risk that Salvadoran immigrants would be deported to face the violence and economic devastation of postwar El Salvador. In the 1990s, the negative connotations of the term *refugee*—being dirty or powerless, fleeing—did not help activists depict Central Americans as a successful community that had set down roots in the United States and that intended to stay. Moreover, activists commented, in the postwar period, it seemed hypocritical to claim that all Salvadorans were refugees. As one activist stated emphatically, "We're calling ourselves immigrants because that's what we are; we're no longer refugees. There's no longer a war in El Salvador." The term was therefore discarded by many as disempowering. Some organizations removed the term *refugee* from their names, while new organizations called themselves Salvadoran-American. Such renamings marked a renewed interest in organizing and empowering Central Americans in the United States. For example, one activist said that his organization was focusing on the question, "What do we want for the future of our generations here, independent of what happens or does not happen in El Salvador?" Activists' rejection of the term *refugee* was not universal, however. In 1996, the director of a significant Central American community agency in Los Angeles told me, "I came to this country as a refugee. I entered *mojado,* 'wetback,' as you say here. And the conditions in my country remain unjust. So I still see my community as a refugee community. We came here as undocumented, and we have achieved a lot. We can be proud."

Although activists redefined Central Americans as an immigrant rather than refugee community, the forms of legal relief available to Salvadorans in the 1990s were based on the political realities of the 1980s. TPS, DED, and ABC were obtained through the solidarity work of the 1980s, and each was designed to meet the needs of people who were unable to return to their homelands due to civil war and human-rights abuses. By the time these remedies were implemented, however, peace accords had been signed, and only those immigrants with the most compelling cases were likely to win political asylum. As a result, activists devised a strategy for using these remedies as a means of obtaining a more appropriate form of legal relief. By registering large numbers of Salvadorans for TPS, DED, and ABC (see chapter 4), activists hoped to enable these Central Americans to remain in the United States long enough to accumulate the seven years of continuous presence required to apply for suspension of deportation. At the same time, activists continued to advocate a grant of residency for all ABC class members and TPS/DED recipients.

Activists' legal strategies were jeopardized in 1996 by the passage of IIRIRA. According to IIRIRA, the clock could be stopped on the accumulation of time by the issuance of a notice to appear in immigration court. In a decision known as *In re N-J-B-*, the Board of Immigration Appeals ruled that orders to show cause were the equivalent of notices to appear. This decision rendered the stoppage of time retroactive, which was particularly damaging to TPS recipients, all of whom were issued orders to show cause in 1993, when their eighteen months of TPS expired. Thus, a Salvadoran who entered the United States in 1989, applied for TPS in 1991, and was issued an order to show cause in 1993 could in 1997 be deemed to have accumulated only four years of continuous residence (from 1989 to 1993) and therefore to be ineligible for suspension of deportation. Even if advocates succeeded in arguing that the TPS orders to show cause—which were never mailed to applicants—did not count, ABC class members whose asylum petitions were denied would face another hurdle: IIRIRA replaced suspension of deportation with cancellation of removal, which required ten years of continuous residence rather than seven and limited grants to individuals who could demonstrate that "removal" (the new term for deportation) would constitute extreme and exceptional hardship not to the applicant but rather to the applicant's U.S. citizen or legal permanent resident spouse, parent, or child. Individuals who did not have a U.S. citizen or legal permanent resident spouse, parent, or child would be ineligible for cancellation. If unchallenged, these higher standards and INS officials' consensus that El Salvador was at peace would result in the deportation of the vast majority of ABC class members.

IIRIRA gave renewed urgency to activists' campaign for a blanket grant of residency to all ABC class members. From January to November 1997, Central American activists lobbied members of the U.S. Congress, wrote letters to President Bill Clinton, organized demonstrations, held fasts and vigils at federal buildings, held press conferences, mobilized solidarity workers, and organized ABC class members. Through alliances with Nicaraguans (who were also affected by IIRIRA), Salvadoran and Guatemalan community leaders sought bipartisan support for residency for all those affected by wars in Central America. Activists took advantage of a May 1997 summit meeting between President Clinton and the Central American presidents to publicize this issue and to obtain Clinton's promise of support for their cause. Activists mobilized multiple sectors of Salvadoran society, including the Salvadoran business community in the United States, Salvadoran religious leaders, Salvadoran government officials, and community organizations. Activists who had once been undocumented met with U.S. congressional aides to discuss legislative proposals, traveled to El Salvador and Guatemala to obtain the support of government officials, and urged ABC applicants to advocate on their own behalf. An activist explained that just as the war effort was outside of the electoral process, so too would undocumented people have to express themselves politically in ways other than voting: "There's no law . . . that they can't make a phone call, that they can't say they support one or another party" (see also Hardy-Fanta 1993). This campaign also created a national coalition of Salvadoran organizations known as the Salvadoran American National Network.

Unlike activists' earlier efforts to obtain refugee status, the campaign for residency for ABC class members not only stressed applicants' need to be outside of their home countries but also staked a claim to membership in the United States. Drawing on the hardship argument that was part of suspension law, activists argued that it would be inhumane to deport Central Americans who have acclimated to the United States. For example, during a speech at the Los Angeles Federal Building in November 1997, an activist noted that many Central Americans have U.S. citizen children as well as jobs, homes, and other property in the United States. Activists also invoked the idea that there is an implicit social contract between migrant workers and the states that employ their labor, which suggests that contributing to society ought to confer legal rights. Activists pointed out that Central Americans pay taxes, take jobs that other people (i.e., Anglos) do not want, pick fruit, baby-sit children, and participate in many social institutions, such as churches. Such activities, organizers argued, entitled Central Americans to residency in the United States. Organizers also pointed out that Central Americans were living in the United States with the permission of the U.S. government and therefore were documented rather than illegal. President Clinton himself echoed this reasoning during his summit meeting with the Central American presidents, as the *Los Angeles Times* reported: "Clinton pointed to a central paradox: Washington allowed the Central Americans to remain here legally, but the 300,000 people affected never qualified as permanent legal immigrants. That prevented them from becoming U.S. citizens, a status that would have shielded them and their families from deportation." (McDonnell 1997b:A32). Such comments redefined the "social construction" of ABC applicants (see Schneider and Ingram 1993), who previously had been considered illegal aliens.

Activists who were involved in the campaign for residency argued that their claims to membership in the United States were justified by their experiences in their homelands. Reminding listeners of the bombings, torture, massacres, and other abuses that pervaded El Salvador during the civil war, activists asserted that Central Americans would have been entitled to asylum during the 1980s had their claims been adjudicated in an unbiased fashion. "I think we already suffered hardship, don't you?" an activist asked his audience rhetorically during a political rally in November 1997. Linking the suffering that is grounds for political asylum to the hardship that is a basis for suspension of deportation, this comment suggested that the past hardship that caused immigration is as relevant to legalization as the future hardship that deportation would pose. Activists also argued that the United States had a moral responsibility to accept Central Americans as residents, given its involvement in the civil war (see Sassen 1989). As one activist stated, "We are a product of a government['s] military aid to El Salvador['s] government that forced us to leave." Finally, just as activists' quest for refugee status had been linked to the war effort in the 1980s, activists' claim to residency in the 1990s was seen as a means of supporting the peace process in El Salvador. Activists argued that mass deportations would destabilize economic and social reconstruction, potentially giving rise to renewed conflict. In the words of one activist, "With or without war in El Salvador, a large deportation would be an economic, social, and political chaos." Noting that remittances fuel the Salvadoran economy, activists defined the expatriate Salvadoran community as critical to the future of El Salvador. Some activists depicted remittances as a substitute for both U.S. foreign aid to El Salvador and for expenditures by the Salvadoran government. One activist explained, "After the peace accords were signed, less money came to the [Salvadoran] government through foreign aid. So now the aid that it receives comes in the form of remittances that private citizens send to their relatives and that therefore enters the economy. These remittances enable people to buy things, which keeps the economy afloat, plus the [Salvadoran] government gets taxes." According to this argument, expatriate Salvadorans, regardless of their organizational status or political affiliations, perform quasi-governmental functions simply through their transnational, social networks.

The campaign for residency for ABC class members led to the passage of NACARA in November 1997 (see chapter 1). NACARA created an amnesty for Nicaraguans who were beneficiaries of the Nicaraguan Review Program and restored the suspension eligibility of ABC class members, TPS recipients, and certain other Salvadoran and Guatemalan asylum seekers. Dissatisfied with the disparate treatment received by Nicaraguans on the one hand and Salvadorans and Guatemalans on the other, activists have continued a grassroots campaign for a blanket grant of residency to all NACARA beneficiaries. This campaign is part of a broader effort to negotiate Central Americans' place in U.S. society.

The Geography of Citizenship

Just as the denial of citizenship forces people into a space of nonexistence, so too does asserting citizenship entail staking a claim to particular places. For Salvadorans, who were persecuted in their homelands, crossed borders clandestinely, lived for years in the United States, and, in some cases, dedicated themselves to revolutionary struggles in El Salvador, such claims have been particularly complicated. A Salvadoran activist and ABC class member described the ways that persecution, flight, and illegality problematized her presence in both El Salvador and the United States:

> Salvadorans have suffered a lot. We're a very suffering people. First, there was the war, and that was terrible. I had to go to school on the bus and come home at night, and I was afraid. Then you have to say goodbye to your friends and to family members, to people you've grown up with. And then coming to another country, where you don't know how things work—it's an emotional shock. And then to find that you're illegal, and to run into problems with Immigration, and to be detained. And then you have to adapt to the country, like it or not. It consumes you. And time passes. Then, suddenly, a time comes when you don't know if you're from here or there. You're not wanted here, but you don't feel that you belong there anymore. And meanwhile they are saying, "We don't know if we'll let you stay or make you go back." They're playing with the destiny of thousands of people. They don't realize what they're doing.

Among the Salvadoran immigrants, activists, and advocates whom I interviewed, there was no consensus regarding the nature of their spatial and national connectedness. It would therefore be too simplistic to say that a sense of transnationalism, assimilation, or exclusive commitment to their homelands predominated among interviewees. What did emerge in these accounts, however, was a common language about belonging, identity, and citizenship. This language used such terms as *blood, roots, flags,* and *food* to mark particular sorts of rights, relationships, and loyalties to national spaces. Immigrants' efforts to articulate their own social locations therefore reveal how they define inclusion and exclusion.

One account of belonging that emerged in Salvadorans' descriptions of their identities was the idea that nationality is an immutable fact of nature, conferred by birth on Salvadoran soil, relationships to Salvadoran family members, and having Salvadoran blood. This fact of nature could be interpreted in various ways, as an unbreakable tie or as something that had been overridden by subsequent social realities. For example, one man quoted a Salvadoran saying, "We'll go back where we left our umbilical cord," to emphasize his continued connections to El Salvador. In contrast, a woman used this idea of birthright and a tie to soil to mark disconnection, commenting that when she dies, she does not want to be buried in El Salvador where, presumably, she would "naturally" belong. Interviewees depicted not only nationality but also such national symbols as flags and anthems as conferred automatically according to birth. One man used the custom of waving flags at soccer matches to describe the multinational origins of his family: "We should bring a U.S. flag for my daughter, because she was born here, and a Salvadoran flag for me, and a Colombian flag for my wife and son, who are from Colombia. We'll be like the whole United Nations!" Such concepts of flags and birth as natural markers of belonging derive belonging from people's origins. One young man, for example, told me, "A Salvadoran is born, not made. Being Salvadoran is your culture, your family, your grandmother who is still in El Salvador and who writes to you all the time." Birth, however, can also mark a disjuncture, as in the example of the Salvadoran father and the U.S. citizen daughter, who would wave different flags at soccer games. When directed toward El Salvador, assertions of jus soli appear nostalgic, but when directed toward the United States, these assertions enable immigrants to claim membership through their children's births on U.S. soil. Such claims are politically significant given that, in 1995, the U.S. Congress was considering proposals that would deny citizenship to the U.S.-born children of undocumented parents (see Chock 1997).

In addition to characterizing national membership as a natural fact, interviewees depicted belonging as subjective, a "structure of feeling" (Williams 1977:128), a sense of connection and being at home or not at home. Unlike "facts of nature," which are immutable, feelings can change. One man who had dedicated his adult life to the Salvadoran revolution described his distress at returning to El Salvador after eight years in exile and discovering that he did not belong:

> I, who had always been conscious that El Salvador is my country and [thought] that "One day I'm going to return, come what may. Not now precisely." . . . I thought I was not accommodating

[to the United States] And when I *go* back [to El Salvador], I miss things, I feel [I'm] in a void. I didn't find the childhood friends that I left behind. My family was no longer the same, El Salvador had completely changed. I thought that that was caught in the past, [but] the one who was caught in the past was me!

In contrast to this activist's distress, a Salvadoran woman who felt that the Salvadoran government had betrayed her by preventing her from living in freedom was pleased to discover that she felt "100 percent American." Although the people with whom I spoke depicted feelings of belonging as products of circumstances and therefore as not under individuals' control, interviewees also suggested that senses of connection can be chosen or constructed, particularly for and by immigrants' children. Salvadoran immigrants described their efforts to transmit Salvadoran culture to their children, so that children—despite the natural fact of having been born in the United States—would "know their roots." Parents, for example, pointed out that their children loved to eat *pupusas* (a popular Salvadoran dish), spoke Spanish, and knew something of Salvadoran music, history, and holidays. One parent described being upset when her daughter came home from school on Cinco de Mayo with a Mexican flag and said, "This is our flag." Immigrants' efforts to promote Salvadoranness within second-generation Salvadoran immigrants look both to a past in El Salvador and a present in which Salvadorans are defining themselves as ethnic minorities in the United States.

Salvadorans' accounts of national membership cite not only birth and feelings as bases for belonging but also substantive actions, such as living in particular territories, paying taxes to particular governments, and working in particular societies (see also Bosniak 1991; Hammar 1990). One Salvadoran activist who, like the man quoted earlier, had dedicated himself to solidarity work, explained how in 1990 he stopped, as he put it, denying that he was in the United States: "I realized, your *patria* [homeland] is that which gives you food, that which gives you work. I realized that we had to stop paying taxes here and living elsewhere emotionally. We had to accept that the United States was our government." This man's juxtaposition of paying taxes and his emotional connections is telling. Taxes—which are cited in court to demonstrate both physical presence and self-sufficiency—are assessed of all residents, regardless of their legal status, and therefore imply that residents are, in some sense, members of the polity that is being governed. Territorial presence and social participation are therefore bases for claiming citizenship. Similarly, territorial absence and lack of social participation on a daily basis can make one "not belong," as this activist notes, despite political connectedness. Assertions of membership that are grounded in social participation draw on the idea of progress that is used to assess suspension claims. For example, one ABC applicant told me, "I think that if I have been living here for twelve years, I work here, I pay my taxes, then I live *here*. I don't have anything to do with El Salvador. I have to do with here, where I work, with this country. Here is where I—or 'we,' right?—have to try to progress, try to make something of ourselves." By shifting to the collective voice, this man, who was involved in the campaign for residency for ABC class members, invokes the promise of the American immigrant story. For some, social incorporation is spatialized in local and national geography. One Salvadoran woman who obtained U.S. citizenship through the amnesty program told me that when she flies into the Los Angeles airport after visiting El Salvador, she thinks, "This is mine. This is part of me."

In contrast to the complexity of their accounts of belonging—as natural attribute, feeling, and ongoing social participation—interviewees characterized formal, legal citizenship as capturing only part of what is entailed in social membership. Some depicted naturalization as a strategic action rather than a substantive, personal transformation. One member of a Salvadoran organization promoting citizenship and civic participation commented, "Becoming citizens, we don't lose anything. We remain Salvadoran at heart." Similarly, an ABC applicant told me, "I will always be Salvadoran, regardless of where my citizenship is or what piece of paper I have. I will never forget my little house or my little town, humble though it is. I am not American." Interviewees who wanted to naturalize (and only a rare few did not) attributed their desire for U.S. citizenship not only to feelings of belonging but also to the practical benefits that citizenship would provide (see also Hagan 1994). Interviewees cited the freedom to travel internationally, the ability to petition for undocumented relatives, the right to vote, and better retirement benefits as the primary advantages of U.S. citizenship. Some pointed out that with legal residency or U.S. citizenship, they would be better connected to families and communities abroad than they are as asylum applicants who jeopardize their chances of legalizing if they leave the United States.[5] Both activists and nonactivists noted that more restrictive immigration policies have sharpened distinctions between U.S. citizens and legal permanent residents. As one woman put it, "The way things are going, in the future, the residents will be treated like illegals." Indeed, since the early 1990s, legal permanent residents have been naturalizing in record numbers, a fact that some analysts attribute to legal immigrants' conclusion that they are threatened by laws, such as California Proposition 187, that make citizenship a prerequisite for an increasing number of rights and services (Paral 1995; G. Sanchez 1997).[6] For example, an ASOSAL staff member commented, "The passage of the 187 law awoke the Latino community to the need to be able to decide, to exercise these rights, because it has been directly affected with the passage of this law. . . . The moment that this law passed, everyone wanted to make themselves a citizen."

The strategic implications of naturalization are apparent to Salvadoran activists, some of whom have dedicated organizational resources to urging Salvadoran legal permanent residents to naturalize. Such promotion of naturalization would not have been possible during the 1980s because most Salvadorans in the United States were undocumented. By the mid-1990s, however, a significant but difficult-to-quantify segment of the Salvadoran community—including the cohort of activists who immigrated in the late 1970s and early 1980s—had obtained permanent residency through the 1986 amnesty program, family visa petitions, or other means. By promoting naturalization, activists hoped to empower immigrants themselves to counter anti-immigrant sentiment through voting. A San Francisco activist explained that the long-term goal of promoting both naturalization and civic participation is another amnesty: "Regarding the people who don't have documents, . . . it's a much more long-term possibility, and that is that we will begin to struggle in favor of a new amnesty. . . . To make changes, you don't work over one or two years, these are matters that take [many] years. . . . But if no one starts, what then?" In addition to addressing the needs of the undocumented, activists see naturalization as a means of defining Salvadorans as a political constituency whose needs deserve attention. A Salvadoran political organizer in Los Angeles explained this strategy: "A politician is not going to give as much importance to a project submitted by the Salvadoran community as residents as a project that the Salvadoran community submits as citizens, because he knows that if he rejects it, he could lose votes." Through naturalization and voting, Salvadoran activists hope to increase Salvadorans' political clout in the United States.

Despite their interest in naturalization, both activists and nonactivists noted that legal citizenship does not guarantee full social rights to those who are racially, economically, and socially marginalized. To make this point, several interviewees told me of a local mayor whose Hispanic appearance and dilapidated vehicle had led INS officials to conclude that he was an illegal alien. The idea that full citizenship is beyond immigrants' reach was echoed by a Salvadoran college student, who told me, "I do feel like I'm a true American, even though I wasn't born here. [It is] like I'm an adopted child, but they will never treat me as a full American." Interviewees linked immigration and racial discrimination to economic marginalization, noting that immigrants and Latinos (categories they saw as interconnected) took the lowest-paying and least-desirable jobs. One activist suggested that the goal of policies such as California Proposition 187 was to "prevent the community from becoming empowered, to not permit it access to higher education. And what does that prevent? That prevents you from occupying high positions, no? In the government, or becoming a lawyer, or becoming a doctor. So that you will always be at their service." Countering depictions of the United States as the land of opportunity, many interviewees noted the economic deprivation they had suffered after immigrating. Gregorio Orozco, who had been a professor in El Salvador and who, at the time of our interview, worked as a janitor, saw marginalization as spatialized along class and racial lines. Describing Latinos as "second-class citizens," Gregorio criticized the crowding and disrepair of buses and other public services in his neighborhood of North Hollywood relative to Beverly Hills. Overwhelmingly, interviewees characterized restrictive immigration policies and anti-immigrant sentiment as directed against minorities in general rather than immigrants in particular.

To counter anti-immigrant sentiment, claim citizenship, obtain political recognition, and assert membership, Central American community organizations sought to define Salvadorans in particular and Central Americans in general as a new ethnic group. Such efforts negotiated rights to public space and culture. Several organizations floated the idea of asking the Los Angeles City Council to name a particular neighborhood in Los Angeles, Little El Salvador or Little Central America. Like Koreatown, Chinatown, and Little Tokyo, such an ethnicization or nationalization of public space would legitimize Central Americans' claims to local and thus legal residency and counter negative depictions of immigrants.[7] Similarly, some community organizations have sought to institutionalize the annual Central American Independence Day on September 15.[8] Like "take back the night" marches or Catholic and Protestant marches in Belfast (Feldman 1991), parades can constitute claims to both territory and time. Both of these claims are explicit in an ASOSAL staff member's description of the Central American parade: "[Mexico]'s independence is on [September] 16, and only the Central American countries are on the fifteenth. And in East L.A., they focus on that date, and on this side, where the Central American community supposedly is, we focus on the fifteenth." Similarly, another activist stressed the importance of "institutionaliz[ing] certain dates for our community. . . . Within a few years it would be good if there were a couple of days that were recognized in the city as days of so-and-so so that we can succeed in getting these celebrated in the schools and elsewhere." Such efforts to publicly institutionalize dates, spaces, and practices as Central American echo states' claims to have encompassed and tamed diversity, thus enriching the cultural wealth of the nation (see Greenhouse 1996). For example, one activist insisted, "What is important is, as a resident community here, we have to move forward, to demonstrate that, yes, we are here, we want to support this country, to give the best of our knowledge, and to show the rest of the ethnic cultures that are here the cultural riches that we have." To be here, to confront racism, and to pass from illegality to legality, immigrants must naturalize their differences by claiming a spot within the array of nationalities that make up immigrant America (see Coutin 1998a).[9]

   My analysis of Central Americans' ideas of belonging only partly coincides with Featherstone's (1995:154) conclusion that global migration "is undermining the once secure fantasy-based 'we- and they-images,' and changing the nature of identity formation to the extent that categories of people are emerging who live more mobile lives and are at ease with more fluid identities." It is true that images of selves and others are being challenged through migration, but this statement seems to celebrate mobility and fluidity. It seems to me that Central American migrants are attempting to construct workable identities in conditions that are simultaneously too fluid and too fixed—that is, these immigrants were forced to move and are in danger of being deported yet are now stuck in legal categories and national spaces. Their ease or unease with fluid identity categories is sort of beside the point, given the power that inheres in constructing identities.

The New Politics of Citizenship

Central Americans' struggle to legalize is part of a wider political struggle over citizens and citizenship in a global era (see, e.g., Hall and Held 1990). It is not a coincidence that as U.S. immigration policy became more restrictive, the Mexican government created dual citizenship, the Salvadoran government intervened on behalf of its citizens in the United States, and Caribbean nations marketed new forms of citizenship to potential investors (Maurer 1998; McMichael 1996). Internationally, political repression, austerity measures, and global restructuring have created both unprecedented movements of people and unprecedented wealth and suffering (Arrighi 1990; Harvey 1989; Ong, Bonacich, and Cheng 1994; Pastor and Wise 1998; Sassen 1988, 1989, 1991; Silbey 1997). To contain the disorder unleashed by these processes,[10] the most powerful states have increasingly restricted membership by reinforcing traditional definitions of citizenship and denying rights and services to outsiders (Freeman 1992; but see also Soysal 1994). At the same time, less powerful nations have sought to reclaim dispersed polities (Schiller, Basch, and Blanc 1995), both to reap some of the benefits of prosperity in financial centers as well as to reconstitute their own markets and spheres of political influence.[11] Migrants, who are situated simultaneously within and between nations, are targets of both of these policies. When they are situated in a space of nonexistence, migrants must devise clandestine modes of being as well as relationships that evade authorized, state-based structures. To legalize, the undocumented must overcome powerful forces that deny their existence and delegitimize their realities. Given their precarious legal status and the family members they may have left behind, migrants also have a continued relationship to their countries of origin and to authorities in those countries. Negotiating these relationships may entail constructing forms of social membership that in some ways contradict the traditional models that are being vigorously reasserted in migrants' countries of residence.

Salvadorans' efforts to obtain political asylum, residency, and citizenship have both manipulated and reinforced existing models of citizenship. Activists' affirmation of substantive citizenship—working, paying taxes, obeying the law—as a basis for membership invokes suspension criteria, but deemphasizes the temporal component. In fact, one Salvadoran paralegal criticized the seven-year requirement, pointing out to me, "Why should someone have to be here seven years in order to prove that they are established? Someone could be here for two weeks and already have established himself, if the person came to rejoin relatives." The notion of substantive citizenship seeks to activate an implicit contract between residents and a government that tacitly tolerates their illegal presence, grants them temporary and limited legality, issues them work permits, and collects both fees and taxes. Salvadorans' invocation of their children's birthrights as U.S. citizens reinforces jus soli as a basis for citizenship but also seeks to transmit minor children's citizenship to their undocumented parents. Such a transmission is not as yet possible within the family visa process (though adult children can petition for their parents) but is recognized in suspension-of-deportation and cancellation-of-removal cases. The argument that the violence of the Salvadoran civil war and the pervasiveness of human rights violations entitle Salvadorans to asylum seeks to broaden the definition of persecution to include the daily terror occasioned by repressive practices and even the economic deprivation caused by civil war. Finally, the idea that the United States has some responsibility for the victims of the Salvadoran civil war manipulates the foreign policy implications of political asylum but directs these implications toward the Salvadoran populace rather than the current Salvadoran state. In other words, activists argue that by supporting a state whose human rights violations rendered it illegitimate, the United States incurred a particular responsibility for the people whose lives were disrupted or destroyed by that state.

In addition to manipulating existing models of citizenship, Salvadorans' political struggles and clandestine existence have produced alternative modes of being that include the absence of citizenship, dual citizenship, and acting as citizens of something other than a state. Clandestinity, of both the political and the immigration varieties, is produced by the denial of citizenship. Thus, individuals whose political activities would trigger repression go underground because their rights as citizens are not respected by their government. Similarly, undocumented immigrants live a clandestine existence because they lack legal status in their countries of residency. People whose existence is denied for political or legal reasons must nonetheless live, work, and interact with others. Such activities create a variety of surprisingly similar illicit relationships and practices, such as working without authorization, transferring funds and goods through unauthorized channels, smuggling people across borders of various sorts, falsifying documents and identities, and locating family members in multiple national spaces. Such clandestine networks and practices create an extrastate order, sort of a "phantom state" (see Thrift 1996) that is the inverse of the known, explicit, official (but contested) state. Activists engaged in revolutionary struggle or in solidarity work created such an order deliberately with the goal of eventually establishing an official but revolutionary state. Attempts to create these structures included the command structures of the FMLN, the FMLN's international diplomacy and solidarity networks, and even the quasi-governmental functions assumed by community organizations that, activists claimed, substituted for the Salvadoran consulate by providing refugee services that the consulate ought to have been offering. Even less-political transactions and networks, such as sending remittances to family members or paying smugglers to bring relatives to the United States, unintentionally created extrastatal linkages and practices. Serving a phantom or revolutionary order (which, like official states, is not unified or coherent) situates individuals in multiple national spaces as dual or multiple citizens. For example, to negotiate Salvadorans' legal status in the United States, Salvadoran activists who were once undocumented have met with U.S. legislators and Department of Justice officials, traveled to El Salvador to petition the Salvadoran Legislative Assembly for a resolution in support of their cause, and fashioned proposals that were adopted by the Central American presidents at their regional summits. Such practices, more than formal dual citizenship, redefine citizenship itself in a transnational context.

Through both their manipulations of traditional models of citizenship and their invention of alternative forms of membership, Salvadoran activists and immigrants advocated a moral order in which citizenship and justice would be linked. According to activists, this order would include liberated spaces in which legal citizenship would be irrelevant to the distribution of rights and services. It would include analysis regarding the connections between neoliberalism and immigration. It would include multilateral policies that address the political and economic injustices that force people into exile. It would include alliances between immigrants and other oppressed groups, such as women, minorities, and gays and lesbians. And it would redefine deservingness so that application deadlines and entry dates were less important than good citizenship (i.e., working, obeying the law, contributing to society). A dream, perhaps, but one that is being realized in certain forms through the ongoing, clandestine practices of immigrants themselves.

Chapter 7
Legitimizing Realities

December 12, 1996. After parking my car, I cross a busy street in Carson to meet Regina Salazar, who is waiting for me near the entrance of her apartment building. I first met Regina a month earlier, at ASOSAL, where she had sought staff members' assistance in applying for permission to leave the United States without losing her rights as an ABC class member. On that occasion, Regina and a younger woman who was also waiting to be attended had reminisced about life in El Salvador. The younger woman had said that she had suffered tremendously in El Salvador and had been traumatized when arrived in the United States. "I don't miss [El Salvador]!" she had shuddered. In contrast, Regina, who had come to the United States in 1980, had said that she wanted to return to El Salvador but could not bring herself to do so. "I lived through the war!" Regina had declared by way of explanation. When an ASOSAL staff member informed her that I was doing a study about Salvadorans, Regina had proceeded to tell me, ASOSAL workers, and other waiting clients the story of her mother's death at the funeral of Archbishop Romero, her own abduction and near death at the hands of Salvadoran security forces, and her cousin's brutal murder (see chapter 2, p. 37). When she finished this account, she was shaking. "I feel scared," she had told us, "remembering all of this."

Now, as we make our way up the staircase to her apartment, I ask Regina about the trip that she just took to El Salvador. She tells me that it was wonderful to see her children and very hard to return to the United States. On entering her apartment, she introduces me to a friend who is staying with her temporarily. The three of us sit down at the kitchen table and chat about children and recent changes in immigration law. The news is on in the background, and whenever something related to immigration comes up, we stop talking to listen. At an opportune moment, I pull out my consent form, a tape recorder, and a notepad. Regina graciously agrees to be recorded.

Regina begins by recounting in greater detail the events that forced her to leave El Salvador—a story that leaves all three of us feeling chilled. When she then describes her trip to the United States as "terrible," I ask her for details. In her account, the U.S.-Mexico border sounds like a war zone: "In Tijuana, in a ravine, all day we were there . . . covering ourselves with some little tree branches, because the helicopters and the airplanes were passing over the ravine." Because Regina had become ill and could barely walk, a *coyote* suggested leaving her in the ravine. But several girls who were in her group refused to leave her side, fearing that without the presence of an older woman—Regina was all of twenty-five at the time—they would be vulnerable to being raped by the *coyotes*. With their assistance, Regina continued on the journey, but the next night, she and one of the *coyotes* became separated from the group: "That man started to touch my hands, and I said, 'Ay! Another trial! Then it's true, what they say, that they rape the women!'" Fortunately, another smuggler signaled that it was time to continue, "and I was saved!"

Because Regina entered the United States in 1980, before employer sanctions were established, I wonder aloud whether it was difficult for her to find work. Regina tells me that it was not, that her cousin's employer was able to get her a job in Los Angeles as a live-in domestic. "But for me, my anguish was that I spent all my time thinking of my children. I was *encerrada* [enclosed, meaning live-in], and I said, '[In El Salvador the security forces] are going to look for my siblings, and my children are there. The same thing could happen [to them]." Because, as an isolated live-in domestic, Regina spent all her time crying, her employer helped her get a day job as a maintenance worker. However, due to lacking papers, Regina worked under a false name. Therefore, when the amnesty program was created, Regina decided not to apply. Not only was she concerned about her work records, but Regina was also afraid of the INS. Friends told her, "Don't go to Immigration, because they'll deport you!" I ask Regina whether she ever considered applying for political asylum, and her friend explains, "According to some men, it was a lie, [asylum] was like a hook to get us to, as they say, enter the wolf's mouth." Regina adds that she was afraid to apply for asylum because the Salvadoran government might learn of her application and would then be able to keep tabs on her.

Longing to see her children again and noting that, with employer sanctions, the legal situation in the United States was becoming more difficult, Regina returned to El Salvador in 1987 and remained there until 1989. When I hear this information, I realize that despite the fact that she was almost killed by Salvadoran authorities in 1980, she has little chance of winning asylum. Her fear, however, was not lessened by her return trip:

> I said, "Could it be that I live on in the thoughts of those who came for me that time?" I lived thinking of this, and for me there was no peace. Because I was always thinking that they were observing me, that they could come for me again, that I heard— in the night I couldn't sleep because I heard steps, I heard that they were knocking on my door, and I heard cries in the street, because I didn't sleep . . . the same fear.

Out of work and living in fear, Regina returned to the United States. Her second crossing was as fraught with discomfort and indignities as was her first: "They put us in a banana truck, and there were thirty-three of us! [We were] sitting, and I was at the back of the truck, open, completely—sitting on the bunches of bananas, open like this." Regina shows me and her friend how she had had to sit, with her legs spread wide, so that another person could sit on her lap. "There was another person sitting here in the same way, and then another, and then another. And like that, [for] twenty-four hours! And here another row of women, the same. Twenty-four hours! . . . I cried, I cried, and I said, 'No more! My legs! No more! No more!' And everyone was like that, crying. You know? They only gave us a plastic bag to do our necessities, . . . but many people did it on themselves, in their clothing." Regina shows us how all night long she lifted first one leg, then the other, trying to rest.

After returning to the United States, Regina again found work, and one day a companion on the bus told her that she could obtain a *permiso* through TPS. This time she did not hesitate to apply: "I thought that I would be more legal here, that this would allow me to not be afraid that they would detain me someplace, right, and be deported." Now, instead of working as a live-in, Regina cleans different people's houses, the best-paid form of domestic employment (Hondagneu-Sotelo and Avila 1997; Salzinger 1991). When her employers try to guess her legal status, she simply shows them her *permiso*.

Even with her *permiso*, Regina still suffers. Fighting back tears, Regina tells me how she reacted when she returned to El Salvador:

> Susan, now that I went, believe me that I almost didn't eat out of sorrow because I didn't see my family eating other food. I went around saying I wasn't eating! Maybe the thought—here everything is an expense, Susan. The money, one thinks—my employers said to me the other day, "You have a lot of money!" And I thought, "What money? If one is trying to see that one's children study." And when I went back, it made me so sad, because I think I didn't even eat, because I said, "My god, I didn't bring enough money." In my house to see only beans and rice, when here, everything can seem fine, I can eat a piece of meat. But my family? . . . Why didn't I apply for amnesty? . . . I would have been able to visit my children! But now, for example, I asked [the INS] for [advanced parole], and they gave it to me. And I said, "One week they're giving me? That's nothing! But it doesn't matter, I want to see my children!" But now, even my children were saying to me, "Ay! *Mamí,* how long will it be [until we see you again]?" "I don't know, I don't know. I don't know how long—"

Regina breaks off in an anguished voice, and I try to show my sympathy, commenting that the problem with just having a work permit is that one cannot travel. Regina then gives me her analysis of her chances of legalizing through ABC. She thinks that she took a big risk in returning to El Salvador, because she may have lost her opportunity to qualify through the law of seven years. The risk, she says, is that the INS will calculate her time in the United States from the date of her most recent entry instead of from her entry in 1989. Her time, she fears, may be erased.

As the interview winds down, Regina tells me of her current predicament. She cannot return to El Salvador due to her fear of the authorities, the crime wave that has struck the country, and her need to support her children. By doing domestic work in the United States, she earns enough to send her children to private school and has had a house built for them. With nothing more than a temporary work permit, however, Regina is unable to visit her children. Her children want to come here but cannot travel legally and, she worries, would face diminished opportunities in the United States. Her oldest son just graduated from high school—she attended the graduation ceremony while she was in El Salvador—and wants to study computers. If he comes to the United States, he will be an "illegal" and, she fears, will be limited to working as a gardener. Her son recently suggested that she marry an American citizen. " 'But,' I told him, 'it's not that easy.' It's not as easy as they say."

As I put away my notebook, Regina's friend suggests, "Why don't you show her your children's pictures?" When Regina shows me a picture of her now eighteen-year-old son taken when she first left El Salvador, I feel sad. The picture shows a very young, very cute child, almost the same age as my son. She then shows me a picture of the same child, taken two weeks previously, as he was being awarded his high school diploma. She had missed most of the intervening years.

Regina walks me downstairs, and she asks me to mention her to any friends who need someone to clean their houses. I agree to do so, uncomfortably aware of our class differences. She then takes her leave of me, saying, "Now I have another friend." Touched, I answer, "Likewise."

Illegitimacies

Regina's account of her flight from political violence, her subsequent efforts to stay alive and to provide for her family, and her legal situation in the United States shed light on the delegitimizing structures within which Regina has had to struggle. One such structure is the complex of practices, institutions, and discourses through which states assert control of international travel. Through travel documents that only certain people can obtain, border checkpoints that can only be traversed by those with these documents, and patrols that hunt out violators, Regina and other people whose words have appeared on these pages are rendered as criminals, fugitives, and illicit. Such practices are violent in that they are complicit in the deaths, rape, deprivation, and dehumanization of those who cross borders illicitly. Because states claim control of international travel, those whose presence is illicit are trapped. Regina's ambivalence about remaining in the United States is complicated by the precariousness of her status in this country: if she could travel more freely, she would not have to choose between here and there. Moreover, because her political asylum application initiated a process of potential legalization, Regina's movement is subjected to even more state control than that of citizens and legal permanent residents. Because she must secure advanced parole to reenter the United States, Regina can only visit her children or respond to a family emergency if INS officials grant her permission to do so. State agents and policies have been inserted into her personal decisions. If her son joins her in the United States, then he too becomes illicit. All of the options through which she and her children could be reunited and survive entail either state control or illegality.

A second delegitimizing structure that Regina has confronted is what Peter Fitzpatrick (1992) terms "the mythology of modern law" (see also Bourdieu 1987). According to Fitzpatrick, modern law is mythic in several senses: (1) law claims an empirical, rational basis, and thus, like other mythical systems, produces unquestionable, taken-for-granted truths (see also Asad 1983); (2) despite its truth claims, law can only appear modern if contrasted to the premodern, mythical, or savage, which means that law's authority depends on constituting another, mythic, nonlegal realm; (3) law can only seem objectively true and modern if it denies its dependence on the premodern; therefore (4) this denial is itself a myth. Regina engaged the mythic character of law when she failed to apply for amnesty before the deadline. Because she did not apply, Regina remained illicit even though she met the requirements for legalization. She thus was constituted yet again as undeserving. Although, like those who had obtained amnesty, she had lived in the United States continuously and illegally since January 1, 1982, she could not obtain work authorization and had to reenter the United States clandestinely. Her stated reason for not applying was that she was afraid of the INS, an agency from which she had earlier hidden in a ravine while search helicopters circled overhead. Similarly, law's mythic nature makes it possible to conclude that having applied for political asylum, setting foot outside U.S. territory without the permission of the U.S. government constitutes an abandonment of one's application. By automatically attributing particular characteristics and motivations to individuals—in this case, undeservingness and disinterest—law creates its own mythic characters (see also Maurer 1997).

Of course, Regina's legal history contains several seeming contradictions: Why, if fear of being deported prevented her from applying for amnesty, did she return to El Salvador just as the amnesty program was being established? Why, if she feared political persecution, did she return to El Salvador at all? And why, if she lived in El Salvador for two years without encountering political problems, does she still claim to be afraid? These seeming contradictions reveal a third delegitimizing structure of power—namely, the notions of narrativity that render particular histories plausible. Because consistency is a legal measure of credibility, inconsistencies delegitimize narratives (Walter Fisher 1987; Greenhouse 1996). Inconsistencies, however, are not simply logical flaws but rather can arise out of the limitations of the plots or discourses through which narratives are interpreted (Matoesian 1995, 1997). It is possible, therefore, that Regina returned to El Salvador in 1987 because she preferred to leave of her own volition before she either was deported (which she thought would occur if she applied for amnesty) or driven out by the enforcement of employer sanctions. It is possible that regardless of her continued fear of persecution, she wanted to be with her children and had concluded that life in the United States was no longer viable. It is possible that her two years in El Salvador convinced her not of her own safety but of her continued danger and that this fear was a significant factor in her decision to return to the United States in 1989. It is also possible that these "inconsistencies" are explained by elements of her story that Regina chose not to reveal during this interview. It is clear, however, that it is difficult to classify Regina exclusively as either an economic immigrant or a political refugee. Regina suffered through traumatic, life-threatening experiences that she, like some of the asylum applicants described in chapter 5, seemingly relives. She also has experienced economic hardships that have necessitated living and working in the United States. Her experiences defy neat categorization or easy narration and therefore, to again quote Carol Greenhouse (1996: 211), risk "falling off the story line."

Although the seeming contradictions in Regina's narrative

might lead INS authorities to dismiss Regina's asylum claim on the grounds that she is an economic immigrant rather than a political refugee, even as an economic immigrant, Regina's life circumstances are not necessarily legally compelling. Her hardship argument is weakened by a fourth delegitimizing structure: legal nationalism. According to what she told me during our interview, Regina needs to be in the United States to support her children, who are in El Salvador. Her children, however, do not have legal status in the United States and therefore do not have legal interests that could be taken into account when assessing whether it would be a hardship for Regina to be deported. Moreover, Regina's family is transnational (Hondagneu-Sotelo and Avila 1997). Like some of the suspension applicants discussed in chapter 5, Regina does not have close family ties to individuals in the United States. Despite her many years of residing in the United States, it will be difficult for her strategy of working in the United States to support her family in El Salvador to be recognized as valid by an immigration court.[1]

For the experiences of Regina and other unauthorized immigrants to be legitimized, these structures of power would have to change. For example, instead of linking national sovereignty to border control, sovereignty could be measured by whether states incorporate their entire populaces into their political systems (see also Hammar 1990; Held 1995; Sassen 1996). As Rainer Bauböck (1994:203) queries, "Do not states of immigration with a large and growing disenfranchised alien population fail to meet the norm of inclusion which characterizes liberal democracy?"[2] If state sovereignty was measured by residents' enfranchisement, then national maps that are riddled with holes occupied by the nonexistent could be replaced by not necessarily national liberated spaces (see chapter 6) in which legal status is not a prerequisite for existence. Such a reconceptualization of both sovereignty and space would eliminate some of the painful dilemmas faced by Regina Salazar and her family. In such a system, she could either travel to visit her children or they could travel to visit or even stay with her. If entire populaces were legally and politically enfranchised, then her son would not have to choose between staying in El Salvador to pursue higher education and coming to the United States to work illegally as a gardener. People could travel as people rather than produce, and the traffic in humans would be, at the very least, curtailed.

Another change that would enable Regina's experiences to be legitimized would be the de- or remythologization of law.[3] In other words, if status was not denied to people simply because they missed a deadline, and if intentions and traits were not ascribed to individuals' assumed natures, then new means of authenticating legal categories and characters might be formulated. According to Fitzpatrick (1993), such a popular justice might be created by seizing the legal instead of by reinventing the informal. The alternative legalities constructed by unauthorized immigrants may be a step in this direction in that these unofficial legalities are based on ideas and practices that derive from immigration law itself. Thus, measuring deservingness according to socially meaningful criteria, such as having lived and worked in the United States for years, seeks to make law live up to its claim that status is allocated according to merit.

To be complete, de- or remythologization would have to be accompanied by a rethinking of the standards that evaluate narrative credibility. As Ewick and Silbey (1995:218–19 emphasis in original) note, "there is a fine, but critical, distinction between generalizing and *emplotting the connections between the particular and the general.*" Such "emplotment" would make it possible for the conditions that shape individuals' lives to become part of their narratives. Nonlinear narratives, such as those of asylum seekers who claim to relive political persecution, might then be considered plausible. Multiple realities— including the political subjectivity created by practices that terrorize populations—could then be recognized. Transnational strategies, such as sending household members abroad to take advantage of job opportunities, could also be accorded legal protection. Transnational allegiances would not necessarily weaken or contradict national claims (Kearney 1995b).

Under what circumstances might such conditions—if they are desirable—be attained? To address this question, I will review the strategies through which Central American immigrants and activists have sought to negotiate their legal identities in the United States.

Legalizing Struggles

This book has set out to reassess both the roles that immigration law plays within the lives of unauthorized immigrants and the roles that unauthorized immigrants play in law. I have argued that even if immigration law does not control unauthorized movement, it is still a powerful and defining social force. Immigrants who live in the United States without authorization are subject to multiple interactions in which identity documents are demanded, rights and services are refused, and existence is denied. The unauthorized are thus located outside of the citizenry in a domain of illegality. Aware of law's power to shape lives, the unauthorized seize the law, applying for papers, claiming legitimacy, and seeking to redefine law itself. Such actions produce law in the form of court hearings, judicial rulings, administrative policies, and even legislation. Within both judicial and legislative proceedings (Chock 1991, 1995), immigrants become protagonists of narratives that have already been written by other authors and performed by other actors. Immigrants sometimes play the role of refugees or deserving suspension applicants, and their cases are approved. At other times, immigrants are cast as not credible or undeserving, and they lose. The play does not end when the curtain falls, however, because such determinations continue to shape respondents' lives. And yet there is also a sense in which the play really is just a play, given that in-absentia deportation orders may not actually be carried out, that people who agree to depart voluntarily may remain, and that legal citizenship may not guarantee full inclusion. The procedures set in motion when the unauthorized pursue legality may have far-reaching effects. The asylum claims filed by Salvadorans and Guatemalans during the 1980s clogged the asylum system, enabling applicants to remain in the United States while their cases were pending. When advocates succeeded in obtaining TPS, DED, and ABC, many of these applicants were able to secure additional protections. The at least temporary documentation of some three hundred thousand ABC class members has affected not only individual applicants but also the Salvadoran economy. The legal system that prohibits their presence can thus be critical to immigrants' individual and collective empowerment.

The relationship between law and immigration makes immigrants' agency quite complex. Within deportation hearings, certain forms of agency are privileged. For example, both asylum applicants who express a difference that occasions persecution and suspension applicants who "progress" and demonstrate "deservingness" can be recognized and legitimized. In contrast, agency of an illegitimate sort is attributed to immigrants who accept public assistance, attempt to "fix" their papers, or operate unlicensed businesses. Because the structures that contribute to these "illegitimate" practices cannot be deemed agentive, individuals' explanations for submitting fraudulent applications, living without insurance, or working under the table appear to be excuses for their own immorality. These ideas of legitimate and illegitimate agency, both of which attribute actions to character, do not take individuals' social positioning into account and therefore cannot describe how immigrants shape policy. To acknowledge the embeddedness of agency, I do not equate agency with autonomy as does legal liberalism (see Collier, Maurer, and Suárez-Navaz 1995; Greenhouse 1996; Fitzpatrick 1992) but rather with maneuvering within a particular set of conditions. People maneuver by going into hiding when they are targeted by death squads, applying for papers when they are undocumented, avoiding legal traps by choosing to remain undocumented, and so forth. Such actions and inactions have multiple consequences and can reproduce as well as challenge structures of power. Nonetheless, when taken collectively, maneuvering can be a potent political force.

Defining agency as maneuvering does not mean that political action cannot be intentional. On the contrary, I contend that political action is both that and more. TPS, DED, ABC, and now NACARA were achieved through many different sorts of actions taken by many different sorts of people. Religious activists formed the sanctuary movement and filed the ABC lawsuit, attorneys represented individual asylum applicants and worked on class-action suits, refugees sought political asylum, activists worked to counter U.S. foreign and refugee policy while supporting political struggles in Central America, immigrants opted to come to the United States despite laws forbidding their presence, and even *notarios* participated by preparing numerous applications for TPS, DED, and asylum under the terms of the ABC settlement agreement. Like everyone else, attorneys and political activists must maneuver within particular sets of conditions. Such maneuverings occasionally result in social change or transformative visions of social existence. For example, activists who have gone into political clandestinity and potential persecution victims who went into exile have created new social realities. Some of these realities—such as transnational family networks, underground economies, and illicit legal systems—may have been created unintentionally, as the effects of other processes. Though they may not, in and of themselves, be counterhegemonic, such illicit realities do call the authority of dominant social institutions into question.

If social realities can be created as the unintentional effects of social maneuvering, then such seemingly objective phenomena as transnationalism, the state, the nation, and immigration become ephemeral. Immigration, for example, is defined as a form of movement across national borders, usually with the purpose of staying instead of merely sojourning or traveling through a particular national space. Immigration is thus a material process that can entail a great deal of hardship and even death for illicit travelers. And yet immigration can be completely dematerialized, as when a citizen immigrates a spouse who is already physically present (see chapter 5). Yet even this dematerialized and stationary movement has material effects in that the individual who "immigrates" is transformed into a legal resident who has the right to live and work in the United States. Similarly, the nation is produced through immigration, the state materializes in the practices that seek to control borders, and transnationalism is an explicit and deliberate business strategy (see Santana 1998). And yet immigration is thought to cause national dissipation, unauthorized border crossings are defined as challenging state sovereignty, and transnational household economies are illegitimate. In some ways materiality is a matter of vantage point: when seen from the perspective of illicitness, the state seems to shimmer. It is both all too real and not there.

Like other seemingly objective phenomena, law too can shimmer. Without law, there could be no such thing as immigration, given that law defines the borders that immigrants cross. And yet unauthorized immigration seems to defy law, throwing into question both its rule and the integrity of the state to which it is linked. Defying law, however, makes the borders that unauthorized immigrants violate even more real. The contest over permitted and illicit entry transforms national borders from mere lines on a map and fences on a terrain into war zones where people undergo hunger, thirst, physical deprivation, and even death. If they withstand such trials, illicit border crossers enter a state of illegality. In this space, they, like criminals and the premodern, become as law's mythic others, beings on whom the differences between law and illegality, merit and undeservingness, citizenship and alienation, are inscribed. Dissatisfied with illicitness, these aliens reconstruct law (and thus themselves) in law's own image. And, perhaps most surprisingly, these delegitimized images of law can sometimes become realities. This has been the experience of Salvadoran asylum seekers.

Beyond NACARA

The passage of NACARA was a victory for ABC class members, Salvadorans and Guatemalans with asylum applications that had been pending since 1990, and beneficiaries of the Nicaraguan Review Program. Although this legislation for the most part simply restored rights that eligible Salvadorans and Guatemalans had enjoyed prior to the passage of IIRIRA, NACARA implicitly recognized these individuals as a protected class, defined them as somewhat documented, and legitimized their strategy of gaining enough time in the United States to become eligible for suspension of deportation.[4] NACARA thus established a precedent for other groups, such as late amnesty applicants (see chapter 3), who hope to obtain legal residency. Since the passage of NACARA, advocates have succeeded in wresting other policy concessions from the INS. The asylum interviews of ABC class members were put on hold until the regulations through which NACARA will be implemented are issued, and the INS may take the unprecedented step of permitting INS asylum officers to hear class members' suspension claims. Such a streamlined procedure would mean that class members who have weak asylum but strong suspension cases could be granted residency at the interview stage. Even with these concessions, however, it is not a foregone conclusion that most class members will obtain residency. As things now stand, their claims will be heard on a case-by-case basis, meaning that each applicant will have to individually demonstrate that he or she merits suspension or asylum. Asylum and suspension cases are not easy to win, as the previous chapters show. Moreover, many applicants will lack adequate legal representation, given that, in Los Angeles for example, there are too few immigration attorneys to represent the approximately 150,000 class members whose cases could be heard in the next few years. Even if there were enough attorneys, low-income applicants might not be able to pay such high legal fees, making NACARA another potential financial bonanza for *notarios*. Technical problems, such as prior deportation orders that needed to be challenged before September 1998, may make it difficult for some applicants to benefit from the legislation (Marrero 1998b). For these reasons, Central American community activists have continued to campaign for residency for NACARA beneficiaries. A march and rally in March 1998 attracted approximately two thousand participants, and a bill that would create parity among Nicaraguan, Guatemalan, and Salvadoran NACARA beneficiaries has already been proposed.[5]

The passage of NACARA may indicate that the tide of immigration reform is turning. Some analysts have attributed this legislation, which only months before was deemed an impossibility, to Republican Party members' fears that immigration reform undermined their appeal to Latino voters. Granting limited relief to particular groups of immigrants, such as Central Americans, could enable Republicans to counter charges of being anti-Latino without discrediting their claim to be tough on illegal immigration. Specific elements of IIRIRA have also been challenged in other forums. For example, advocates have characterized expedited removal proceedings and limitations on judicial review as violations of due process and therefore as possibly unconstitutional (ACLU Immigrants Rights Project et al. 1996). Citizens and legal permanent residents who discover that their ability to petition for relatives is curtailed by the creation of "illegal time" and the elimination of 245(i) may demand waivers or legislative change. Yet it is too soon to conclude that restrictive policies will be eased for most immigrants. The INS's budget and personnel have increased, and proposals for counterfeit-resistant work permits and machine-readable identity documents are circulating. An era of increased surveillance could be around the corner.

While immigration law is being negotiated in Congress and elsewhere, the Salvadoran community in Los Angeles is becoming established. The first convention of Salvadoran and Los Angeles businesspeople was held in June 1998 (Santana 1998), Salvadoran hometown associations are flourishing, and new organizations such as the Salvadoran American Leadership and Education Fund continue to arise. Community organizations that were created to serve a transitory refugee population have seemingly become permanent institutions. CARECEN, for example, has relocated to a building that it purchased, and El Rescate has operated for more than seventeen years.

FIG. 4.   March demanding parity in the treatment of
NACARA beneficiaries, Los Angeles, February 1999. (Photo
by Joaquín Romero.)

ABC class members' campaign for residency has become a grassroots
movement, creating new coalitions and incorporating new members.
In recognition of the economic and political potential of Salvadoran
expatriates, businesses, politicians, and others are seeking Salvadoran support. A possible Salvadoran presidential candidate recently
visited Los Angeles to meet with community members, local businesses target Salvadoran consumers in their advertising, and a Salvadoran official recently told a reporter, "We want this community to
feel that being outside of the country does not mean that it is not part
of [the country]. That they feel that they are a part of us, that we can
give them information that helps them to advance and helps them to
organize" (Marrero 1998c) Community organizations that are promoting naturalization and civic education may succeed in creating
specifically Central American constituencies.

Despite their growing strength, Central Americans' efforts to
claim rights and space (Flores and Benmayor 1997) confront a
resignified politics of race (see Gregory and Sanjek 1994; Smith and

Feagin 1995; Wilmsen and McAllister 1996). In California, the 1990s have witnessed the acquittal of police officers accused of using excessive force against Rodney King (see Gooding-Williams 1993), the rioting that followed this verdict, the passage of Proposition 187, searing debates about race and domestic violence during the O. J. Simpson trial, the elimination of affirmative action in major universities, and the dismantling of bilingual education. Virginia Sapiro's (1984:3–4) observation that "racism, sexism, and xenophobia do not merely exist in parallel but rather are systematically interrelated" seems to be borne out. Not only have support systems that targeted the marginalized been undermined, but in addition the acceptability of publicly displaying nongeneric difference has been challenged. Language use, ways of dressing, and public groupings have become politicized (see also Davis 1992).[6] With Proposition 209, which couched attacks on affirmative action in the language of civil rights, claims to common rights have become means of legitimizing exclusions. The legal categories that in immigration court treat poverty or unemployment as an aspect of character also define public personhood with the result that subordination is erased of political content or collective responsibility (Crenshaw and Peller 1993). Seemingly, in public, persons are to be individuals, with ethnic or other national backgrounds to be sure but without histories that redefine the categories that they occupy.

Central Americans and other historically marginalized groups face formidable challenges in negotiating identities, space, and rights in the United States. If the past two decades are any indication, Central Americans will meet these challenges by claiming, reconstituting, and even bypassing structures of power. Through such struggles, perhaps the conditions that delimit existence itself can be transformed.

Notes

Chapter 1

1. PL 105-100 (H.R. 2607), November 19, 1997.

2. The Salvadorans and Guatemalans who benefited from NACARA included individuals who applied for political asylum as beneficiaries of a lawsuit that charged the INS with discriminating against Salvadoran and Guatemalan asylum seekers, relatives of these asylum applicants, or asylum applicants who were not beneficiaries of the lawsuit but who submitted their applications prior to April 1, 1990, and whose cases have not yet been adjudicated. Under NACARA, eligible Salvadorans and Guatemalans were permitted to apply for suspension of deportation (referred to as "special rule for cancellation of removal") in the event that their asylum applications were denied. To be granted suspension of deportation, an individual must demonstrate seven years of continuous presence in the United States, good moral character, and that being deported would constitute an extreme hardship for the applicant or for the applicant's family members who have legal status in the United States. An individual who is awarded suspension of deportation becomes a legal permanent resident at the time of the judge's decision to grant the suspension. Suspension of deportation was eliminated by IIRIRA.

3. P.L. 101-649, 104 Stat. 4978, November 29, 1990.

4. *American Baptist Churches v. Thornburgh*, 1991, 760 F.Supp. 796 (N.D. Cal.).

5. *Mendez v. Reno*, no. CV-88-04995-TJH, C.D. Cal., August 12, 1993.

6. PL 104-208 (H.R. 3610), September 30, 1996. For a summary and analysis of IIRIRA's provisions, see ACLU et al. 1996.

7. I use the word *asylee* to differentiate individuals who enter the United States and then are granted asylum from those who are granted refugee status outside U.S. borders and enter as refugees. The latter enjoy potentially permanent legal status from their time of entry. The former usually enter the country on a tourist visa or as illegal aliens. See Churgin 1996; INS 1997:77–80; and USCR 1986 for discussions of this distinction.

8. California Proposition 187, which was passed by voters but largely forestalled in the courts, would have expanded the range of individuals who are legally accountable for others' immigration statuses to include teachers and medical personnel (Martin 1995).

9. The political implications of law have been the subject of some debate in recent years. Some have seen law as a tool of capitalism, others have argued that law limits the actions of the powerful, and still others have pursued a more complex view, noting that law can be both repressive and counterhegemonic. See Althusser 1971; Hunt 1985; Kairys 1990; Lazarus-Black and Hirsch 1994; Merry 1990; Starr and Collier 1989; Thompson 1975; Yngvesson 1993b.

10. *Agency* is notoriously difficult to define (Greenhouse 1996). *Agency* can refer to activeness, in the sense that individuals participate in constructing the conditions of their own existence (Bourdieu 1977; Collier 1988) or to actions that are creative (Limon 1983), that are not "overdetermined" (Giddens 1976), that demonstrate individuals' and groups' capacity for choice and innovation (see Collier, Maurer, and Suárez-Navaz 1995). *Agency* as activeness is not necessarily counterhegemonic, as people can actively participate in reproducing repressive systems. Likewise, innovation is not intrinsically subversive, given that torturers and dictators are skilled in devising new repressive mechanisms.

11. But note that the situation was not tolerable for those who were deported during this period and perished as a result. In Los Angeles, a community organization was named after Santana Chirino Amaya, a Salvadoran who was deported and subsequently assassinated. As Cover (1992b:203) notes, "Legal interpretation takes place in a field of pain and death."

12. P.L. 99-603, 100 Stat. 3359, November 6, 1986.

13. Some scholars have argued that IRCA actually increased illegal immigration, as strengthened border enforcement led seasonal migrants who would normally have returned to Mexico to remain in the United States and to send for their families. See Cornelius 1990 for further details.

14. Jobs in the primary labor market are long term and well paid and have benefits and opportunities for advancement. Jobs in the secondary labor market tend to be temporary, more poorly paid, dead end, and without benefits. See Delgado 1993; J. Craig Jenkins 1978.

15. INS policy regarding the issuance of work permits to asylum applicants has not been uniform. After IRCA was passed, immigrant advocates in New York had to take the INS to court to ensure that asylum applicants received work permits while their cases were pending. Even now, it is not uncommon for the INS to lose immigrants' work permit applications, issue work permits with incorrect names or photos, or to make other mistakes that delay applicants' receipt of work permits to which they are entitled by law.

16. In 1995, the INS closed a loophole in immigration law that made it possible to obtain a work permit by applying for political asylum. According to regulations that went into effect in 1995, asylum applicants must wait six months before they are entitled to work permits. At the same time, the INS adopted a last-in/first-out policy in adjudicating asylum claims, so that in most cases, decisions are rendered within the first six months. As a result, applying for asylum is no longer a viable means of obtaining a work permit unless the case is deemed meritorious and asylum is granted.

17. Just over half of my interviews were tape-recorded. Some activists who were seemingly accustomed to speaking to journalists asked to go off the record and turned off the tape recorder when discussing issues that they deemed sensitive. Most activists and legal-service providers agreed to be recorded. Individuals with pending legalization cases were sometimes reluctant to be recorded. Often I, rather than the interviewee, decided not to tape-record an interview. When I anticipated that a tape recorder would either make the interviewee uncomfortable or make the interview itself overly formal, I did not broach the subject and instead decided to forgo taping the interview.

18. I did not feel ethically comfortable interviewing public notaries when some of the community organizations with which I worked were suing them for consumer fraud. I did interview several immigration officials near the conclusion of my research, but I did not work with the INS in the way that I worked with community organizations. Because I was interviewing people who had pending legalization cases, and because I also met and worked with individuals who were undocumented, I avoided contact with the INS. I did not want to create any appearance that I might be giving the INS information (see Feldman 1991) or to lead immigration officials to anyone. See Cornelius 1982 for a discussion of the precautions necessary when doing research among the undocumented.

Chapter 2

1. The official term is not *illegal time* but rather *unlawful presence*. Section 301 of IIRIRA defines *unlawful presence* as follows: "For the purposes of this paragraph, an alien is deemed unlawfully present in the United States if the alien is present in the United States after the expiration of the period of stay authorized by the Attorney General or is present in the United States without being admitted or paroled." Minors, asylees, family unity beneficiaries, and battered women and children are exempted from this provision (*Interpreter Releases* 1996a).

2. Regarding contests over such categories as "employer," "employee," "contractor," and "consumer," see Gonos 1997.

3. Work, presence, time, and legalization are interconnected. For example, in suspension cases, check stubs count as proof of residence, evidence of continuous employment indicates that aliens' time in the United States has been well spent, and proof of employment also helps to demonstrate that aliens are not public charges.

4. Though technically, no travel documents are required to leave the Los Angeles area, this migrant correctly observes that when they leave Los Angeles, migrants encounter INS officials at checkpoints, bus stops, train stations, and so forth. As these officials may, in fact, request proof of legal presence, the speaker's comment is accurate.

5. I do not mean to suggest that unauthorized immigrants and legal res-

idents/visitors are evenly distributed throughout Los Angeles. There is obviously a great deal of segregation along not only legal but also class, ethnic, and racial lines (Davis 1992). As Teresa Caldeira (1996:319) notes, cities like Los Angeles are structured "to insure that different social worlds meet as infrequently as possible in city space, i.e., that they belong to different spaces." My point is rather that terms such as *underground* and *outside* suggest that the undocumented in no way share the spaces occupied by those who are legal, when, in fact, legal and illegal individuals live in the same apartment complexes, eat at the same restaurants, shop in the same stores, are members of the same families, and so forth.

6. At the time of the interview, Maria, her husband, and their two daughters were sharing a one-bedroom apartment in Los Angeles, a step up from their initial residence, which was shared with fifteen other migrants and therefore afforded even less privacy.

7. Taylor's (1997:74) account of political violence in Argentina suggests that like those who fear becoming victims of death squads, torturers cut off their social ties, denying that they have mothers or children and characterizing themselves as nonhuman.

8. By citing this analogy, I do not mean to imply that the United States was solely responsible for the violence and human-rights abuses that occurred during the Salvadoran civil war. Salvadoran government officials, death-squad members, informers, guerrilla group members, and others clearly are also at fault. For additional information regarding the nature of and responsibility for human rights abuses, see Americas Watch 1991; United Nations Commission on the Truth 1993.

9. I am grateful to Rosemary Coombe and Richard Perry for this point.

10. Though it is important to note that the undocumented may pay more in taxes than they receive in benefits. This imbalance occurs because aliens who work under false social security numbers sometimes have taxes withheld from their paychecks but do not file tax returns or claim refunds. See Simon 1989 for further discussion of this point.

11. Some have argued that far from being potentially subversive, legal clandestinity disciplines workers by making them work hard and scared. See J. Craig Jenkins 1978; Portes 1978.

12. A newspaper article about the 1986 amnesty program begins, "A state agency trying to count the uncountable has concluded that there are 1.7 million illegal immigrants in California who qualify" (McLeod 1987:8).

13. PL 104-132, April 24, 1996. The antiterrorism bill placed aliens who had entered the United States without inspection in exclusion proceedings rather than in deportation proceedings. Individuals in exclusion proceedings are ineligible to apply for suspension of deportation as they are deemed to be outside of the United States seeking entry and therefore cannot accrue years of continuous residence within the United States (*Interpreter Releases* 1996b). AEDPA was superseded by IIRIRA.

Chapter 3

1. An immigration attorney made a related distinction during an interview: "One thing that I try to get across to public defenders—and it's always difficult for them to understand—is that there are only two types of humans who walk the earth: citizens and aliens. It doesn't matter if you're a legal permanent resident or an illegal alien: as long as you're an alien, you have less rights and you're deportable. It's worse for a permanent resident to enter without inspection than it is to sell drugs!"

2. My discussion here is an initial response to Annelise Riles's (1998:378) invitation to "visualize the forms latent in the norms." The norm that everyone has some sort of immigration status is realized in INS forms that have blanks where individuals are to fill in their "present nationality" and "current immigration status." See, for example, INS Form I-589 (Rev. 11/16/94), "Application for Asylum and for Withholding of Deportation," questions 11 and 14.

3. The point of my analogy between marital status and immigration status is that, theoretically at least, there are a finite number of possible statuses that one can have, and everyone ought to be able to check a box on forms that list these possibilities. There are obviously situations in which individuals' marital status is ambiguous not because their records are missing but because their relationship is not legally recognizable. For example, heterosexual couples who live together for years are more or less married, though they may or may not be legally recognized as married in states that do not recognize common-law unions. Similarly, gay or lesbian couples may be unable to formally marry in a legal sense, regardless of the length of their relationship.

4. For example, after one immigration hearing that I attended, an attorney confessed to me that his client's nationality was unclear: "She was born in Honduras, but her parents were Salvadoran, and she has a Salvadoran birth certificate." Had the INS attorney chosen to challenge this attorney's assertion that his client was Salvadoran, he explained, he would have had to investigate the matter further to determine her true nationality or nationalities.

5. Asylum applicants concede deportability by admitting to the charges contained in the order to show cause. They then petition for the right to remain in the United States on the grounds that they face persecution in their countries of citizenship. There are sometimes circumstances in which individuals who are in deportation proceedings do not concede deportability, as when the INS obtained its evidence against them illegally. If the evidence is successfully suppressed, then the individual may be released, even though he or she will remain undocumented.

6. Though policies vary from judge to judge, most judges give individuals more time to prepare their applications. After several chances, however, unprepared applicants may be required to go forward with their cases.

7. Maria Bonilla, a Salvadoran ABC class member, explained why she

and her husband had entered the United States without authorization: "Susan, do you know what you have to have to get a visa? You have to have two cars, three houses, and five thousand dollars in the bank—things that we could never even dream of getting, especially back in 1985."

8. The INS clothes detainees in color-coded uniforms that correspond to their procedural status. Individuals who are in exclusion proceedings wear orange suits.

9. The undocumented are defined by their means of mobility as "feet people" and "boat people," and aquatic metaphors referring to illegal immigration as a "stream," "flood," "torrent," or "trickle" also stress movement. Note that the means of movement ascribed to the undocumented are the least technologically advanced—traveling by boat and by foot (compare to Thrift's (1996) discussion of mobility in the postmodern era).

10. Individuals who benefited from what has come to be known as *amnistía tardía* (late amnesty) are in a similar situation. Several class-action lawsuits have charged that the INS erroneously denied amnesty to individuals who would have qualified but who left the United States briefly. Such individuals have been permitted to open or reopen amnesty cases. While their cases were pending, these late amnesty applicants have received work permits and been able to remain in the United States. Like ABC class members, late amnesty applicants assert that they deserve permanent residency, both on the basis of their original amnesty applications and because of living in the United States in a documented status while their applications were pending. See Marrero 1998a, 1998d.

11. The use of papers to establish rights to presence is not limited to the undocumented. Elijah Anderson (1990:198) notes that "many lower-class blacks, who continue to find it necessary to campaign for civil rights denied them because of skin color, believe that carrying an identification card brings them better treatment than is meted out to their less fortunate brothers and sisters." I am grateful to Michael Musheno for drawing this similarity to my attention.

12. As Engel and Munger (1996:16) note, "In American society, where independence and self-sufficiency are particularly prized, employment is a fundamental element of social identity. . . . Supporting oneself by earning and spending money legitimates one's status as a full-fledged, adult member of the community."

13. Of course, citizens do not need time to "count" in the same way that immigrants do.

14. The two payments that Mario mentions total $750, so Mario may have paid $750 instead of $850. It is also possible that the $850 figure is correct and that one of the two payments was larger than Mario remembers or that there was an additional $100 fee that Mario did not mention.

15. The *Diccionario Jurídio Mexicano* (Instituto de Investigaciones Jurídicas 1988:2217–18, translation mine) explains the difference between U.S. and Latin American concepts of notaries as follows: "In the United States, the Anglo Saxon or private notary only authenticates signatures, without this

action referring to the background of the respective document. [This contrasts with] the Latino type of notary, like that of [Mexico], in which the notary is at the same time an official of public record and an attorney who illustrates the parts, composes the document, authorizes it, sends out certified copies, and keeps the original."

16. In January 1995, the INS instituted a six-month delay in issuing work permits to asylum applicants and also adopted a last-in/first-out policy in scheduling asylum interviews. Since January 1995, most asylum applicants receive interviews within the six-month period and if their applications are denied are placed in deportation prior to becoming eligible for a work permit. Even prior to January 1995, some asylum applicants had difficulty obtaining work permits, as INS offices varied regionally in their willingness to grant work authorization to individuals with pending asylum applications.

17. This comment is borne out by my experiences accompanying a CARECEN attorney who was interviewing detainees at the San Pedro detention facility. I noticed that the detainees sometimes complained, "Why am I in here? My card didn't even expire yet."

18. Hagan's (1994) study of the Houston Mayan community reported that undocumented Mayans who were technically ineligible for amnesty sometimes applied anyway, reasoning that it was worthwhile to obtain a work permit for several months even though their applications would eventually be denied.

19. Beatriz Sandoval, for example, supplied the following account of document forgery: "You can falsify a *mica* [green card], but not a [California?] ID or *permiso*. . . . There are some people who work at the place that distributes the *micas*, and they'll give you other people's numbers. You have to supply the photos and the fingerprints yourself. And you have to be about the same age as the person whose *mica* it is or else they'll figure it out. For instance, I couldn't use my photo for someone who's five years younger than I am. Then sometimes the people whose numbers are being used come back from abroad or from wherever they are, and those who are using their numbers get caught."

20. See Rose 1989 for a discussion of the politics of charging fees for public services.

21. Homi Bhabha's discussion of the "partiality" of colonial subjects' presence is relevant here. Bhabha (1997:154) writes, "It is as if the very emergence of the 'colonial' is dependent for its representation upon some strategic limitation or prohibition *within* the authoritative discourse itself." The same could be said of the "illegal." The incomplete authority of U.S. immigration law permits the production of illegal aliens, who are only "partly" present (see chapter 2). Though partial, this illegal presence reauthorizes immigration law as an attempt to close the borders.

22. As Bruner (1986:109) notes, "We know the world in different ways, from different stances, and each of the ways in which we know it produces different structures or representations, or, indeed, 'realities.'"

23. This man had lived in the United States for eleven years before this

incident and was potentially eligible for suspension of deportation if he could demonstrate that his departure was "brief, casual, and innocent."

24. Mahler (1995:173) reports that asylum applications rose from 26,512 in 1980 to 101,697 in 1989. She states that 86 percent of the applications filed in 1989 were from Central Americans. See also INS 1991, 1997.

25. See Mahler 1995 for a discussion of the ways that IRCA fueled an industry in fake documents and unethical legal practices.

26. Not all INS offices were equally forthcoming with work permits for individuals with pending asylum applications. The New York office was particularly reluctant to grant permits to asylum applicants (Mahler 1995:187).

27. At a 1997 meeting, INS asylum officials and immigrant advocates discussed "problematic" work permit cases, such as the situation of a dependent of an ABC applicant. In certain instances (as when the dependent was added to the applicant's case after the deadline), the dependent would not be eligible for a work permit. Officials noted that because this is a complicated situation that the people who process work-permit renewal requests might not understand, the dependent might be issued a work permit despite being ineligible. "But," an official pointed out, "if the person was caught, the person would lose his asylum benefits and could be put into deportation proceedings." An immigrant advocate immediately observed, "But as a practical matter, they don't detain them if they have a work permit," thus confirming the notion that a *permiso* grants some permission to remain in the United States.

Chapter 4

The title for this chapter is excerpted from an El Rescate attorney's weekly presentation on immigration law.

1. These five organizations include the Fuerzas Populares de Liberación (FPL, Popular Forces of Liberation), the Resistencia Nacional (RN, National Resistance), the Partido de la Revolución Salvadoreña (PRS, Party of the Salvadoran Revolution) which was associated with the Ejército Revolucionario del Pueblo (ERP People's Revolutionary Army), the Partido Comunista de El Salvador (PCS, Communist Party of El Salvador), and the Partido Revolucionario de los Trabajadores Centroamericanos (PRTC, Revolutionary Party of Central American Workers) (Montgomery 1995:102; see Gordon 1989 for an account of the formation of the FMLN). For reasons of confidentiality, I cannot identify the political roots of Los Angeles–based organizations.

2. The CARECEN office in Los Angeles is part of a network of CARECEN offices around the United States.

3. In 1996 and 1997, El Rescate and CARECEN explored the possibility of merging their legal-services departments to better coordinate their work and to improve their funding. I was asked to facilitate the merger by acting as a liaison to educate each group about the other's organizational culture.

I declined to accept this offer, as the merger was a controversial proposition, and playing a role in the decision-making process could have jeopardized my relationship with certain staff members. In the end, the groups decided not to merge.

4. Although the INS was denying 98 percent of the asylum applications filed by Salvadorans and Guatemalans (USCR 1986), such defensive asylum applications could delay deportation, especially if denials were appealed, and could thus buy the applicant more time in the United States, during which conditions in El Salvador might improve. In addition to defending Central Americans in deportation proceedings, El Rescate and CARECEN raised bail funds for immigrants in detention, represented detainees in bond-reduction hearings, created legal guardianships for detained minors so that undocumented parents did not have to turn themselves in to free their children, and filed affirmative (i.e., nondefensive) asylum applications for individuals who had particularly strong cases.

5. The 1990 Immigration Act gave Salvadorans who had been in the United States since September 19, 1990, the right to apply for eighteen months of TPS. When the eighteen months expired, TPS recipients were permitted to register for DED status. And when DED expired, both DED and TPS recipients were eligible to apply for asylum under the terms of the ABC agreement (see chapter 1). Guatemalans, who never received TPS status, also benefited from the ABC settlement. Approximately 80,000 Guatemalans and 180,000 Salvadorans applied for asylum under the terms of the ABC agreement. These figures do not include dependants who have been included in class members' asylum applications.

6. Despite their extensive legal programs, it would be incorrect to view El Rescate, CARECEN, and ASOSAL exclusively as legal-service agencies, as each was also involved in a variety of other projects. El Rescate has provided social services—including a shelter, food bank, clothing distribution, and bus tokens—to Pico-Union residents. El Rescate also offered ESL classes to immigrants, sponsored cultural and political events, supported the work of Salvadoran hometown associations, worked with a sister organization in El Salvador to monitor the implementation of the peace accords, organized delegations to El Salvador, and launched a transnational credit union intended to promote economic development both locally and in El Salvador. CARECEN has organized youth programs, a public market, international student exchanges, leadership training, earthquake-preparedness training, conferences, and cultural events. And ASOSAL sponsored a folkloric dance group, organized community events and fund-raisers (such as dances and picnics), helped to plan the annual Central American Independence Day parade in Los Angeles, promoted citizenship and voter registration, and supported Salvadoran hometown associations. Legal services were nonetheless a critical and in some ways defining component of the organizations' work.

7. For example, each of these organizations hired extra staff members when Salvadoran ABC class members were applying for political asylum.

8. One student intern compared the difficulty of winning a legalization case to the difficulty of being represented by a community organization: "I think a lot of [immigrants] are screened out at certain levels. I mean like even when you come to a service [organization], like El Rescate, you're screened out, because there's a limited amount of cases they can handle here, a limited amount of resources. So if [the attorney] decides that we've had enough suspension, we need to do political asylum, the suspension [cases] for that week are screened out—you know, if the caseload's too much."

9. Of course, precedent-setting cases could potentially affect large numbers of people.

10. One client whom I interviewed compared legal advocacy to fixing a car. Regarding his prior, largely negative, experiences with a notary, he commented, "We know nothing of law. We left the legal matters in [the notary's] hands, just like when you take your car to be repaired, you entrust it to the mechanic." When I told an attorney about this man's comment, the attorney replied, "That's an interesting comparison—just like, until recently, people didn't question their doctors."

11. Medical matters are actually an issue in people's immigration cases. Vaccinations are required for adjustment, medical problems can constitute hardship for purposes of suspension of deportation, and people can be excluded from immigrating for medical reasons. And of course, medical reports ascertain the extent of damage caused by torture and other abuses and therefore can be significant within asylum cases. As one attorney commented during a training on asylum and suspension, "Everybody has *some* problem!" This comment indicates that to legalize, one must simultaneously pathologize. Asylum applicants must depict themselves as needy, and suspension applicants must have a problem if they are to demonstrate hardship.

12. One student intern described these multiple roles as follows: "We're very much human when we deal with our clients and very much machines when we deal with the court." The student's description of how he transformed clients' stories into legal cases echoes Sally Merry's (1990:97) discussion of the differences between a "case" and a "problem." Merry describes problems as "emotionally intense" and cases as "a cool difference of interest."

13. An alternative means of learning the status of a client's case was to dial an 800 number provided by the INS, enter the client's alien number, and listen to recorded information about the case. This method was particularly important if clients failed to attend prior court hearings and might have been ordered deported in absentia.

14. To illustrate this difference, the legal worker contrasted a three-inch-thick folder containing the supporting documentation that she had photocopied for another suspension applicant's case with the slender envelope that the client in this case had brought along as proof of his claim.

15. The family visa petition process became more difficult after the passage of IIRIRA, which instituted new deeming requirements, thereby mak-

ing it more difficult for petitioners to demonstrate that they had the financial resources to support the relatives for whom they were petitioning. Additionally, IIRIRA created three- and ten-year bars on the reentry of individuals who had been in the United States without authorization for 180 days or one year, respectively. A program that permitted individuals to adjust their status in the United States instead of outside the country, 245(i), expired in 1998, meaning that individuals who were the beneficiaries of family visa petitions and who had been in the United States without authorization would have to leave the country to claim their visas. If they had accumulated sufficient illegal time, then the three- or ten-year bar would be triggered, making it impossible for them to reenter the country. It is as yet unclear who, if anyone, will qualify for waivers under these circumstances.

16. The Violence against Women Act acknowledged that immigrant women sometimes remain in abusive relationships simply because their spouses are their tickets to green cards. The act therefore permits victims of domestic violence to self-petition and to file for suspension of deportation after only three years of residency in the United States. In contrast to other sorts of family visa petitions, self-petitions under this legislation transfer the right to immigrate from the petitioner to the petitionee and recognize that the content of kin relations (in this case, spousal relations) may differ from that implied by the legal relationship alone. The legal relationship is nonetheless necessary in these cases, as women who are in abusive nonmarital relationships cannot self-petition and may stay in the relationship in hopes of a marriage that will result in a green card.

17. As one attorney advised audience members during a charla on immigration law, "Sometimes the oldest child is already over age, he already has a girlfriend, they're already living together, and the parents say, 'Why isn't there a legal marriage?' And the attorney has to say, 'No, wait, don't marry now.' Why? Because a visa is pending."

18. Between 1995 and 1997, community organizations prepared two sorts of asylum applications for clients: relatively skeletal ABC applications under the terms of the settlement agreement, and regular asylum applications involving clients who were not ABC class members. Regular asylum cases were accepted through the case evaluation process described previously, whereas ABC asylum applications were prepared for almost all clients who met the minimum eligibility requirements: Salvadoran citizenship, continuous presence in the United States since September 19, 1990, and prior registration for TPS. (By the time of my fieldwork, the registration period for Guatemalan ABC class members had already expired.) Because community organizations sought to maintain TPS recipients' documented status, legal staff filled out as many asylum applications for the approximately ninety thousand Salvadoran ABC class members living in Los Angeles as were possible before the January 31, 1996, deadline. Unlike regular clients, the thousands of ABC clients whose asylum applications were completed by ASOSAL, El Rescate, and CARECEN were not promised legal representation but only assistance with the application process, legal advice, and advocacy for the

ABC class as a whole. Only the few ABC class members who had what advocates considered strong asylum cases were promised more extensive services, such as legal representation.

19. A legal worker who had prepared ABC asylum applications told me, "That's what's good about the law. There are always ways that you can stretch it. Social class can indicate membership in a social group. Or the fact that you're a family member of someone who was killed, and there were very many people who had family members who in turn were killed or persecuted also. That could make them a member of a social group. They were family members." The other three grounds for claiming asylum are having a well-founded fear of being persecuted on the basis of one's race, religion, or nationality.

20. In addition, legal workers at all three organizations included such statements as "Although peace accords have been signed in my country, there is still political instability" in almost all narratives to address the diminished likelihood of persecution in postwar El Salvador.

21. One ABC applicant described her asylum narrative as follows: "'Refugee' is just an excuse, something that we call ourselves from time to time in order to get support from the government. For instance, I had to put this in the papers that I filled out in order to get this status, . . . saying everything that had happened to me during the war and that I was afraid to go back." In contrast to this woman, most of the ABC class members with whose cases I was familiar seemed genuinely fearful due to their experiences during the civil war.

22. Service providers did avoid information that would prevent them from being able to certify that the data on the form were true and correct to the best of their knowledge. For example, one legal worker told me that when TPS recipients began to tell her that since applying for TPS, they had left and reentered the United States without authorization, she immediately stopped them. Such unauthorized departures interrupted their stays and could make them ineligible for the benefits of the ABC settlement agreement.

23. Former California Governor Pete Wilson has been a leading proponent of restrictive immigration measures, such as the state's Proposition 187, which would have required a range of public servants to report suspected illegal aliens to the INS. Proposition 187 was approved by California's electorate in 1994 but has largely been struck down by the courts. See Martin 1995.

Chapter 5

The title of this chapter derives from a comment made by a Salvadoran man who was listening in as I interviewed his friend. When I asked the interviewee—a Salvadoran woman—why she did not apply for asylum during the 1980s, this man explained that many of his peers viewed asylum as "a hook" to get them into "the wolf's mouth"—that is, into the clutches of the INS. See chapter 7 for additional discussion of this comment.

1. Such erasures occur regardless of and despite judges' and officials' intentions. Some judges are fairly sympathetic to immigrants and let their sympathies be known publicly through both their comments and their rulings. Nonetheless, officials, like advocates, are still limited in the justice that they are able to render through law and in the sorts of "persons" that they can construct and recognize during proceedings.

2. Immigrants' narratives are judged according to legal standards of logical argument, narrative consistency, and empirical proof. At the same time, because immigrants' cases can be approved on the basis of testimony that is sufficiently clear and convincing, these narratives must be good stories.

3. For descriptions of immigration proceedings, see Aleinikoff, Martin, and Motomura 1995; Anker 1991, 1992; NILC 1994.

4. The process of subjugation actually begins before this entry into the formal legal arena, through requests for identity documents and so forth. I refer here to the particular legal subjugation that occurs through formal proceedings. In addition, individuals are called in for other sorts of proceedings, such as interviews regarding their applications for adjustment of status. I limit my analysis to asylum interviews and court hearings because I was able to observe these proceedings, not because they exhaust the possible forms that legal proceedings can take in an immigration context.

5. In 1997, the court was moved to 606 South Olive Street, also in downtown Los Angeles. The courtrooms are on floors 14 through 17 and remain difficult to reach. Many people have to arrive at the same time, which means that the elevators are slow and crowded at peak times. The court schedules are posted on the fifteenth floor rather than the ground floor, which means that two elevator rides can be necessary to arrive in court. Security checks are now quicker, however, as security is posted on each floor instead of only at the entrance to the building.

6. The more liberal judges sometimes direct their ire at attorneys who are associated with notaries or who are less than thorough in the services they provide to immigrants. The same judge who criticized in-absentia deportations, for example, rather rudely asked a private attorney when he had last spoken to his client: "Was it in the cellar or on an airplane or where?" The judge also accused this attorney of working for an outfit that "promises what it can't deliver."

7. In fact, it is impossible for people who do not speak English to state with certainty that the English translations of their testimony are accurate and complete. See Berk-Seligson 1990 for an analysis of the role that interpreters play in legal proceedings.

8. This is the only case in my sample in which the person applying for legal status was in detention. The applicant in this case had been detained at the airport and placed in exclusion hearings. El Rescate had accepted his case and had helped him apply for political asylum. His hearing was held in a courtroom at the San Pedro detention facility rather than in downtown Los

Angeles. When inaccuracies arose during his asylum hearing, the applicant—who spoke several languages—asked if he could simply testify in English. The judge encouraged him to postpone the hearing, fearing that testifying in English would impair his ability to present his case. The hearing was postponed for several months. At the next hearing, the same court interpreter appeared, meaning that the delay had been for naught. Testimony was nonetheless taken at this hearing, and the applicant's asylum request was approved.

9. For example, children are sometimes told, "You get to your room right now, sir! You are in trouble!"

10. These prototypes have also been the focus of recent anti-immigrant sentiment. See Bosniak 1996; Calavita 1996; Chavez 1997 for a discussion of these ideas.

11. Fitting multiple prototypes does not always prevent being deemed a refugee. In one Ethiopian asylum applicant's hearing, the judge acknowledged that the applicant had been persecuted due to both his political opinion and a conflict with his employer and then approved the asylum petition.

12. In fact, one of the ways that repression terrorizes is by making it difficult for populaces to understand how death squads select victims and which actions put one at risk (Green 1994; Taussig 1984; Taylor 1997). To demonstrate that they are singled out, asylum applicants also have to be able to identify those who are doing the persecuting, another difficult task given the nature of political persecution. When, at a master calendar hearing, a Guatemalan man testified that he had received anonymous threats, the judge quickly concluded that the man was ineligible for asylum and granted him voluntary departure. Similarly, the case of an applicant who told an asylum official that she feared the "situation" in El Salvador was referred to court instead of granted.

13. The Violence against Women Act created special protections for battering victims, including the right for battered spouses to apply for suspension of deportation after only three years of continuous presence. The purpose of this provision is to allow victims of domestic abuse to leave abusive relationships without facing the prospect of losing green cards that batterers promised to provide.

14. A Guatemalan asylum seeker encountered this problem when he testified that Guatemalan authorities had abducted him, beaten him, forced him to sign a confession, and then released him. To the judge, this testimony contained a plot hole: why would the applicant fear future persecution if the authorities had had the opportunity to kill him but had released him? The applicant's inability to account for his persecutors' motives in releasing him was a factor in the judge's decision to deny the asylum petition.

15. Suspension cases are an interesting context in which to evaluate the differential impact of immigration and welfare reform on immigrant men and women. The stigmatization of welfare use falls more heavily on women than on men, as women are more likely to have received public assistance to bear or care for U.S. citizen children. In contrast to the welfare debate at

large, however, which stigmatizes mothers rather than fathers (Delaney 1997), immigration judges hold immigrant fathers accountable for paying child support and for the public assistance that anyone may have received on behalf of his children. Interestingly, though, when the legal tie between spouses has been severed through divorce, a man is able to argue that he is not responsible for his ex-wife's decision to apply for public assistance. Of course, if he were paying sufficient child support, it might not be necessary for her to seek public benefits. At the same time, custody arrangements seem to give both mothers and fathers rights that immigration courts respect. For example, one divorced mother who had been granted custody of her daughter argued that because the divorce decree required her daughter to live in the vicinity of her ex-husband, she had to remain in the United States. Similarly, a divorced father who had legal visitation rights but not custody of his children argued that if he were deported, he would be unable to avail himself of these rights, creating a hardship for both himself and his children.

16. Definitions of family are also at issue during asylum hearings, as a legal worker who had prepared ABC asylum applications explained: "The definition of family in El Salvador is very different from the definition of family here. It includes uncles, it includes cousins, it includes nieces and nephews. And [INS] officials may not understand this notion of family. So if you go into the interview and say, 'My cousin was killed,' the official won't understand that this is like your brother being killed. . . . In my own town, I saw, before I left, a case in which three cousins were killed at the same time in the same town, just because one of those cousins was accused of being a guerrilla. The other two weren't accused of anything. This is what it means to be a family in El Salvador."

17. The need to individualize an account while matching a prototype may derive from conventions of narrativity. In her study of prolife and pro-choice activities, Faye Ginsburg (1989:142) notes that life stories have both plots and stories. The story, which would be analogous to a prototype, is a conventional framing, and the plot, which would be analogous to the individualization of a prototype, is the way that people's own lives differ from the conventions of the story.

18. This requirement is a strange twist on the liberal logic that excludes through the gap between notions of universal human capacities and "the specific cultural and psychological conditions woven in as preconditions for the actualization of these capacities" (Mehta 1997:61). In essence, potential persecution victims can only be recognized as such if their persecutors realize their capacity to persecute and thus make victims actual rather than potential targets.

19. The exchange that occurred during this hearing was as follows:

Trial attorney: Are the death squads part of the army?

Respondent: Yes.

Judge: How do you know that the death squads and the army are connected?

Respondent: Eighty percent of the Salvadoran population knows this, with the exception of very young children.

Judge: Well, perhaps I'm like a baby, but, since I'm the person who is going to decide where you'll spend your future, perhaps it would be best if you humored me and answered my question. I don't care about the other 80 percent of the population. How do you know that the death squads and the military are connected?

The respondent then explained that he had seen cadavers with "EM" and "FAS" emblazoned on their chests. "EM," he related, stood for *escuadrones de la muerte* (death squads), and "FAS" stood for Fuerzas Armadas Salvadoreñas (Salvadoran Armed Forces). The judge found this answer satisfactory.

20. Regarding what he terms "characterological coherence," Walter Fisher (1987:16) writes, "Central to all stories is character. Whether or not a story is believable depends on the reliability of characters, both as narrators and as actors. Determination of one's character is made by interpretations of a person's decisions and actions that reflect values. In other words, character may be considered an organized set of actional tendencies. If these tendencies contradict one another, change significantly, or alter in 'strange' ways, the result is a questioning of character. Coherence in life and in literature requires that characters behave characteristically. Without this kind of predictability, there is no trust, no community, no rational order."

21. I do not mean to suggest that apprehensions do not occur. One attorney told me of an instance in which the INS apprehended an undocumented woman and her one-year-old U.S. citizen child in their home in Los Angeles at 5:00 A.M., when they were in bed asleep. Both were deported. Though the child had the legal right to remain in the United States, officials permitted the mother and child to remain together.

22. I attended one adjustment interview at which there was great confusion regarding the number of times a woman had been deported. The woman stated that she had been physically removed from the United States by U.S. officials one time. The interviewer noticed that a deportation order had been issued some time earlier, suggesting that the woman had been ordered deported twice, though she had only been removed from the country once. The woman's attorney finally figured out that there was only one deportation order, because the actual removal from U.S. territory had been an execution of the prior deportation order rather than a new order.

23. As Engel and Munger (1996:10) note, "Civil rights . . . concern themselves not only with the legal interests of those who belong to civil society but also with the issue of membership itself."

24. Consider, for example, the contested election of Loretta Sanchez. When Sanchez beat Representative Robert Dornan by a close margin in the 1996 congressional elections, Dornan supporters immediately suggested that some of the voters in this increasingly Latino district were not citizens and were not entitled to vote.

25. For example, when asked whether he would agree to depart voluntarily, one asylum applicant replied, "I can't return to Guatemala because my life would be in danger. That's why I'm seeking asylum here."

Chapter 6

1. My description is deliberately vague. I was asked not to reveal such details as the names of organizations and organizations' affiliations with Salvadoran political groups.

2. Activists in El Salvador made similar sacrifices. A man who served in the political branch of one of the groups that made up the FMLN described the dedication demanded of activists in El Salvador during the civil war: "You had to give up everything else, including your studies, your family, and everything. Later, supposedly, you were going to take these up again, when the revolution triumphed. And that was another ideology, because there was a type of certainty that yes, the revolution was going to triumph, right? So that was a matter, a mystique, as we said, that was spread through the group. 'You have to prepare yourself, you have to give up many things, you have to sacrifice many things, your family, your studies, your children, all that you love, to dedicate yourself to the moment that the fight ends, if we win. And if we don't win, well, we have offered our lives, or our sacrifice to the new generations.' That was the mystique that, in general, the revolution followed."

3. Solidarity groups in the United States were infiltrated by the U.S. INS, the U.S. FBI, and Salvadoran right-wing informers (Coutin 1995; Gelbspan 1991; U.S. Senate 1989). A Salvadoran woman who was active in the solidarity movement described the persecution that she experienced in Los Angeles: "There were death threats and my name was on the list, and Padre Olivares, and lots of other people. . . . I had received death threats, and then one day, I was on Olympic, and I was driving across the intersection, when we suddenly heard gunshots. One of the bullets lodged in the gasoline tank, and none of them hit me. We were lucky. But I had received death threats, so I know that this was not a common crime."

4. See also Malkki 1995a, regarding the multiple identities claimed by the Hutu in Tanzania.

5. If asylum applicants leave the United States without the permission of the U.S. government, they are deemed to have abandoned their applications. Asylum applicants who have to travel due to an emergency, such as the imminent death of a close relative, can sometimes obtain advanced parole from U.S. immigration officials. Advanced parole allows applicants to reenter the United States if their travel is completed before a certain date. Returning to one's country of origin can weaken an asylum claim, as the applicant's willingness to return suggests an absence of fear. Moreover, the absence of difficulties encountered on the return trip can be taken as evidence that the applicant is not, in fact, in danger of persecution.

6. Proposition 187 would have required public schoolteachers, health-care workers, and benefits counselors to verify the legal status of students, patients, and applicants for public assistance and to report illegal immigrants to the INS. This proposition, which was passed by California voters, has largely been stalled in the courts (Martin 1995). Besides Proposition 187, other explanations for record naturalization rates include the fact that the beneficiaries of the 1986 amnesty program have now become eligible for naturalization, the promotion of naturalization on the part of community organizations and U.S. immigration officials, and the Mexican government's approval of dual citizenship (see Coutin 1998a).

7. An ASOSAL staff member noted that in common parlance, the term *el pequeño centroamerica* refers to Pico Union and implies prostitution and drug use.

8. Not all Central American community groups emphasize Central American Independence Day. One activist told me that this difference is rooted in political divisions within the Salvadoran Left: some organizations that made up the FMLN promoted this date, whereas others did not.

9. James Clifford (1994:313, emphasis original) draws attention to the political ambivalence of such a project, commenting, "While clearly necessary, making *cultural* room for Salvadorans, Samoans, Sikhs, Haitians, Khmers, and so forth, does not, of itself, produce a living wage, decent housing, or health care." At least some Salvadoran activists see their efforts to claim cultural space, promote naturalization, become a political constituency, and improve housing and health care as interconnected.

10. I owe this idea of containing disorder to conversations with David Goldberg.

11. A Salvadoran community leader described the Salvadoran government's recent overtures to the immigrant community as follows: "The Salvadoran government has suddenly identified the Salvadoran community in places like Los Angeles, and they're investing thousands upon thousands of dollars to (1) develop this market [and] (2) support their main investors. Funny, a big market is also one of the main investors through the remittances." Another activist from a different political group gave a similar analysis: "There is no article in which they don't mention that family remittances are a sustaining source in the Salvadoran economy. That means that the Salvadoran businesspeople and the very same party in power have to cast political lines to see what to do with the Salvadoran community in Los Angeles, to try to capture family remittances in their favor."

Chapter 7

1. Regina could, however, argue that if her children suffered economically, she would suffer emotionally. As hardship to the applicant is relevant to a suspension case, Regina could claim that she needs to remain in the

United States in order to avoid the distress of being unable to support her children.

2. For example, some nonnaturalized immigrants have told me of their frustration that they could not vote on California Proposition 187, an initiative that directly affected both them and their family members.

3. My discussion of the de- or remythologization of law is not inconsistent with Engel's analysis of the "origin myths" recounted by parents of children with disabilities. Engel (1993:792) points out that these origin myths—parents' accounts of their children's initial diagnoses—transcend linear time in that they "not only regenerate themselves but also reaffirm and 'reactualize' the cosmic order that they find encoded in the myths." Engel contrasts these origin myths with law. This contrast does not, however, mean that law is not a *mythology* in Fitzpatrick's sense of the term. For example, as Engel's article effectively demonstrates, law also "'creates a character' for children with disabilities" (1993:790), a characterization that parents challenge as they construct their own origin myths and seek justice for their children.

4. I do not mean to suggest that ABC class members were merely trying to gain time or that their asylum applications were without merit. The INS clearly bears some responsibility for not adjudicating asylum petitions in a timely and fair manner.

5. Representative Christopher H. Smith introduced H.R. 2722, the Central American and Haitian Adjustment Act, in the House of Representatives on August 5, 1999. This act would permit certain Salvadorans, Guatemalans, Hondurans, and Haitians to apply for permanent residency.

6. The University of California Regents for example, recently criticized "ethnic" and other distinctive graduation ceremonies (Weiss 1998).

References

Cases and Statutes Cited

1990 Immigration Act. P.L. 101-649, 104 Stat. 4978, November 29, 1990.
American Baptist Churches v. Thornburgh. 1991. 760 F.Supp. 796 (N.D. Cal.).
Antiterrorism and Effective Death Penalty Act. P.L. 104–132, 110 Stat. 1214, April 24, 1996.
Illegal Immigration Reform and Immigrant Responsibility Act. P.L. 104-208, 110 Stat. 3009, September 30, 1996.
Immigration Reform and Control Act. P.L. 99-603, 100 Stat. 3359, November 6, 1986.
In re N-J-B-, Int. Dec. 3309 (BIA 1997).
Mendez v. Reno, no. CV-88-04995-TJH, C.D. Cal., August 12, 1993.
Nicaraguan Adjustment and Central American Relief Act. P.L. 105-100, 111 Stat. 2193, November 19, 1997.
Violence against Women Act of 1994. P.L. 103-322, 108 Stat. 1796.

Books and Articles Cited

Abu-Lughod, Lila. 1986. *Veiled Sentiments: Honor and Poetry in a Bedouin Society.* Berkeley: University of California Press.
Abu-Lughod, Lila. 1990. "The Romance of Resistance." *American Ethnologist* 17:41–55.
ACLU Immigrants Rights Project; Catholic Legal Immigration Network, Inc.; Immigrant Legal Resource Center; National Immigration Law Center; National Immigration Project of the National Lawyers Guild. 1996. *Background Materials: The 1996 Immigration Law.* Los Angeles: National Immigration Law Center.
Aguayo, Sergio, and Patricia Weiss Fagen. 1988. *Central Americans in Mexico and the United States: Unilateral, Bilateral, and Regional Perspectives.* Washington, D.C.: Center for Immigration Policy and Refugee Assistance, Georgetown University.
Aguilera Peralta, Gabriel. 1988. "Esquipulas y el conflicto interno en Centroamérica." *Cuadernos de Trabajo* 11 (January): 9–28.
Aleinikoff, T. Alexander, David A. Martin, and Hiroshi Motomura. 1995. *Immigration, Process and Policy.* 3d ed. St. Paul, Minn.: West Publishing.
Alonso, Ana Maria. 1988. "The Effects of Truth: Re-Presentations of the Past

and the Imagining of Community." *Journal of Historical Sociology* 1 (1): 33–56.

Althusser, Louis. 1971. "Ideology and Ideological State Apparatuses (Notes towards an Investigation)." In *Lenin and Philosophy, and Other Essays*, trans. Ben Brewster, 127–86. New York: Monthly Review Press.

American Friends Service Committee. 1992. *Sealing Our Borders: The Human Toll. Third Report of the Immigration Law Enforcement Monitoring Project (ILEMP). A Project of the Mexico-U.S. Border Program*. Philadelphia: American Friends Service Committee.

Americas Watch. 1991. *El Salvador's Decade of Terror: Human Rights since the Assassination of Archbishop Romero*. New Haven: Yale University Press.

Americas Watch. 1993. "United States Frontier Injustice: Human Rights Abuses along the U.S. Border with Mexico Persist amid Climate of Impunity." *News from Americas Watch* 5 (4): 1–48.

Anderson, Benedict. 1991. *Imagined Communities: Reflections on the Origin and Spread of Nationalism*. Rev. ed. London: Verso.

Anderson, Elijah. 1990. *Streetwise: Race, Class, and Change in an Urban Community*. Chicago: University of Chicago Press.

Anker, Deborah E. 1991. *The Law of Asylum in the United States*. Washington, D.C.: American Immigration Law Foundation.

Anker, Deborah E. 1992. "Determining Asylum Claims in the United States: A Case Study on the Implementation of Legal Norms in an Unstructured Adjudicatory Environment." *New York University Review of Law and Social Change* 19 (3): 433–528.

Anzaldua, Gloria. 1987. *Borderlands/La Frontera*. San Francisco: Spinsters/Aunt Lute.

Appadurai, Arjun. 1991. "Global Ethnoscapes: Notes and Queries for a Transnational Anthropology." In *Recapturing Anthropology: Working in the Present*, ed. Richard G. Fox, 191–210. Santa Fe, N.M.: School of American Research Press.

Arrighi, Giovanni. 1990. "The Developmentalist Illusion: A Reconceptualization of the Semiperiphery." In *Semiperipheral States in the World-Economy*, ed. William G. Martin, 11–42. New York: Greenwood.

Asad, Talal. 1983. "Anthropological Conceptions of Religion: Reflections on Geertz." *Man* 18 (2): 237–59.

Asad, Talal. 1990. "Multiculturalism and British Identity in the Wake of the Rushdie Affair." *Politics and Society* 18 (4): 455–80.

Bach, Robert L. 1978. "Mexican Immigration and the American State." *International Migration Review* 12 (4): 536–58.

Bach, Robert L. 1990. "Immigration and U.S. Foreign Policy in Latin America and the Caribbean." In *Immigration and U.S. Foreign Policy*, ed. Robert W. Tucker, Charles B. Keely, and Linda Wrigley, 123–49. Boulder, Colo.: Westview Press.

Baldus, David C., George Woodworth, and Charles A. Pulaski Jr. 1990. *Equal Justice and the Death Penalty: A Legal and Empirical Analysis*. Boston: Northeastern University Press.

Barbalet, J. M. 1988. *Citizenship: Rights, Struggle and Class Inequality.* Milton Keynes, Eng.: Open University Press.

Basch, Linda, Nina Glick Schiller, and Cristina Szanton Blanc. 1994. *Nations Unbound: Transnational Projects, Postcolonial Predicaments, and Deterritorialized Nation-States.* Langhorne, Pa.: Gordon and Breach.

Bau, Ignatius. 1985. *This Ground Is Holy: Church Sanctuary and Central American Refugees.* New York: Paulist Press.

Bauböck, Rainer, ed. 1994. *From Aliens to Citizens: Redefining the Status of Immigrants in Europe.* Aldershot, England: Avebury.

Bean, Frank D., Barry Edmonston, and Jeffrey S. Passel, eds. 1990. *Undocumented Migration to the United States: IRCA and the Experience of the 1980s.* Washington, D.C.: Urban Institute Press.

Benítez, Raúl. 1990. "El Salvador 1980–1990: Guerra, política y perspectivas." *Cuadernos de Trabajo* 13 (December): 78–99.

Benmayor, Rina, Rosa M. Torruellas, and Ana L. Juarbe. 1997. "Claiming Cultural Citizenship in East Harlem: 'Si Esto Puede Ayudar a la Comunidad Mía . . .'" In *Latino Cultural Citizenship,* ed. Flores and Benmayor, 152–209. Boston: Beacon.

Bennett, W. Lance, and Martha S. Feldman. 1981. *Reconstructing Reality in the Courtroom: Justice and Judgment in American Culture.* New Brunswick, N.J.: Rutgers University Press.

Berk-Seligson, Susan. 1990. *The Bilingual Courtroom: Court Interpreters in the Judicial Process.* Chicago: University of Chicago Press.

Berryman, Phillip. 1984. *The Religious Roots of Rebellion.* Maryknoll, N.Y.: Orbis.

Bhabha, Homi. 1997. "Of Mimicry and Man." In *Tensions of Empire: Colonial Cultures in a Bourgeois World,* ed. Frederick Cooper and Ann Laura Stoler, 152–60. Berkeley: University of California Press.

Bhabha, Jacqueline. 1996. "Embodied Rights: Gender Persecution, State Sovereignty, and Refugees." *Public Culture* 9 (1): 3–32.

Blum, Carolyn Patty. 1991. "The Settlement of *American Baptist Churches v. Thornburgh:* Landmark Victory for Central American Asylum Seekers." *International Journal of Refugee Law* 3 (2): 347–56.

Bogoch, Bryna. 1997. "Gendered Lawyering: Difference and Dominance in Lawyer-Client Interaction." *Law and Society Review* 31 (4): 677–712.

Bosniak, Linda S. 1991. "Human Rights, State Sovereignty and the Protection of Undocumented Migrants under the International Migrant Workers Convention." *International Migration Review* 25 (4): 737–70.

Bosniak, Linda S. 1996. "Opposing Prop. 187: Undocumented Immigrants and the National Imagination." *Connecticut Law Review* 28 (3): 555–619.

Bourdieu, Pierre. 1977. *Outline of a Theory of Practice.* Trans. Richard Nice. Cambridge: Cambridge University Press.

Bourdieu, Pierre. 1984. *Distinction: A Social Critique of the Judgment of Taste.* Trans. Richard Nice. Cambridge: Harvard University Press.

Bourdieu, Pierre. 1987. "The Force of Law: Toward a Sociology of the Juridical Field." Trans. Richard Terdiman. *Hastings Law Journal* 38 (July): 805–53.

Bousquet, Gisele L. 1991. *Behind the Bamboo Hedge: The Impact of Homeland Politics in the Parisian Vietnamese Community.* Ann Arbor: University of Michigan Press.

Brady, Katherine, and Dan Kesselbrenner. 1996. "Recent Developments in the Immigration Consequences of Crimes." In ACLU Immigrants Rights Project et al., *Background Materials*, 55–81. Los Angeles: National Immigration Law Center.

Briggs, Vernon M., Jr. 1984. *Immigration Policy and the American Labor Force.* Baltimore: Johns Hopkins University Press.

Brubaker, Rogers. 1992. *Citizenship and Nationhood in France and Germany.* Cambridge: Harvard University Press.

Bruner, Jerome. 1986. *Actual Minds, Possible Worlds.* Cambridge: Harvard University Press.

Bumiller, Kristin. 1991. "Fallen Angels: The Representation of Violence against Women in Legal Culture." In *At the Boundaries of Law: Feminism and Legal Theory*, ed. Martha A. Fineman and Nancy S. Thomadsen, 95–112. New York: Routledge.

Burns, Allan F. 1993. *Maya in Exile: Guatemalans in Florida.* Philadelphia: Temple University Press.

Byrne, Hugh. 1996. *El Salvador's Civil War: A Study of Revolution.* Boulder, Colo.: Lynne Rienner.

Calavita, Kitty. 1990. "Employer Sanctions Violations: Toward a Dialectical Model of White-Collar Crime." *Law and Society Review* 24 (4): 1041–69.

Calavita, Kitty. 1992. *Inside the State: The Bracero Program, Immigration, and the I.N.S.* New York: Routledge.

Calavita, Kitty. 1994. "U.S. Immigration and Policy Responses: The Limits of Legislation." In *Controlling Immigration: A Global Perspective*, ed. Wayne A. Cornelius, Philip L. Martin, and James F. Hollifield, 55–82. Stanford, Calif.: Stanford University Press.

Calavita, Kitty. 1996. "The New Politics of Immigration: 'Balanced-Budget Conservatism' and the Symbolism of Proposition 187." *Social Problems* 43 (3): 284–305.

Caldeira, Teresa P. R. 1996. "Fortified Enclaves: The New Urban Segregation." *Public Culture* 8 (2): 303–28.

Cardenal, Ernesto. 1976. *The Gospel in Solentiname.* Maryknoll, N.Y.: Orbis Books.

Castaneda, Jorge G. 1995. *The Mexican Shock: Its Meaning for the United States.* New York: New Press.

Castles, Stephen, and Mark J. Miller. 1993. *The Age of Migration: International Population Movements in the Modern World.* New York: Guilford Press.

Chavez, Leo. 1991. "Outside the Imagined Community: Undocumented Settlers and Experiences of Incorporation." *American Ethnologist* 18 (2): 257–78.

Chavez, Leo. 1992. *Shadowed Lives: Undocumented Immigrants in American Society*. Fort Worth, Tex.: Harcourt Brace Jovanovich.

Chavez, Leo. 1997. "Immigration Reform and Nativism: The Nationalist Response to the Transnationalist Challenge." In *Immigrants Out! The New Nativism and the Anti-Immigrant Impulse in the United States*, ed. Juan F. Perea, 61–77. New York: New York University Press.

Chock, Phyllis Pease. 1991. "'Illegal Aliens' and 'Opportunity': Myth-Making in Congressional Testimony." *American Ethnologist* 18 (2): 279–94.

Chock, Phyllis Pease. 1995. "Ambiguity in Policy Discourse: Congressional Talk about Immigration." *Policy Sciences* 28 (2): 165–84.

Chock, Phyllis Pease. 1997. "'A Very Bright Line': Kinship and Nationality in U.S. Congressional Hearings on Immigration." Paper presented at the annual meeting of the American Ethnological Society, Seattle.

Churgin, Michael J. 1996. "Mass Exoduses: The Response of the United States." *International Migration Review* 30 (1): 310–25.

Clifford, James. 1988. "Identity in Mashpee." In *The Predicament of Culture: Twentieth-Century Ethnography, Literature, and Art*, 277–348. Cambridge: Harvard University Press.

Clifford, James. 1994. "Diasporas." *Cultural Anthropology* 9 (3): 302–38.

Clifford, James. 1997. *Routes: Travel and Translation in the Late Twentieth Century*. Cambridge: Harvard University Press.

Collier, Jane F. 1988. *Marriage and Inequality in Classless Societies*. Stanford, Calif.: Stanford University Press.

Collier, Jane F., Bill Maurer, and Liliana Suárez-Navaz. 1995. "Sanctioned Identities: Legal Constructions of Modern Personhood." *Identities* 2 (1–2): 1–27.

Conklin, Beth A. 1997. "Body Paint, Feathers, and VCRs: Aesthetics and Authenticity in Amazonian Activism." *American Ethnologist* 24 (4): 711–37.

Conley, John M., and William M. O'Barr. 1990. *Rules versus Relationships: The Ethnography of Legal Discourse*. Chicago: University of Chicago Press.

Coombe, Rosemary J. 1997. "The Demonic Place of the 'Not There': Trademark Rumors in the Postindustrial Imaginary." In *Culture, Power, Place: Explorations in Critical Anthropology*, ed. Akhil Gupta and James Ferguson, 249–76. Durham, N.C.: Duke University Press.

Córdova Macías, Ricardo. 1988. "El Salvador: Perspectivas de paz." *Cuadernos de Trabajo* 11 (January): 29–52.

Córdova Macías, Ricardo. 1993. *El Salvador: Las negociacions de paz y los retos de la postguerra*. San Salvador, El Salvador: Institute de Estudios Latino Americanos.

Cornelius, Wayne A. 1982. "Interviewing Undocumented Immigrants: Methodological Reflections Based on Fieldwork in Mexico and the United States." *International Migration Review* 16 (2): 378–411.

Cornelius, Wayne A. 1990. "Impacts of the 1986 U.S. Immigration Law on Emigration from Rural Mexican Sending Communities." In *Undocumented Migration to the United States*, ed. Bean, Edmonston, and Passel, 227–49. Washington, D.C.: Urban Institute Press.

Coutin, Susan Bibler. 1993. *The Culture of Protest: Religious Activism and the U.S. Sanctuary Movement*. Boulder, Colo.: Westview Press.

Coutin, Susan Bibler. 1995. "Smugglers or Samaritans in Tucson, Arizona: Producing and Contesting Legal Truth." *American Ethnologist* 22 (3): 549–71.

Coutin, Susan Bibler. 1996. "Differences within Accounts of U.S. Immigration Law." *PoLAR: Political and Legal Anthropology Review* 19 (1): 11–19.

Coutin, Susan Bibler. 1998a. "The 'Real' Americans: Citizenship and Belonging with Mass Naturalization Ceremonies in Los Angeles." Paper presented at the annual meeting of the Law and Society Association, Aspen, Colo.

Coutin, Susan Bibler. 1998b. "From Refugees to Immigrants: The Legalization Strategies of Salvadoran Immigrants and Activists." *International Migration Review* 32 (4): 901–25.

Coutin, Susan Bibler. Forthcoming. "The Oppressed, the Suspect, and the Citizen: Subjectivity in Competing Accounts of Political Violence." *Law and Social Inquiry*.

Coutin, Susan Bibler, and Phyllis Pease Chock. 1995. " 'Your Friend, the Illegal': Definition and Paradox in Newspaper Accounts of Immigration Reform." *Identities* 2 (1–2): 123–48.

Coutin, Susan Bibler, and Susan F. Hirsch. 1998. "Naming Resistance: Ethnographers, Dissidents, and States." *Anthropological Quarterly* 71 (1): 1–17.

Cover, Robert. 1992a. "Nomos and Narrative." In *Narrative, Violence, and the Law: The Essays of Robert Cover*, ed. Martha Minow, Michael Ryan, and Austin Sarat, 95–172. Ann Arbor: University of Michigan Press.

Cover, Robert. 1992b. "Violence and the Word." In *Narrative, Violence, and the Law: The Essays of Robert Cover*, ed. Martha Minow, Michael Ryan, and Austin Sarat, 203–38. Ann Arbor: University of Michigan Press.

Crenshaw, Kimberlé, and Gary Peller. 1993. "Reel Time/Real Justice." In *Reading Rodney King*, ed. Gooding-Williams, 56–70. New York: Routledge.

Darling, Juanita. 1996. "U.S. Dollars Sent South Now Fuel Salvador Economy." *Los Angeles Times*, January 28, A1, A6.

Davis, Michael. 1992. "Fortress Los Angeles: The Militarization of Urban Space." In *Variations on a Theme Park*, ed. Sorkin, 154–80. New York: Hill and Wang.

Delaney, Carol. 1997. "The Presence and Absence of Fathers in the Welfare Debate." Maxine Van de Wetering Endowed Lecture, University of Montana.

Delgado, Hector. 1993. *New Immigrants, Old Unions: Organizing Undocumented Workers in Los Angeles*. Philadelphia: Temple University Press.

EBSC (East Bay Sanctuary Covenant). 1997. "Expanded INS Endangering Lives, Threatening Civil Liberties." *Exodus* 16 (7): 1, 4.

Eisenstein, James, and Herbert Jacob. 1977. *Felony Justice: An Organizational Analysis of Criminal Courts*. Boston: Little, Brown.

Ellingwood, Ken. 1998. "Plan Seeks to Save Lives of Illegal Immigrants." *Los Angeles Times,* June 16, A3, A18.

Ellis, Virginia. 1998. "Study Says More Immigrants Are Going Hungry." *Los Angeles Times,* May 27, A1, A22.

Engel, David. 1993. "Origin Myths: Narratives of Authority, Resistance, Disability, and Law." *Law and Society Review* 27 (4): 785–826.

Engel, David M., and Frank W. Munger. 1996. "Rights, Remembrance, and the Reconciliation of Difference." *Law and Society Review* 30 (1): 7–53.

Evans, Sara M., and Harry C. Boyte. 1986. *Free Spaces: The Sources of Democratic Change in America.* New York: Harper and Row.

Ewick, Patricia, and Susan S. Silbey. 1995. "Subversive Stories and Hegemonic Tales: Toward a Sociology of Narrative." *Law and Society Review* 29 (2): 197–226.

FAIR (Federation for American Immigration Reform). 1997. "Congressional Background Briefing Paper: Has the INS Prepared for Large-Scale Deportations When It Begins Re-Screening ABC Asylum Applicants?" News release, March 18. Washington, D.C.: FAIR.

Featherstone, Mike. 1995. *Undoing Culture: Globalization, Postmodernism and Identity.* London: Sage.

Feldman, Allen. 1991. *Formations of Violence: The Narrative of the Body and Political Terror in Northern Ireland.* Chicago: University of Chicago Press.

Fiederlein, Suzanne Leone. 1991. "Interpreting International and Domestic Law Concerning Refugees: The U.S. Government vs. the Sanctuary Movement." *Journal of Borderlands Studies* 6 (1): 23–50.

Fiederlein, Suzanne Leone. 1992. "Responding to Central American Refugees: Comparing Policy Design in Mexico and the United States." Ph.D. diss., University of Arizona.

Fisher, Walter R. 1987. "Technical Logic, Rhetorical Logic, and Narrative Rationality." *Argumentation* 1 (1): 3–21.

Fisher, William F. 1997. "Doing Good? The Politics and Antipolitics of NGO Practices." *Annual Review of Anthropology* 26:439–64.

Fitzpatrick, Peter. 1992. *The Mythology of Modern Law.* New York: Routledge.

Fitzpatrick, Peter. 1993. "The Impossibility of Popular Justice." In *The Possibility of Popular Justice,* ed. Merry and Milner, 453–74. Ann Arbor: University of Michigan Press.

Flores, William V., and Rina Benmayor. 1997. *Latino Cultural Citizenship: Claiming Identity, Space, and Rights.* Boston: Beacon.

Foucault, Michel. 1977. *Discipline and Punish: The Birth of the Prison.* Trans. Alan Sheridan. New York: Pantheon.

Foucault, Michel. 1978. *The History of Sexuality.* Vol. 1, *An Introduction.* Trans. Robert Hurley. New York: Random House.

Foucault, Michel. 1980. *Power/Knowledge.* Ed. Colin Gordon. New York: Pantheon.

Freeman, Gary P. 1992. "Migration Policy and Politics in the Receiving States." *International Migration Review* 26 (4): 1144–66.

Frelick, Bill, and Barbara Kohnen. 1994. "Filling the Gap: Temporary Protected Status." Washington, D.C.: U.S. Committee for Refugees.

Fuchs, Lawrence H. 1985. "The Search for a Sound Immigration Policy: A Personal View." In *Clamor at the Gates: The New American Immigration*, ed. Nathan Glazer, 17–48. San Francisco: Institute for Contemporary Studies.

Gelbspan, Ross. 1991. *Break-Ins, Death Threats and the FBI: The Covert War against the Central America Movement.* Boston: South End Press.

Giddens, Anthony. 1976. *New Rules of the Sociological Method: A Positive Critique of Interpretative Sociologies.* London: Hutchinson.

Gilroy, Paul. 1987. *"There Ain't No Black in the Union Jack": The Cultural Politics of Race and Nation.* Chicago: University of Chicago Press.

Ginsburg, Faye D. 1989. *Contested Lives: The Abortion Debate in an American Community.* Berkeley: University of California Press.

Gonos, George. 1997. "The Contest over 'Employer' Status in the Postwar United States: The Case of Temporary Help Firms." *Law and Society Review* 31 (1): 81–110.

Gooding-Williams, Robert, ed. 1993. *Reading Rodney King/Reading Urban Uprising.* New York: Routledge.

Gordon, Sara. 1989. *Crisis política y guerra in El Salvador.* Distrito Federal, Mexico: Siglo veintiuno.

Green, Linda. 1994. "Fear as a Way of Life." *Cultural Anthropology* 9 (2): 227–56.

Greenhouse, Carol J. 1996. *A Moment's Notice: Time Politics across Cultures.* Ithaca: Cornell University Press.

Gregory, Steven, and Roger Sanjek, eds. 1994. *Race.* New Brunswick, N.J.: Rutgers University Press.

Gupta, Akhil. 1992. "The Song of the Nonaligned World: Transnational Identities and the Reinscription of Space in Late Capitalism." *Cultural Anthropology* 7 (1): 63–79.

Gupta, Akhil, and James Ferguson. 1992. "Beyond 'Culture': Space, Identity, and the Politics of Difference." *Cultural Anthropology* 7 (1): 6–24.

Gupta, Akhil, and James Ferguson. 1997. "Beyond 'Culture': Space, Identity, and the Politics of Difference." In *Culture, Power, Place: Explorations in Critical Anthropology*, ed. Akhil Gupta and James Ferguson, 33–51. Durham, N.C.: Duke University Press.

Gutierrez, Gustavo. 1973. *A Theology of Liberation: History, Politics, and Salvation.* Trans. Sister Caridad Inda and John Eagleson. Maryknoll, N.Y.: Orbis Books.

Hagan, Jacqueline Maria. 1994. *Deciding to Be Legal: A Maya Community in Houston.* Philadelphia: Temple University Press.

Hagan, Jacqueline Maria, and Susan Gonzalez Baker. 1993. "Implementing the U.S. Legalization Program: The Influence of Immigrant Communities and Local Agencies on Immigration Policy Reform." *International Migration Review* 27 (3): 513–36.

Hall, Stuart, and David Held. 1990. "Citizens and Citizenship." In *New Times:*

The Changing Face of Politics in the 1990s, ed. Stuart Hall and Martin Jacques, 173–88. London: Verso.

Hamilton, Nora, and Norma Stoltz Chinchilla. 1991. "Central American Migration: A Framework for Analysis." *Latin American Research Review* 26 (1): 75–110.

Hammar, Tomas. 1990. *Democracy and the Nation State: Aliens, Denizens and Citizens in a World of International Migration.* Aldershot, Eng.: Avebury.

Hammar, Tomas. 1994. "Legal Time of Residence and the Status of Immigrants." In *From Aliens to Citizens: Redefining the Status of Immigrants in Europe,* ed. Rainer Bauböck, 187–97. Aldershot, Eng.: Avebury.

Haraway, Donna J. 1991. *Simians, Cyborgs, and Women: The Reinvention of Nature.* New York: Routledge.

Hardy-Fanta, Carol. 1993. *Latina Politics, Latino Politics: Gender, Culture, and Political Participation in Boston.* Philadelphia: Temple University Press.

Harvey, David. 1989. *The Condition of Postmodernity.* Cambridge: Blackwell.

Harwood, Edwin. 1984. "Arrests without Warrant: The Legal and Organizational Environment of Immigration Law Enforcement." *University of California, Davis, Law Review* 17 (2): 505–48.

Harwood, Edwin. 1985. "How Should We Enforce Immigration Law?" In *Clamor at the Gates: The New American Immigration,* ed. Nathan Glazer, 73–91. San Francisco: Institute for Contemporary Studies.

Harwood, Edwin. 1986. *In Liberty's Shadow: Illegal Aliens and Immigration Law Enforcement.* Stanford, Calif.: Stanford University Press.

Held, David. 1995. *Democracy and the Global Order: From the Modern State to Cosmopolitan Governance.* Stanford, Calif.: Stanford University Press.

Heyman, Josiah McC. 1991. *Life and Labor on the Border: Working People of Northeastern Sonora, Mexico, 1886–1986.* Tucson: University of Arizona Press.

Heyman, Josiah McC. 1995. "Putting Power in the Anthropology of Bureaucracy: The Immigration and Naturalization Service at the Mexico–United States Border." *Current Anthropology* 36 (2): 261–87.

Hing, Bill Ong. 1986. *The Immigration Reform and Control Act of 1986: Its Provisions, Applications, and Effect on Immigration Practice.* San Francisco: Immigrant Legal Resource Center.

Holston, James. 1991. "The Misrule of Law: Land and Usurpation in Brazil." *Comparative Studies in Society and History* 33 (4): 695–725.

Holston, James, and Arjun Appadurai. 1996. "Cities and Citizenship." *Public Culture* 8 (2): 187–204.

Hondagneu-Sotelo, Pierrette. 1994. *Gendered Transitions: Mexican Experiences of Immigration.* Berkeley: University of California Press.

Hondagneu-Sotelo, Pierrette, and Ernestine Avila. 1997. "'I'm Here, but I'm There': The Meanings of Latina Transnational Motherhood." *Gender and Society* 11 (5): 548–71.

Hull, Elizabeth. 1985. *Without Justice for All: The Constitutional Rights of Aliens.* Westport, Conn.: Greenwood.

Hunt, Alan. 1985. "The Ideology of Law: Advances and Problems in Recent

Applications of the Concept of Ideology to the Analysis of Law." *Law and Society Review* 19 (1): 11–37.

Hunt, Alan. 1993. *Explorations in Law and Society: Toward a Constitutive Theory of Law.* New York: Routledge.

INS (Immigration and Naturalization Service, U.S. Department of Justice). 1991. *Statistical Yearbook of the Immigration and Naturalization Service, 1990.* Washington, D.C.: U.S. Government Printing Office.

INS (Immigration and Naturalization Service, U.S. Department of Justice). 1997. *Statistical Yearbook of the Immigration and Naturalization Service, 1996.* Washington, D.C.: U.S. Government Printing Office.

INS (Immigration and Naturalization Service, U.S. Department of Justice). 1998. "INS Seeks Public Comment on Proposed Rule to Simplify Employment Verification Process for Employers." News release dated January 30. Washington, D.C.: INS.

Instituto de Investigaciones Jurídicas. 1988. *Diccionario Jurídico Mexicano.* 2d ed. Mexico City: Editorial Porrúa.

Interpreter Releases. 1990a. "Congress Approves Major Immigration Reform." *Interpreter Releases* 67 (41): 1209–15.

Interpreter Releases. 1990b. "Section-by-Section Summary of the 'Immigration Act of 1990.'" 67 (42): 1277–92.

Interpreter Releases. 1996a. "Appendix II: Congressional Record—House." 73 (October 7):1360–1406.

Interpreter Releases. 1996b. "Final Anti-Terrorism Bill Contains Major Immigration Changes." 73 (April 22): 521–30.

Ishay, Micheline R., ed. 1997. *The Human Rights Reader: Major Political Writings, Essays, Speeches, and Documents from the Bible to the Present.* New York: Routledge.

Jacob, Herbert. 1992. "The Elusive Shadow of the Law." *Law and Society Review* 26 (3): 565–90.

Jenkins, J. Craig. 1978. "The Demand for Immigrant Workers: Labor Scarcity or Social Control?" *International Migration Review* 12 (4): 514–35.

Jenkins, Janis Hunter. 1991. "The State Construction of Affect: Political Ethos and Mental Health among Salvadoran Refugees." *Culture, Medicine and Psychiatry* 15 (2): 139–65.

Jenkins, Janis Hunter. 1996. "The Impress of Extremity: Women's Experience of Trauma and Political Violence." In *Gender and Health: An International Perspective,* ed. Carolyn F. Sargent and Caroline B. Brettell, 278–91. Upper Saddle River, N.J.: Prentice Hall.

Jenkins, Janis Hunter, and Martha Valiente. 1994. "Bodily Transactions of the Passions: *el calor* among Salvadoran Women Refugees." In *Embodiment and Experience: The Existential Ground of Culture and Self,* ed. Thomas J. Csordas, 163–82. Cambridge: Cambridge University Press.

Kairys, David, ed. 1990. *The Politics of Law: A Progressive Critique.* Rev. ed. New York: Pantheon.

Kearney, Michael. 1991. "Borders and Boundaries of State and Self at the End of Empire." *Journal of Historical Sociology* 4 (1): 52–74.

Kearney, Michael. 1995a. "The Effects of Transnational Culture, Economy, and Migration on Mixtec Identity in Oaxacalifornia." In *The Bubbling Cauldron*, ed. Smith and Feagin, 226–43. Minneapolis: University of Minnesota Press.

Kearney, Michael. 1995b. "The Local and the Global: The Anthropology of Globalization and Transnationalism." *Annual Review of Anthropology* 24:547–65.

Lazarus-Black, Mindie. 1997. "The Rites of Domination: Practice, Process, and Structure in Lower Courts." *American Ethnologist* 24 (3): 628–51.

Lazarus-Black, Mindie, and Susan F. Hirsch, eds. 1994. *Contested States: Law, Hegemony and Resistance*. New York: Routledge.

Lernoux, Penny. 1982. *Cry of the People*. New York: Doubleday.

Levy, Daniel. 1995. *Naturalization Handbook*. Deerfield, Ill.: Clark, Boardman, Callaghan.

Limon, Jose E. 1983. "Western Marxism and Folklore: A Critical Introduction." *Journal of American Folklore* 96 (3): 34–52.

Lopez, David E., Eric Popkin, and Edward Telles. 1996. "Central Americans: At the Bottom, Struggling to Get Ahead." In *Ethnic Los Angeles*, ed. Roger Waldinger and Mehdi Bozorgmehr, 279–304. New York: Russell Sage Foundation.

López Casanova, Alfredo. 1995. *El Salvador por el camino de la paz y la esperanza. Testimonios de excombatientes insurgentes*. Tlaquepaque, Mexico: Instituto Tecnológico y de Estudios Superiores de Occidente.

MacEoin, Gary, ed. 1985. *Sanctuary: A Resource Guide for Understanding and Participating in the Central American Refugees' Struggle*. San Francisco: Harper and Row.

Macpherson, C. B. 1962. *The Political Theory of Possessive Individualism: Hobbes to Locke*. Oxford: Oxford University Press.

Maher, Kristen Hill. 1997. "Space, Race, Class, and Immigrant Labor: Latino Workers in Fortressed Middle-Class Neighborhoods." Paper presented at the annual meeting of the American Political Science Association, Washington, D.C.

Mahler, Sarah J. 1995. *American Dreaming: Immigrant Life on the Margins*. Princeton: Princeton University Press.

Malkki, Liisa. 1992. "National Geographic: The Rooting of Peoples and the Territorialization of National Identity among Scholars and Refugees." *Cultural Anthropology* 7 (1): 24–44.

Malkki, Liisa. 1995a. *Purity and Exile: Violence, Memory, and National Cosmology among Hutu Refugees in Tanzania*. Chicago: University of Chicago Press.

Malkki, Liisa. 1995b. "Refugees and Exile: From 'Refugee Studies' to the National Order of Things." *Annual Review of Anthropology* 24:495–523.

Marrero, María del Pilar. 1998a. "Detienen deportaciones." *La Opinión*, June 6, 1A, 6A.

Marrero, María del Pilar. 1998b. "Más problemas con la ley NACARA." *La Opinión*, June 18, 1A, 8A.

Marrero, María del Pilar. 1998c. "Ministro Salvadoreño promueve su país." *La Opinión,* June 26, 9B.

Marrero, María del Pilar. 1998d. "No consuela decisión sobre 'amnistía tardía.'" *La Opinión,* June 9, 1A, 6A.

Marrus, Michael R. 1985. *The Unwanted: European Refugees in the Twentieth Century.* New York: Oxford University Press.

Martin, Philip. 1995. "Proposition 187 in California." *International Migration Review* 29 (1): 255–63.

Mather, Lynn, and Barbara Yngvesson. 1980–81. "Language, Audience, and the Transformation of Disputes." *Law and Society Review* 15 (3–4): 775–821.

Matoesian, Gregory M. 1995. "Language, Law, and Society: Policy Implications of the Kennedy Smith Rape Trial." *Law and Society Review* 29 (4): 669–701.

Matoesian, Gregory M. 1997. "'You Were Interested in Him as a Person?': Rhythms of Domination in the Kennedy Smith Rape Trial." *Law and Social Inquiry* 22 (1): 55–96.

Maurer, Bill. 1995. "Orderly Families for the New Economic Order: Belonging and Citizenship in the British Virgin Islands." *Identities* 2 (1–2): 149–72.

Maurer, Bill. 1997. *Recharting the Caribbean: Land, Law, and Citizenship in the British Virgin Islands.* Ann Arbor: University of Michigan Press.

Maurer, Bill. 1998. "Cyberspatial Sovereignties: Offshore Finance, Digital Cash, and the Limits of Liberalism." *Indiana Journal of Global Legal Studies* 5 (2): 493–519.

McBarnet, Doreen. 1984. "Law and Capital: The Role of Legal Form and Legal Actors." *International Journal of the Sociology of Law* 12 (August): 231–38.

McDonnell, Patrick J. 1997a. "Hunting a Way In: Illegal Immigrants Grapple with Law that Will Speed Deportation." *Los Angeles Times,* March 9, A3.

McDonnell, Patrick J. 1997b. "Immigrants' Plight at Issue in Costa Rica Talks." *Los Angeles Times,* May 8, A32.

McKinley, Michelle. 1997. "Life Stories, Disclosure and the Law." *PoLAR: Political and Legal Anthropology Review* 20 (2): 70–82.

McLeod, Ramon G. 1987. "1.7 Million Aliens in State May Be Eligible for Amnesty." *San Francisco Chronicle,* July 7, 8.

McMichael, Philip. 1996. "Globalization: Myths and Realities." *Rural Sociology* 61 (1): 25–55.

Mehta, Uday S. 1997. "Liberal Strategies of Exclusion." In *Tensions of Empire: Colonial Cultures in a Bourgeois World,* ed. Frederick Cooper and Ann Laura Stoler, 59–86. Berkeley: University of California Press.

Menjívar, Cecilia, Julie DaVanzo, Lisa Greenwell, and R. Burciaga Valdez. 1998. "Remittance Behavior among Salvadoran and Filipino Immigrants in Los Angeles." *International Migration Review* 32 (1): 97–126

Merry, Sally Engle. 1990. *Getting Justice and Getting Even: Legal Consciousness among Working-Class Americans.* Chicago: University of Chicago Press.

Merry, Sally Engle. 1994a. "Courts and Performances: Domestic Violence Hearings in a Hawai'i Family Court." In *Contested States: Law, Hegemony and Resistance,* ed. M. Lazarus-Black and S. F. Hirsch, 35–58. New York: Routledge.

Merry, Sally Engle. 1994b. "Narrating Domestic Violence: Producing the 'Truth' of Violence in 19th- and 20th-Century Hawaiian Courts." *Law and Social Inquiry* 19 (4): 967–94.

Merry, Sally Engle. 1995. "Gender Violence and Legally Engendered Selves." *Identities: Global Studies in Culture and Power* 2 (1–2): 49–74.

Merry, Sally Engle, and Neal Milner, eds. 1993. *The Possibility of Popular Justice: A Case Study of Community Mediation in the United States.* Ann Arbor: University of Michigan Press.

Mertz, Elizabeth. 1994. "A New Social Constructionism for Sociolegal Studies." *Law and Society Review* 28 (5): 1243–65.

Miller, Mark J. 1981. *Foreign Workers in Western Europe: An Emerging Political Force.* New York: Praeger.

Minow, Martha. 1990. *Making All the Difference: Inclusion, Exclusion, and American Law.* Ithaca: Cornell University Press.

Mnookin, Robert H., and Lewis Kornhauser. 1979. "Bargaining in the Shadow of the Law: The Case of Divorce." *Yale Law Journal* 88 (5): 950–97.

Montgomery, Tommie Sue. 1995. *Revolution in El Salvador: From Civil Strife to Civil Peace.* 2d ed. Boulder, Colo.: Westview.

Morales, Alfonso. N.d. "Tax Problems of New Immigrants: Merchants of Chicago's Maxwell Street Market." Working paper no. 9126. Chicago: American Bar Foundation.

Murphy, Kim. 1989. "Deportations Blocked until INS Gives New Interviews to 23,000." *Los Angeles Times,* May 16, I, 3, 26.

Nagengast, Carole. 1994. "Violence, Terror, and the Crisis of the State." *Annual Review of Anthropology* 23:109–36.

Nelson, Barbara J. 1984. "Women's Poverty and Women's Citizenship: Some Political Consequences of Economic Marginality." *SIGNS* 10 (2): 209–31.

Neuman, Gerald L. 1996. *Strangers to the Constitution: Immigrants, Borders, and Fundamental Law.* Princeton: Princeton University Press.

NILC (National Immigration Law Center). 1994. *Immigrants' Rights Manual.* 2d ed. Los Angeles: NILC.

NILC (National Immigration Law Center). 1996. *Immigrants and the '96 Welfare Law: A Resource Manual.* Los Angeles: NILC.

O'Barr, William M., and John M. Conley. 1985. "Litigant Satisfaction versus Legal Adequacy in Small Claims Court Narratives." *Law and Society Review* 19 (4): 661–701.

Oliver, Myrna. 1989. "INS Sued on Handling of Political Asylum Requests." *Los Angeles Times,* January 31, I, 17.

Ong, Paul, Edna Bonacich, and Lucie Cheng. 1994. *The New Asian Immigration in Los Angeles and Global Restructuring.* Philadelphia: Temple University Press.

La Opinión. 1998. "Buscan restablecer la Sección 245i." July 7, 1A, 6A.

Paral, Rob. 1995. "Naturalization: New Demands and New Directions at the INS." *Interpreter Releases* 72 (27): 937–43.

Pastor, Manuel, Jr., and Carol Wise. 1998. "Trading Places: U.S. Latinos and Trade Liberalization in the Americas." In *Borderless Borders: U.S. Latinos, Latin Americans, and the Paradox of Interdependence,* ed. Frank Bonilla, Edwin Meléndez, Rebecca Morales, and María de los Angeles Torres, 35–51. Philadelphia: Temple University Press.

Paul, Benjamin D., and William J. Demarest. 1988. "The Operation of a Death Squad in San Pedro la Laguna." In *Harvest of Violence: The Maya Indians and the Guatemalan Crisis,* ed. Robert M. Carmack, 119–54. Norman: University of Oklahoma Press.

Peteet, Julie M. 1991. *Gender in Crisis: Women and the Palestinian Resistance Movement.* New York: Columbia University Press.

Pirie, Sophie H. 1990. "The Origins of a Political Trial: The Sanctuary Movement and Political Justice." *Yale Journal of Law and the Humanities* 2 (2): 381–416.

Poitras, Guy. 1983. "Through the Revolving Door: Central American Manpower in the United States." *Inter-American Economic Affairs* 36 (4): 63–78.

Portes, Alejandro. 1978. "Toward a Structural Analysis of Illegal (Undocumented) Immigration." *International Migration Review* 12 (4): 469–84.

Portes, Alejandro. 1981. "Modes of Structural Incorporation and Present Theories of Labor Immigration." In *Global Trends in Migration: Theory and Research on International Population Movements,* ed. Mary M. Kritz, Charles B. Keely, and Silvano M. Tomasi, 279–97. Staten Island, N.Y.: Center for Migration Studies.

Pratt, Mary Louise. 1990. "Women, Literature, and National Brotherhood." In *Women, Culture and Politics in Latin America,* by Emilie Bergmann et al., 48–73. Berkeley: University of California Press.

Riles, Annelise. 1998. "Infinity within the Brackets." *American Ethnologist* 25 (3): 378–98.

Robertson, Roland. 1995. "Glocalization: Time-Space and Homogeneity-Heterogeneity." In *Global Modernities,* ed. Mike Featherstone, Scott Lash, and Roland Robertson, 25–44. London: Sage.

Rocco, Raymond. 1997. "Citizenship, Culture, and Community: Restructuring in Southeast Los Angeles." In *Latino Cultural Citizenship,* ed. Flores and Benmayor, 97–123. Boston: Beacon.

Rosaldo, Renato. 1989. *Culture and Truth: The Remaking of Social Analysis.* Boston: Beacon.

Rose, Richard. 1989. "Charges as Contested Signals." *Journal of Public Policy* 9 (3): 261–86.

Rouse, Roger. 1991. "Mexican Migration and the Social Space of Postmodernism." *Diaspora* 1 (1): 8–23.

Rubin, Robert. 1991. "Ten Years After: Vindication for Salvadorans and New Promises for Safe Haven and Refugee Protection." *Interpreter Releases* 68 (4): 97–109.

Salzinger, Leslie. 1991. "A Maid by Any Other Name: The Transformation of 'Dirty Work' by Central American Immigrants." In *Ethnography Unbound: Power and Resistance in the Modern Metropolis,* by Michael Burawoy et al., 139–60. Berkeley: University of California Press.

Sanchez, George J. 1997. "Face the Nation: Race, Immigration, and the Rise of Nativism in Late Twentieth Century America." *International Migration Review* 31 (4): 1009–30.

Sanchez, Lisa. 1998. "Boundaries of Legitimacy: Sex, Violence, Citizenship and Community in a Local Sexual Economy." *Law and Social Inquiry* 22 (3): 543–80.

Santana, Alfredo. 1998. "El Salvador se hace presente en Los Angeles." *La Opinión,* June 23, 2D.

Sapiro, Virginia. 1984. "Women, Citizenship, and Nationality: Immigration and Naturalization Policies in the United States." *Politics and Society* 13 (1): 1–26.

Sarat, Austin. 1990. "'. . . The Law Is All Over': Power, Resistance, and the Legal Consciousness of the Welfare Poor." *Yale Journal of Law and the Humanities* 2 (2): 343–80.

Sassen, Saskia. 1988. *The Mobility of Labor and Capital: A Study in International Investment and Labor Flow.* New York: Cambridge University Press.

Sassen, Saskia. 1989. "America's Immigration 'Problem': The Real Causes." *World Policy Journal* 6 (4): 811–31.

Sassen, Saskia. 1991. *The Global City: New York, London, Tokyo.* Princeton: Princeton University Press.

Sassen, Saskia. 1996. *Losing Control? Sovereignty in an Age of Globalization.* New York: Columbia University Press.

Schiller, Nina Glick, Linda Basch, and Cristina Szanton Blanc. 1995. "From Immigrant to Transmigrant: Theorizing Transnational Migration." *Anthropological Quarterly* 68 (1): 48–63.

Schirmer, Jennifer G. 1985. "A Different Reality: The Central American Refugee and the Lawyer." *Immigration Newsletter* 14 (5): 6–9.

Schirmer, Jennifer G. 1988. "'Those Who Die for Life Cannot Be Called Dead:' Women and Human Rights Protest in Latin America." *Human Rights Yearbook* 1:41–76.

Schneider, Anne, and Helen Ingram. 1993. "Social Construction of Target Populations: Implications for Politics and Policy." *American Political Science Review* 87 (2): 334–47.

Scott, James. 1990. *Domination and the Arts of Resistance: Hidden Transcripts.* New Haven: Yale University Press.

Shapiro, Michael J. 1988. "The Constitution of the Central American Other: The Case of 'Guatemala.'" In his *The Politics of Representation: Writing Practices in Biography, Photography, and Policy Analysis,* 89–123. Madison: University of Wisconsin Press.

Sierra, Maria Teresa. 1995. "Indian Rights and Customary Law in Mexico: A Study of the Nahuas in the Sierra de Puebla." *Law and Society Review* 29 (2): 227–54.

Silbey, Susan S. 1997. "'Let them Eat Cake': Globalization, Postmodern Colonialism, and the Possibilities of Justice." *Law and Society Review* 31 (2): 207–35.

Simon, Julian Lincoln. 1989. *The Economic Consequences of Immigration.* Oxford: Blackwell.

Singer, Joseph William. 1988. "The Reliance Interest in Property." *Stanford Law Review* 40 (3): 611–751.

Smith, Michael Peter, and Joe R. Feagin, eds. 1995. *The Bubbling Cauldron: Race, Ethnicity, and the Urban Crisis.* Minneapolis: University of Minnesota Press.

Sorkin, Michael, ed. 1992. *Variations on a Theme Park: The New American City and the End of Public Space.* New York: Hill and Wang.

Soysal, Yasemin Nuhoglu. 1994. *Limits of Citizenship: Migrants and Postnational Membership in Europe.* Chicago: University of Chicago Press.

Starr, June, and Jane F. Collier, eds. 1989. *History and Power in the Study of Law: New Directions in Legal Anthropology.* Ithaca: Cornell University Press.

Stephen, Lynn. 1995. "Women's Rights Are Human Rights: The Merging of Feminine and Feminist Interests among El Salvador's Mothers of the Disappeared (CO-MADRES)." *American Ethnologist* 22 (4): 807–27.

Stoler, Ann Laura, and Frederick Cooper. 1997. "Between Metropole and Colony: Rethinking a Research Agenda." In *Tensions of Empire: Colonial Cultures in a Bourgeois World,* ed. Frederick Cooper and Ann Laura Stoler, 1–56. Berkeley: University of California Press.

Taussig, Michael. 1984. "Culture of Terror—Space of Death: Roger Casement's Putumayo Report and the Explanation of Torture." *Comparative Studies in Society and History* 26 (3): 467–97.

Taylor, Diana. 1997. *Disappearing Acts: Spectacles of Gender and Nationalism in Argentina's "Dirty War."* Durham, N.C.: Duke University Press.

Thomas, Robert J. 1985. *Citizenship, Gender, and Work: Social Organization of Industrial Agriculture.* Berkeley: University of California Press.

Thompson, E. P. 1967. "Time, Work-Discipline, and Industrial Capitalism." *Past and Present* 38 (December): 56–97.

Thompson, E. P. 1975. *Whigs and Hunters: The Origins of the Black Act.* London: Allen Lane, Penguin.

Thrift, Nigel. 1996. *Spatial Formations.* Thousand Oaks, Calif.: Sage.

Tucson Citizen. 1987. "Amnesty: At 1 Million." November 23, 1A.

Turner, Victor. 1969. *The Ritual Process: Structure and Anti-Structure.* Ithaca: Cornell University Press.

United Nations Commission on the Truth. 1993. *De la locura a la esperanza: La guerra de 12 años en El Salvador: Informe de la Comisión de la Verdad para El Salvador (1992–1993).* San Salvador, El Salvador: Editorial Arcoiris.

USCR (U. S. Committee for Refugees). 1986. *Despite a Generous Spirit: Deny-*

ing Asylum in the United States. Washington, D.C.: American Council for Nationalities Service.

U.S. Senate, Select Committee on Intelligence. 1989. *The FBI and CISPES.* Washington, D.C.: U.S. Government Printing Office.

Wagner-Pacifici, Robin. 1994. *Discourse and Destruction: The City of Philadelphia versus MOVE.* Chicago: University of Chicago Press.

Waldinger, Roger, and Mehdi Bozorgmehr, eds. 1996. *Ethnic Los Angeles.* New York: Russell Sage Foundation.

Wasem, Ruth Ellen. N.d. "Temporary Protections under U.S. Immigration Law." Washington, D.C.: Congressional Research Service, Library of Congress.

Weiss, Kenneth R. 1998. "Mixing Commencement and Culture." *Los Angeles Times,* June 20, A1, A21.

Weissbourd, Bernard, and Elizabeth Mertz. 1985. "Rule-Centrism versus Legal Creativity: The Skewing of Legal Ideology through Language." *Law and Society Review* 19 (4): 623–59.

Weissinger, George. 1996. *Law Enforcement and the INS: A Participant Observation Study of Control Agents.* Lanham, Md.: University Press of America.

White, James Boyd. 1985. *Heracles' Bow: Essays on the Rhetoric and Poetics of the Law.* Madison: University of Wisconsin Press.

Wilgoren, Jodi, and Patrick J. McDonnell. 1997. "House Approves Nicaraguan and Cuban Amnesty." *Los Angeles Times,* November 13, A1, A29.

Williams, Raymond. 1977. *Marxism and Literature.* Oxford: Oxford University Press.

Wilmsen, Edwin N., and Patrick McAllister, eds. 1996. *The Politics of Difference: Ethnic Premises in a World of Power.* Chicago: University of Chicago Press.

Wilson, Tamar Diana. 1993. "Theoretical Approaches to Mexican Wage Labor Migration." *Latin American Perspectives* 20 (3): 93–129.

Yanagisako, Sylvia, and Carol Delaney, eds. 1995. *Naturalizing Power: Essays in Feminist Cultural Analysis.* New York: Routledge.

Yngvesson, Barbara. 1993a. "Local People, Local Problems, and Neighborhood Justice: The Discourse of 'Community' in San Francisco Community Boards." In *The Possibility of Popular Justice,* ed. Merry and Milner, 379–400. Ann Arbor: University of Michigan Press.

Yngvesson, Barbara. 1993b. *Virtuous Citizens, Disruptive Subjects: Order and Complaint in a New England Court.* New York: Routledge.

Yngvesson, Barbara. 1997. "Negotiating Motherhood: Identity and Difference in 'Open' Adoptions." *Law and Society Review* 31 (1): 31–80.

Zolberg, Aristide R. 1990. "The Roots of U.S. Refugee Policy." In *Immigration and U.S. Foreign Policy,* ed. Robert W. Tucker, Charles B. Keely, and Linda Wrigley, 99–120. Boulder, Colo.: Westview.

Index